HERE TO STAY

Five Plays from the Women's Project

edited by Julia Miles

APPLAUSE
NEW YORK • LONDON

An Applause Original

HERE TO STAY: FIVE PLAYS FROM THE WOMEN'S PROJECT

Copyright ©1997 by Applause Theatre Book Publishers
All Rights Reserved
ISBN 1-55783-315-X (paper)

Here to stay: five plays from the Women's Project / edited by Julia Miles.
     p.   cm.
     Contents: Frida, the story of Frida Kahlo / Hilary Blecher -- Why we have a body / Claire Chafee-- Dream of a common language / Heather MacDonald -- Black / Joyce Carol Oates -- Aye aye aye I'm integrated / Anna Deavere Smith.
     ISBN 1-55783-315x (pbk.)
     1. American drama--Woman authors.   2. American drama--20th century.
3. Women--United States--Drama. I. Miles, Julia. II. Women's Project (New York, N.Y.)
PS628.W6H47   1997
812'.540809287--dc21   97-28470
                                          CIP

Applause Theatre Book Publishers
     211 West 71st Street
     New York, NY 10023
     Phone: (212) 595-4735
     Fax: (212) 721-2856
First Applause Printing, 1997

A & C Black
Howard Road, Eaton Socon
Huntingdon, Cambs PC19 3CZ
Phone: 01480-212666
Fax: 01480-405014

HERE TO STAY

Five Plays from the Women's Project

Other Plays by Women from Applause

PLAYS BY AMERICAN WOMEN 1900-1930
edited by Judith Barlow

PLAYS BY AMERICAN WOMEN 1930-1960
edited by Judith Barlow

WOMEN ON THE VERGE edited by Rosette Lamont

WOMENSWORK edited by Julia Miles

WOMEN HEROES edited by Julia Miles

AMAZON ALL-STARS edited by Rosemary Keefe Curb

DEAR by Rosalyn Drexler

THE MOTHERS by Lavonne Mueller

WELCOME TO AMERICA: MEMORIES OF A BINTEL BRIEF by Barbara Lesser

Edith Wharton's **THE CUSTOM OF THE COUNTRY**
adapted by Jane Stanton Hitchcock

I AM A WOMAN by Viveca Lindfors and Paul Austin

CONTENTS

INTRODUCTION

by *Julia Miles*

What better way to celebrate twenty years of the Women's Project & Productions than to bring to readers five outstanding plays from the ninety-five we have produced — they have made me proud, and many have been published in our past anthologies.

The question I asked in 1978, "Where are the women playwrights?" has been answered with soft and loud voices of women on our stages — where they belong. Women are telling their stories, through their characters' dialogue and onstage action. And in the process they learn that theatre is a collaborative roller-coaster ride and you must hold on.

Rewriting is part of rehearsing a play. Sometimes the actors do not sound like the voices in playwrights' heads; however, they often sound stronger! They frequently surprise the playwrights.

The plays in this volume are as varied as the playwrights. Two of them are by distinguished women who also are known for other forms of writing. Anna Deavere Smith is best known for the verbatim interviews that she so powerfully performs about race in America, and Joyce Carol Oates is best known for her stories, poems, essays, and, of course, novels.

Aye Aye Aye I'm Integrated is a short, early play by Anna Deavere Smith, produced in 1984, as part of our "Festival of Six One-Act Plays." It is funny, endearing, and sophisticated in its look at the absurdist aspects of racial discrimination in America.

A young black woman wants to be an actress and perform on television and in the theatre in the same way as her best friend, a white boy with whom she grew up. However, she's a light-skinned black woman, and the agent tells her: "There's no room in show business for racial ambivalence." So she becomes a doctor. (The playwright, unlike her character, has found a unique place as a writer and performer in "show business" and also acts in theatre, film, and television.)

Black, which was produced in 1994, embodies the theme that Oates maintains is the major preoccupation of her work. "I am concerned with only one thing: the moral and social conditions of my generation." Certainly, *Black* embraces this concern. A white man is coming home to take his possessions after a divorce. He has been invited by his former wife, also white, to have dinner with her and her fiancé, a black man. He is "the highest ranking black appointee in the state of New Jersey," a former Southerner, graduate of Yale, and former Rutgers professor. Boyd, the ex-husband, remarks to Debra, "You've come back to life." We later learn that Boyd is a drunk, a wife-beater, and a Pulitzer Prize-winning photographer—and he wants his wife back. He's also boyish, charming, thinks himself a liberal, and carries a gun. There is a hateful confrontation between the men and masks are discarded. But murder is not committed, and we are left wondering if Debra (who at thirteen could not be hypnotized) gets or does not get what she wants.

In 1992, we shared an AT&T: OnStage award with Berkeley Repertory Theatre for Heather McDonald's play about women artists' struggle to have a place at the first Impressionist table and be wives and mothers. *Dream of a Common Language* (the title is from a poem, "Origins and History of Consciousness", by Adrienne Rich) is the love story of a married couple, both painters, in France in 1874. The husband is hosting a party for the male painters who will have their works shown at the first Impressionist exhibition. No women are invited to the dinner. They were left out. Because they are women?

Clovis, the wife, has given up painting. She realized that the objects she chose to paint because she loved them were not taken seriously. They are girls' things. The women hold their own "Soprano" party, and Clovis awakens to her absolute need to paint. She persuades her husband to pose nude for her, which is against the rules of the art world. This act opens a way to connect to and share a common language with her husband and her art.

In 1993, we were invited to be a partner in a complex opera/theatre piece about Frida Kahlo. In her lifetime, Mexican painter Frida Kahlo had only two one-woman shows. It took twenty-five years for her to be rediscovered, honored, and exhibited. And, certainly, the women's movement can take credit for some of her deserved popularity. *Frida*, conceived and directed by Hilary Blecher, is the story of her life told with music, images from her paintings, and puppets.

Frida Kahlo was a tomboy as a child and political all her life. When she was eighteen, a bus accident almost killed her; her spinal column, collarbone, and pelvis were broken, and her right leg and foot were crushed. While recuperating, she began to paint, lying on her back with a mirror over her head and herself as subject.

She courts and marries Diego Rivera, and they fight, paint, marry, divorce, and remarry until her death at the age of 44. Much of *Frida* is sung to composer Robert Rodriguez' original and haunting music and Migdalia Cruz's lyrics. We co-produced *Frida* with the American Music Theatre Festival and the Houston Grand Opera, and I, a fan of Kahlo's work, was proud to help bring her life to theatre and music audiences.

Why We Have A Body is similar to a piece of music you like and want to hear again. When I first heard a reading of the play, I was hooked. I loved it, maybe because I'm the mother of daughters, and certainly because the language is strong and epigramatic and the form is uniquely its own, wise and right.

The playwright, Claire Chafee, does warn us to listen and pay attention. Mary, the youngest daughter and a stick-up artist who has feminist nightmares, says in her opening monologue: "There will be no pitons on which to hook your rope, no themes, no easy contradictions." She depends on and loves her older sister, a lesbian private investigator, and tells her, when the sister falls in love with a married woman: "You always pick someone busy not noticing you." Their mother, an explorer, is convinced that the female psyche is stuck. "Women just don't think it's our turn...we haven't thought big enough." Her daughters finally realize that she isn't coming home, when Mary is told by the heart of Joan of Arc: "Fish somewhere else." For all of us, "that is a sentence in the sky." Indeed!

These writers have created plays in which their characters "fish somewhere else," or as Ibsen wrote in *Peer Gynt*: "Backward or forward it's just as far, out or in the way's as narrow, go round." They "go round," and they go forward. I admire them and cheer them on.

Conceived by Hilary Blecher

Monologues and lyrics by Migdalia Cruz

Music by Robert X. Rodriguez

FRIDA: THE STORY OF
FRIDA KAHLO

Frida: The Story of Frida Kahlo was produced by the Women's Project & Productions, American Music Theater Festival, and Houston Grand Opera and premiered at A.R.T. Fall Festival in Cambridge, Massachussetts, September 16-27, 1992. It was directed by Hilary Blecher with the following cast:

FRIDA   Helen Schneider

DIEGO   William Rhodes

With Chris Fields, Karen Hale, Andrea Kane, Stephen Kaplin, Barbara Pollitt, Alba Quezada, Michael Romanyshyn, David Toney, Byron Utley, and Andrew Varela

Book: Hilary Blecher

Monologues and Lyrics: Migdalia Cruz

Music: Robert Xavier Rodriguez

Scenic Design by Andrew Jackness

Costume Design by Ann Roth and Robert de Mora

Lighting Design by Robert Wierzel

Musical Director and Conductor: Robert Kapilow

Choreographer: Hope Clarke

Sound Design by Theater Sound

Puppetry Director: Michael Romanyshyn

Production Stage Manager: Erica Schwartz

CHARACTERS

FRIDA KAHLO   mezzosoprano

DIEGO RIVERA   baritone

An ensemble of four players who form the Quartet:

WOMAN 1   soprano; CRISTINA KAHLO (Frida's younger sister), The voice of MRS. FORD

WOMAN 2   mezzosoprano; The voice of the MOTHER, LUPE MARIN** (Diego's wife when he met Frida), The voice of MRS. ROCKEFELLER, NATALIA TROTSKY**

MAN 1   tenor; ALEJANDRO (Frida's teenage boyfriend), the voice of FORD, LEON TROTSKY**

MAN 2   bass; The voice of the PETATE VENDOR, a CACHUCHA, GUILLERMO KAHLO** (Frida's father), The voice of MR. ROCKEFELLER, The voice of EDWARD G. ROBINSON

The six puppeteers play:

**THREE CALAVERAS (Death figures inspired by the Day of the Dead and Posada)

*MOTHER, a peasant

*DIMAS, the peasant woman's dead son

*TOWNSPEOPLE, including a PETATE VENDOR and a PINOLE VENDOR

*PEASANTS

*SCHOOLGIRLS, Frida's teenage enemies

*CACHUCHAS, Frida's teenage schoolchums

*BUS PASSENGERS

*WEDDING GUESTS

*MR. AND MRS. JOHN ROCKEFELLER, SR.

*MR. AND MRS. HENRY FORD

*DIEGO'S LOVERS, a parade of women

*EDWARD G. ROBINSON

NURSE

FRIDA'S LOVER

*Indicates a puppet

**Indicates a masked actor

> FRIDA: The Story of Frida Kahlo *is an opera with actor/singers and puppets. All the visual elements are inspired by the work of Frida Kahlo and Diego Rivera. The Music and the Puppetry are powerful elements essential in creating the full impact of the work.*
>
> *NOTES: The puppets range from huge to tiny 3-dimensional figures to flat puppets, shadow puppets, and actors wearing masks. The puppets and masks are based on people and scenes depicted in the work of Frida Kahlo and Diego Rivera.*
>
> *The voices of the puppet characters are sung by members of the chorus strategically placed onstage so that the puppets and voices are identified.*
>
> *All words in capital letters are sung.*

ACT ONE

SCENE 1

FRIDA AT THE NATIONAL PREPARATORY SCHOOL — LA PREPARATORIA — ON THE DAY FRIDA LEARNS WHAT DEATH LOOKS LIKE AND THE REVOLUTION COMES TO AN END.

OVERTURE: The figure of a CALAVERA *(a traditional Mexican death figure) is spotlit on a dark empty stage, his face hidden in shadows beneath a large sombrero. He plays an accordion with increasingly exaggerated movements. As he looks up at the audience and grins, we recognize the presence of* DEATH. *He makes a presentational gesture, which seems to summon up the events that are to follow, and exits.*

The lights come up to reveal a Mexican street scene created by various puppets, actors in masks, and set pieces derived from Diego Rivera's murals, such as the PETATE SELLER, WOMAN WITH ARUM LILIES, *etc. A bright blue wall extends across the stage. In the center of the wall are green gates above which appears the inscription* PREPARATORIA *and the motto "Love, Order and Progress." Brightly colored Mexican birds fill the air. The school gates open, and a perfect line of pious* TEENAGE SCHOOLGIRLS*, *identically dressed in school uniform, file out.*

SCHOOLGIRLS*: SOMOS HIJAS DE LA PREPARATORIA.

HIJAS BUENAS Y LLENAS DE GLORIA!

SCHOOLGIRLS, SWEET AND CLEVER—

AND OH, SO PRETTY AND SLIM!

WE DON'T SPEAK TO THE CACHUCHAS

NOR TO THAT GIRL WHO ACTS JUST LIKE THEM!

SOMOS HIJAS DE LA QUERIDA PREPARATORIA...

TENEMOS PARA SIEMPRE DECENTES MEMORIAS!

[*Loud noise/disturbance offstage. Suddenly a wild group of bicy-*

clists—FRIDA, ALEJANDRO *and their gang, the* CACHUCHAS* *enter and ride through the* SCHOOLGIRLS*, *shouting their school war cry and totally upsetting the girls' demeanor.* FRIDA *is dressed like the boys. She wears striped skull cap, and her hair is cropped short. The air current from the bicycles makes the* SCHOOLGIRLS'* *skirts fly up and they spin around in disorder.*]

SCHOOLGIRLS: [*As they see the* CACHUCHAS *approaching.*] Oh, no! Los malotes Cachuchas! La banda de Frida!

CACHUCHAS: [*SHOUTING.*] Shi...ts...pum

Jooya, jooya

Ca-chun, ca-chun, ra, ra,

Joooya, joooya,

Preparatoria!

FRIDA: STUPID ESCUINCLAS! LITTLE DOGS WITHOUT HAIR!

COME RUN WITH FRIDA. USE YOUR BRAINS—IF YOU DARE!

NIÑITAS DE LA PREPARATORIA—

DON'T JUST SING HOSANNA Y GLORIA!

SCHOOLGIRLS*: What a monster! What disgusting behavior for a girl!

FRIDA: [*Imitating the girls.*] "Oh, what a monster! Oh, how disgusting!"

CRISTI: Frida! You shouldn't!

FRIDA: [*Laughs.*] I can't believe a sister of mine could be such a girl!

[*Sings, mocking schoolgirls.*] WHERE THEY SHOULD HAVE BRAINS—ALL THEY HAVE ARE CURLS.

ALEJANDRO: [*To* FRIDA.] I LOVE YOU...

FRIDA: [*Shooting* ALEJANDRO *a look of amusement.*] AND NOTHING IS MORE BORING THAN YOU STUPID, GIRLY GIRLS!

ALEJANDRO: I MEAN...YOUR MIND!

[*During the following* CRISTI *tries to restrain* FRIDA, *who boldly encourages* CRISTI *to join in the proceedings.*]

FRIDA & ALEJANDRO: WHEN YOU LOOK AT YOUR RE-FLECTIONS,

AREN'T YOU SHOCKED AT WHAT YOU SEE?

UGLY GIRLS WITH EMPTY EYES AND THE BRAIN STEM OF A TREE.

CACHUCHAS: NOT LIKE US—WE'RE CACHUCHAS—THE GREATEST MINDS OF MEXICO!

WE DEVOUR ARISTOTLE, COPERNICUS, AND MARX.

FRIDA: WE'LL CLIMB THE HIMALAYAS, WALK THE MOON

AND SWIM WITH SHARKS!

CRISTI: FRIDA? HOW WILL YOU EVER DO THAT?!

FRIDA: YOU'LL SEE!

[FRIDA *pulls* CRISTI *towards her.* CRISTI *reluctantly joins in.*]

CACHUCHAS: WE'RE CACHUCHAS—THE GREATEST MINDS OF MEXICO!

WE HAVE A MISSION—TO RISE ABOVE IGNO-RANCE—

TO LEARN TO MAKE OUR COUNTRY GREAT.

[FRIDA *lights a firecracker; the other* CACHUCHAS* *follow suit.*]

CRISTI: Frida, no!

[FRIDA *and the* CACHUCHAS* *throw firecrackers at the feet of the* GIRLS*, *who are startled and jump high in the air with fright.*]

GIRLS*: [*Throwing their hands into the air and running away.*] Anarchists! Subversives! Monsters!

[FRIDA *and the* CACHUCHAS* *laugh as they continue to throw fire-crackers at the fleeing girls. The* CACHUCHAS *exit after the girls, leaving* FRIDA *momentarily alone. The music changes abruptly as a* *huge, peasant* MOTHER *puppet enters. Her movements are wild and erratic with grief. In her arms, she holds a child swaddled in rags.*]

MOTHER*: [*In anguish.*] NOTHING... NOTHING...

LIFELESS EYES... EMPTY FACES...

I WALK CIRCLES THROUGH THE CITY—

LOOKING FOR GOD... LOOKING...

TO ASK, TO PRAY FOR MERCY...

WHAT ELSE?

WHAT ELSE...

[*With great urgency, she turns towards the rolls/stacks of petates and begins rummaging frantically through them.*]

PETATE VENDOR*: Oye! — What the hell — Those aren't free —

MOTHER*: My son... please... a place to rest his —

PETATE VENDOR*: You want a petate, lady, then híjole — You pay for it!

[MOTHER* *suddenly becomes aware that her child is dead.*]

MOTHER*: MY SWEET DIMAS...

MY SWEET DIMAS IS DEAD. MY SWEET SON.

ALL LIGHT HAS DIED WITH HIM.

CHORUS: DARKNESS IS MEXICO.

MOTHER*: [*In great anguish.*] Bread could have saved him!

PETATE VENDOR*: You let him starve?!

MOTHER* You must pay for CHORUS: DARKNESS   IS
bread and I have nothing!   MEXICO.

FRIDA: That's where our fight begins... Children must have bread!

MOTHER*: I would have cut my own flesh to feed him — but he's gone from me... too late... too late.

[*The* PETATE VENDOR* *takes the body of* DIMAS* *and places it on a petate.* FRIDA *places flowers, predominantly marigolds, around the body.*]

CHORUS: NOW HE IS DRESSED FOR PARADISE. NOW DI-MAS IS DRESSED FOR GOD.

FRIDA: I 'LL NEVER FORGET THOSE STARING, BROWN EYES.

I'LL SEE THEM IN MY SLEEP.

[*The* PETATE VENDOR* *crosses himself and begins to sing the Lord's Prayer in Spanish.*]

PETATE VENDOR: PADRE NUESTRO QUE ESTÁS EN LOS CIELOS, SANTIFICADO SEA TU NOMBRE...

EVERYONE: MEXICO—YOU'RE STEALING YOUR OWN BREATH.

MOTHER*: It is enough...

CHORUS: [*With revolutionary fervor.*] It is enough! It is enough!

PETATE VENDOR*: Why do the rich live while the rest of us die?

FRIDA: THE ONLY ROAD TO HEAVEN SHOULDN'T BE THROUGH HELL ON EARTH!

WE MUST STOP THE CHILDREN DYING...

PETATE VENDOR*: In this world there is never enough—life is God's lie!

CHORUS: EL PAN NUESTRO DE CADA DÍA DÁNOSLO HOY...

FRIDA: [*Softly.*] MEXICO, YOU'RE STEALING YOUR OWN BREATH.

[FRIDA *speaks to* DIMAS*.] I will remember you. Those honest eyes—

FRIDA: [*Cont'd.*] The eyes of death. Those eyes on a yellow-green straw mat. A ribbon of pink to prove that you're a gift to the Earth...and surrounded by yellow marigolds...yellow and green are death.

CHORUS: NOW HE IS DRESSED FOR PARADISE. NOW DIMAS IS DRESSED FOR GOD.

[*The* MOTHER* *exits, followed by a grieving procession of all the other characters, including* FRIDA. *A moment of silence for the dead child is shattered by the sound of distant gunfire and bullets. Flat puppets appear above the blue wall and enact a scene depicting the execution of Zapatista peasant revolutionaries by government soldiers. As the bodies of the dead peasant soldiers are shot down, a small figure of the revolutionary leader, Zapata, on a white horse, rises up in their place, leading his army of other* ZAPATISTAS. *These small figures are replaced by identical large ones as the blue wall opens to reveal a large, victorious throng consisting of Zapata on his horse,* ZAPATISTAS, *the* MOTHER, *the* PETATE SELLER, FRIDA, CRISTI, ALEJANDRO, *the* CACHUCHAS, *who all sing a victorious anthem of liberation.*]

EVERYONE: [*With patriotic fervor.*] ¡Viva la revolución! ¡Viva Zapata!

[*REVOLUTIONARY PARADE SONG:*]

ZAPATISTAS*: WE WANT WHAT WE'VE EARNED WITH THE SWEAT OFF OUR BACKS.

LAND WILL SET US FREE. LAND IS LIBERTY!

ALL: GLORIOUS MEXICO—THE COUNTRY WHERE OUR FATHERS DIED—

GIVE US BACK OUR HISTORY, FILLED WITH STRENGTH AND PRIDE.

WE WILL FIGHT FOR OUR FREEDOM, WE WILL FIGHT FOR OUR LAND.

LAND!—TO THOSE UNAFRAID OF HARD WORK AND DIRTY FINGERNAILS.

LAND!—AWAY FROM THE THIEVING RICH WHO RIDE ON FOREIGN SAILS.

CACHUCHAS*: WE ARE THE FUTURE, CREATING LIFE FROM THE DEATH OF OUR FATHERS.

CHORUS: VIVA, VIVA, VIVA ZAPATA.

CACHUCHAS*: A NEW GENERATION—RAISING OUR VOICES!

CHORUS: VIVA, VIVAN TIERRA Y LIBERTAD.

CACHUCHAS*: PROUD OF THE AZTEC DUST BENEATH OUR FEET.

CHORUS: VIVA, VIVA, VIVA ZAPATA.

CACHUCHAS*: MEXICANS FOR MEXICO, STANDING TO-GETHER, OUR LOVE IS COMPLETE.

CHORUS: VIVA, VIVAN TIERRA Y LIBERTAD.

ALL: VIVA, VIVA, VIVA ZAPATA! VIVA, VIVAN TIERRA Y LIBERTAD!

VIVA, VIVA, VIVA ZAPATA! VIVA, VIVAN TIERRA Y LIBERTAD!

FRIDA: [*To the* CACHUCHAS.] I was born the same day as the revolution.

CRISTI: No, Frida you were—

[FRIDA *puts her hand over* CRISTI's *mouth to prevent her true birth date from being revealed. The parade breaks into a celebration of flag-waving and jubilation.*]

ALL: Viva Zapata! Vivan Tierra y Libertad! Land for the People! Down with the Rich!

[*The parade exits. Lights cross fade to Scene 2.*]

SCENE 2

FRIDA BECOMES A WOMAN.

FRIDA *is having her first period. She stands, very clinically watching the blood run down her thighs as* CRISTI *looks on, fascinated.*

FRIDA: It's so amazing. A part of myself is running down my thighs. In this blood is an egg which, if I had been "lista" enough to catch one, a sperm could have penetrated and made into a baby. A little me and somebody. Alex is the only one handsome enough for me. It has to be his sperm...

I thought it would never come. I must be the last girl in Coyoacan to become a woman...

CRISTI: You shouldn't have worried so much about it, Frida. It's not such a big thing.

FRIDA: It was for me . . . Eighteen and still like a boy.

CRISTI: Frida! The things you say!

FRIDA: Today my bathwater will be pink. I'll wash the blood from my legs into the water and the water will take it to new, foreign places. Into the ocean . . . into the mouths of a school of tuna . . . onto a beach in San Francisco. I'm going to run away to San Francisco . . . That's where life is — for bohemians . . . and artist-philosophers. And only intelligent people are allowed to live there.

[*Pause.*] Oh, Cristi, do you think he'll still love me even though I'll have blood coming out of me all the time now?

CRISTI: Of course, he will.

FRIDA: My children will have my brains and their father's beauty . . . Or maybe my beauty and — my brains. Anyway, one thing is for sure — they have to be wild and unpredictable —

CRISTI: [*Teasing.*] And nothing like you!

[*They laugh.* CRISTI *exits. Lights cross fade as* FRIDA *moves across the stage to* ALEX *to begin Scene 3.*]

SCENE 3

THE BUS STOP, SEPTEMBER, 1925.

FRIDA'S ACCIDENT

(*cf Frida:* The Autobus, *drawings of the accident.*) *The accident is enacted by the* CALAVERAS *using puppets and models on a smaller scale than reality.*

Soft sounds of conversation.

FRIDA: Look, I'm not some stupid little whore who'll drop her pants for anybody who asks me. [*She looks at him intently, suddenly serious.*] It was the first time for me, Alex.

ALEX: Mine too . . .

[*They look at each other in silence for a moment.*]

FRIDA: [*Seriously.*] Promise you'll love me forever.

ALEX: Forever...

FRIDA: Kiss me.

[*He smiles, grabs her and kisses her passionately. As they kiss the BUS arrives, the* PASSENGERS* *get on.*]

ALEX: [*Pulling himself, laughing, from her tight embrace.*] Frida, the bus!

FRIDA: [*Shouts.*] Hey wait! We're coming!

[*As the BUS SONG begins, a* CALAVERA *holding the bus and another, holding the trolley, appear and dance slowly towards each other until they collide in a climax of music, sounds, and light effects.*]

[*The doors of the bus are about to close.* FRIDA* *and* ALEX* *jump on. The doors close. The bus moves off leaving the Mexican landscape empty.*]

WOMEN'S CHORUS:

AQUI YO HE VENIDO,	[Here I've come,
PORQUE YA HE LLEGADO	because I've arrived
Y VENGO MUY DES-CANSADA,	and I'm very much rested,
CANTANDO CANCIONES	since by singing songs,
ME PASO LA VIDA	spend my life
UN POCO MAS DIVERTIDA.	a bit more amused.]

CHORUS:

EL AUTOBUS CORRIA	[The bus ran
SOBRE LA ESTRECHA VIA	down the narrow street
DE PRONTO SE FUE A ES-TRELLAR	and suddenly it crashed
CONTRA UN TRANVÍA	into a streetcar

CHORUS: [*Cont'd.*] A TODO DAR   going too fast down the middle
POR EL MEDIO

DE ESA CALLE, SIN PARAR.   of that steet, without stopping.]

FUE EN EL AÑO VEINTE —   [It was in the year of '20—

SEPTIEMBRE, EL VEINTE Y   September, the 25th,
CINCO,

CUANDO MURIERON VAR-   when some people died—
IOS —

PERO NO FRIDA DE COYOA-   but not Frida of Coyoacan.]
CAN.

LLEGO LA CRUZ BLANCA,   [The White Cross arrived,

LLEGO LA CRUZ ROJA,   the Red Cross arrived,

A AUXILIAR A LOS HERIDOS,   to help the wounded,

Y ALLI ENCONTRARON   and there they found

QUE   FRIDA   NO   HABÍA   that Frida hadn't died—
MUERTO —

PERO SU CUERPO ESTABA   but her body was broken.]
ROTO…

[*The following happens in very slow motion. As bus and trolley collide, the bus breaks open, and the naked broken body of puppet* FRIDA* *falls out. An* ANGEL* *flies in from above and sprinkles gold paint dust over it. At the moment of impact, the actors* FRIDA *and* ALEJANDRO *are thrown onstage and witness the accident. A* CALAVERA *moves to grab the puppet* FRIDA* *away, but is stopped by the real* FRIDA, *who snatches back the broken doll representing her damaged body.*]

CHILDREN'S VOICES: [*Offstage.*]

DALE DALE DALE.   [Hit it, hit it, hit it,

NO PIERDAS EL TINO.   Don't lose your touch.

MIDE LA DISTANCIA   Measure the distance

QUE HAY EN EL CAMINO.   of your path.]

ALEJANDRO: A house-painter had been carrying a packet of powdered gold.

ALEJANDRO: [*Cont'd.*] The packet broke and the gold fell over her like rain.

PASSENGERS*: [*In awe of her naked, golden body.*] La bailarina! La bailarina! [The ballerina! The ballerina!]

ALEJANDRO: With the gold on her body they thought she was a dancer...

[*The* CALAVERAS *exit slowly.*]

[ALEJANDRO *moves downstage as he repeats his speech as a litany, almost inaudibly, as if by speaking it quietly he could avoid reliving the horror of the moment.*]

ALEJANDRO: Frida had a piece of iron in her body. Her spinal column was broken in three places. Her collarbone was broken, and her third and fourth ribs. Her right leg had eleven fractures and her right foot was dislocated and crushed. Her left shoulder was out of joint, her pelvis broken in three places. The steel handrail had literally skewered her body at the level of the abdomen. Entering on the left side, it had come out through the vagina. Frida said she had lost her virginity on the bus.

[*The lighting becomes very white. A* CALAVERA *moves* FRIDA's *bed on stage.* FRIDA *hangs the "broken"* FRIDA* *puppet on the bed.*]

FRIDA: I WAS ONCE FULL OF LIFE

DANCING IN A WORLD OF HIDDEN COLORS.

NOW MY STEPS ARE SLOW AND PAINFUL

OVER SHARDS OF CRIMSON GLASS.

ALEX: I was certain she was going to die.

FRIDA: DEATH DANCES AROUND MY BED AT NIGHT—

GOLD-SPECKLED REDNESS ON NAKED FLESH.

MY FRIENDS WILL BE WOMEN SLOWLY...

I'M OLD IN AN INSTANT.

ALEJANDRO: The doctors were certain she was going to die...

FRIDA: MY FAITHFUL COMPANION, THE DARKNESS—

ITS SHADOW CARESSES MY HAIR.

FRIDA: [*Cont'd.*] REMEMBER? WE WERE TO CLIMB THE HIMALAYAS?

DON'T TOUCH THE SUN WITHOUT ME, MI VIDA!

REMEMBER ME AS I WAS—NOT SHATTERED LIKE THIS.

TELL ME SOMETHING NEW, MI AMOR.

DIMÉ QUE ME QUIERES PARA SIEMPRE ... PARA SIEMPRE.

ALEJANDRO: We were all certain she was going to die.

[FRIDA *gazes longingly after him as he exits.*]

FRIDA: TODAY STILL GOES ON ...

I FEEL THE WIND OF MY PLAYFUL "PELONA" ...

WHAT IS AHEAD OF ME? WILL MY LIFE ONCE AGAIN BE COMPLETE?

WHEN I LOOK IN A MIRROR, ONE FRIDA LOOKS OUT ... ONE FRIDA LOOKS IN.

I'LL WEAR A MASK TO COVER MY PAIN. I'LL LIVE MY LIFE UPSIDE DOWN.

DEATH DANCES AROUND MY BED AT NIGHT BUT I REFUSE TO CRY.

DEATH DANCES AROUND MY BED AT NIGHT BUT I REFUSE TO DIE ...

[*During the following speech, a* CALAVERA *enters bringing* FRIDA *an easel and some paints.* FRIDA *begins to paint.*]

FRIDA: [*Cont'd.*] Dear Alejandro: I stole some oil paints from my father. And my mother ordered a special easel for me so I can paint lying down in bed ...

THE FRIDAS I SEE IN THESE FACES ROAM THE WORLD—

WHILE I LIE HERE DIPPING BRUSHES INTO PAINT THE COLOR OF MY HEART

TO CREATE THE FRIDA I WANT TO BE ...

FRIDA: [*Cont'd.*] WHAT I HOPE, WHAT I AM, WHAT I KNOW.

So Alex, I am painting this for you—my breasts and nipples. A magic talisman. So that one day soon, very soon, you will come back to me.

[*Musical interlude, representing* FRIDA's *gradual recovery. She slowly begins to walk—at first painfully, and then, as she becomes stronger, with great ease and exuberance.*]

SCENE 4

FRIDA MEETS DIEGO. 1927

DIEGO *is high up on a scaffold working on his mural in the* PREPARATORIA. LUPE MARIN**, *his wife at that time, poses for him.* DIEGO *is very intent on his work.* FRIDA *enters, dragging a reluctant* CRISTINA *behind her.* FRIDA *walks with a slight limp on her right side. They hide behind a column.* LUPE** *becomes restless with posing and tries to get* DIEGO's *attention by singing a seductive tango.*

CRISTINA: Is that HIM!?

FRIDA: Yes . . . the greatest painter in the world . . .

CRISTINA: [*Incredulously, as the words spill out too loudly.*] That's Diego Rivera!??

FRIDA: Shh!

[LUPE** *begins to sing, moving seductively around* DIEGO*.]

DIEGO: Lupe, can't you hold still?!

LUPE**: DIEGO . . . CAN'T YOU STOP TO LOOK INTO MY EYES?

IF I DANCE FOR YOU? WILL YOU LOOK AT LUPE THEN?

DIEGO: I look at you all the time, Lupe.

LUPE**: WILL YOU LET ME PAINT MY NAME ON YOUR LIPS WITH MY TONGUE?

LUPE: [*Cont'd.*] WILL YOU LET ME TASTE YOUR MILK WHITE, BABY SKIN?

[*Suddenly spotting another woman's face in the mural; outraged.*] WHO IS THAT WOMAN YOU'RE SO BUSY PAINTING IN YOUR MURAL?

WHO IS THAT WOMAN — SHE ISN'T ME?!

I'VE SEEN HER BEFORE, SNIFFING AROUND OUR BACKDOOR —

LIKE A CAT IN HEAT...HANGING AROUND YOU LIKE A WHORE!

DIEGO: FOR A PAINTER...NEW MODELS ARE ESSEN-TIAL—

FRESH BLOOD TO MIX IN WITH HIS PAINTS.

A PAINTER LIVES FOR INSPIRATION,

THAT DOESN'T MEAN I DON'T LOVE YOU, LUPE.

LUPE**: It's hard to believe you could need more woman than me for your satisfaction.

DIEGO: You distract me. You're too beautiful. Go away, niña, go play cards, and then later we'll make love.

LUPE**: ¡MIRAME, SEÑOR PINTOR!

[*They kiss.*]

LUPE**: [*Cont'd.*] Mmmm...you always taste like fresh-cooked chicken.

DIEGO: My women never go hungry!

[*He becomes more passionate.* FRIDA *and* CRISTI *begin to giggle.*]

FRIDA: [*Full of high energy.*] Isn't he adorable?

CRISTINA: He looks so dirty!

FRIDA: So what? I'll bathe him!

CRISTINA: And he's got such a big pot-belly! Oooey!

[*Score #4B*]

FRIDA: Cristi! Don't you understand?! It doesn't matter what he

FRIDA: [*Cont'd.*] looks like—he's a genius...Imagine life with a man like that! He could teach me everything! Everything I need to know...

I'm going to tell him "Diego Rivera, look at me! You don't know who I am now, but one day I'll have your son!"

CRISTINA: What about Alejandro?

FRIDA: We're just pals now. I need love "con un hombre!"

CRISTINA: ¡Ay qué atrevida!! But he's so old! You wouldn't dare!

FRIDA: Wouldn't I? [*She approaches the scaffold and shouts up to* DIEGO.] Diego Rivera! Diego Rivera!

CRISTINA: ¡Qué sinvergüenza! Come back! ¡Ay Dios mío! Be careful!

[*The four sing a quartet.*]

FRIDA: DIEGO RIVERA!

LUPE**: I THINK WE HAVE AN AUDIENCE.

CRISTINA: FRIDA, YOU'RE CRAZY!

LUPE**: LET'S GIVE THEM A LITTLE SHOW.

[LUPE** *lunges at* DIEGO *who turns to* FRIDA *instead.* CRISTINA *runs to hide behind the scaffold.*]

DIEGO: YES?

FRIDA: COULD YOU PLEASE COME DOWN TO ME?

CRISTINA: BE CAREFUL...

DIEGO: WHAT DO YOU WANT? I'M WORKING?

LUPE**: GO AWAY!

FRIDA: I HAVE SOMETHING IMPORTANT TO SHOW YOU!

CRISTINA: YOU CAN'T TELL FRIDA WHAT TO DO ABOUT ANYTHING!

I'M JUST HER BABY SISTER—WHAT DO I KNOW ABOUT MEN?!

LUPE**: YES . . . HURRY DOWN. MAYBE SHE'S NOT WEAR-ING ANY PANTIES!

DIEGO: LUPE! YOUR SUSPICIONS!

THERE IS SOMETHING IN HER VOICE.

FRIDA: I HAVE SOMETHING I WANT YOU TO SEE.

LUPE**: SO WHAT AM I, DIEGO!? DON'T YOU DARE TO LEAVE ME UP HERE! DIEGO!

FRIDA: JUST COME DOWN FOR A MOMENT.

DIEGO: [To FRIDA.] ALL RIGHT. ONE MOMENT . . .

[He begins to descend the scaffold slowly.]

I'LL BE RIGHT DOWN.

LUPE**: [To DIEGO.] COME BACK HERE!

[To FRIDA.] HOW DARE YOU!

CRISTINA: [With admiration.] I KNOW ONE THING MY DEAR SISTER, MY DEAR FRIDA . . .

FRIDA: [To LUPE.] I'M NOT AFRAID OF YOU.

CRISTINA: I WISH I COULD BE MORE LIKE YOU —

LUPE**: [Shouting to FRIDA.] I could tear your little tits off with my teeth!

CRISTINA: — EVERY NOW AND THEN!

FRIDA: [To LUPE.] DON'T BE MY ENEMY —

LUPE**: GOOD FOR YOU.

CRISTINA: [To audience.] ABOUT CONVENTION, FRIDA COULDN'T CARE LESS—

FRIDA: YOU'RE MUCH TOO BEAUTIFUL FOR THAT.

LUPE**: [To FRIDA] YOU'RE NOT AFRAID OF ME . . .

CRISTINA: TO TEST THE WATERS SHE PLUNGES IN HEADFIRST!

CRISTI TAKES A LITTLE LONGER—

LUPE**: SHE REMINDS ME OF MYSELF.

CRISTINA: I DON'T BELIEVE IN CHANCE OR FATE.

LUPE**: [*To* FRIDA.] Watch out, little one. He's the enemy... he'll break your heart. [LUPE** *exits.*]

CRISTINA: I TAKE MY TIME SO I CAN CHANGE MY MIND BEFORE IT IS TOO LATE.

Come on, Frida, let's go before—

[DIEGO *appears from behind the scaffold and sees the girls. He seems surprised by how young they are.*]

DIEGO: Little girls?! Shouldn't you be in school?

[CRISTINA *runs off, intimidated by* DIEGO's *presence.*]

FRIDA: I'm not here to flirt with you or anything stupid like that! I brought some of my paintings and I just need you to tell me, if they're any good!

[FRIDA *lays the paintings down on the ground.* DIEGO *looks at them carefully, in silence.*]

FRIDA: [*Cont'd.*] Look, I'm serious. I have to be able to support myself. So I need to know—do I paint or do I do something else?

DIEGO: [*With admiration for both* FRIDA *and her paintings.*] You should paint.

FRIDA: [*With growing excitement.*] Really? D'you mean that?

DIEGO: [*Laughs, enjoying* FRIDA.] Yes... I do.

[FRIDA *looks hesitant.*]

DIEGO: [*Cont'd.*] Now what's the matter?

FRIDA: What if you're just trying to sweet-talk me?

DIEGO: Why would I?

FRIDA: [*Provocatively.*] To get me in bed. They say you'll sleep with any woman who's not an absolute dog.

DIEGO: [*Amused.*] Go and paint some more, niña. I'll try to come to your house next Sunday to see what you've done and tell you what I think.

FRIDA: [*Elated.*] Okay! I live in Coyoacan, Avenida Londres, number 126. [*She starts to exit.*] My name is Frida.

[*She begins to exit, but then turns back.*] Kahlo. [*She exits.*]

[*A door appears, representing the Kahlo home.* DIEGO *knocks. It opens.* GUILLERMO KAHLO**, FRIDA's *father, steps out.*]

GUILLERMO KAHLO**: So now it's every Sunday. [*Pause.*] You're not in love with my daughter, are you?

DIEGO: Why else would I come all this way?

GUILLERMO KAHLO**: [*Trying to warn* DIEGO *off* FRIDA.] You do know that she'll need special care . . . she could be an invalid for most of her life . . .

[DIEGO *nods.*]

GUILLERMO KAHLO**: [*Cont'd.*] She's not pretty, but she is very intelligent.

[DIEGO *is amused.*]

GUILLERMO KAHLO**: [*Cont'd.*] Also, she's a devil!

[DIEGO's *smile gets broader.*]

DIEGO: I know! That's why I love her!

GUILLERMO KAHLO**: Well, I've warned you!

[KAHLO** *closes door. They exit. Door moves up/out revealing* FRIDA *and* DIEGO *who stand some distance apart. They move closer and closer during the duet, to represent their growing intimacy, until they are standing together as if at a wedding ceremony.*]

DIEGO: PALOMA DE MI ALMA, NIÑA DE MI CORAZON . . .

FRIDA: CONTIGO SOY COMPLETA, MIS PENAS DESAPARECEN.

I FEEL YOUR POWER LIKE THE WALL OF A TEMPLE ON MY BACK

HOLDING ME UP, STRAIGHTENING MY LEGS.

DIEGO: FRIDA—A BOLD BEAUTY BORN OF PAIN

JOIN ME IN A LOVE BEYOND CONVENTION—

UNAFRAID OF LIFE'S DARKER TINTS

YOU CREATE YOUR LIFE IN COLORS

NO ONE ELSE DARE TOUCH.

FRIDA: DIEGO . . .   DIEGO: LIKE A RIPE FRUIT
WITH HIS WARM EYES —   OF A SINGULAR TREE
HIS GENTLE BREATH —   I'LL DEVOUR HER.
HE TASTED ME.

FRIDA: TAKE ME AWAY AND TEACH ME THE WONDERS
OF YOUR WORLD.

DIEGO: SAVOUR LIFE LIKE A RIPE PEACH:

FOLLOW VOICES TO UNKNOWN PLACES.

FRIDA: YOUR WARM, SWEATY HANDS, STAINED PLAS-
TER WHITE,

WILL LEAD ME WHERE I COULD NEVER GO
ALONE.

DIEGO: LET ME AWAKEN TO THE SOUND OF YOUR
LAUGH—

THAT SOUND MAKES AN OLD MAN YOUNG
AGAIN.

FRIDA: MI ALMA, YOU TAKE MY SICKNESS AWAY, YO SOY
COMPLETA.

DIEGO: ¡PALOMA DE MI ALMA, NIÑA DE MI CORAZON!

FRIDA & DIEGO: ¡MI CORAZON!

[*THE WEDDING:* FRIDA *and* DIEGO *kiss as the* WEDDING
GUESTS** *enter and sing a lusty, mariachi-style wedding serenade.
Birds fly on with a ribbon retablo announcing the wedding. (cf.
Kahlo:* Frida and Diego Rivera, 1931). *The wedding party in-
cludes* GUILLERMO**, ALEJANDRO, CRISTINA *and a bizarre pro-
cession of other guests** wearing masks based on* FRIDA'S *paintings*
Magnolias, The Flower of Life, *and* Diego and I.]

WEDDING GUESTS: ¡FELICIDADES! ¡FELICIDADES! QUE
DIOS LOS CUIDE TODOS SUS DIAS. (TODA LA VIDA.)

¡FELICIDADES! ¡FELICIDADES! QUE DIOS LOS
GUARDE SIEMPRE FELIZ.

WEDDING GUESTS: [*Cont'd.*]¡FELICIDADES! ¡FELICIDADES! DIOS LOS BENDIGA EN ESTE DIA.

VIVAN LOS NOVIOS Y LA ALEGRIA. QUE DIOS LOS GUARDE SIEMPRE FELIZ.

[*As the ceremony begins, two* CALAVERAS *enter carrying a moon and a sun. They enact a parody of the ceremony in which the moon and the sun symbolize the union between* FRIDA *and* DIEGO.]

FRIDA: YOU ARE THE SUN TO MY MOON

FRIDA & DIEGO: TOGETHER THE PERFECT UNIVERSE

FRIDA: WHERE LOVE WILL SHINE FROM YOUR FACE ONTO MINE.

A MAN WHO'S A BOY I WANT FOR MY OWN.

DIEGO: REMEMBER MY SWEET FRIDA

TOGETHER THE SUN AND THE MOON MAY LIGHT UP THE SKY

BUT EACH MUST FOLLOW ITS OWN ORBIT—

NEVER THE SAME SIZE.

FRIDA & DIEGO: TOGETHER OUR BRUSHES WILL BRING GODS BACK TO THE TEMPLES.

TOGETHER WE'LL PAINT A GOLDEN RING AROUND THE WORLD.

[*The following lines overlap.*]

CRISTINA: I WARNED HER...I KNEW SHE'D FALL IN LOVE TOO FAST.

ALEJANDRO: I WAS HER FIRST LOVE...IS DIEGO MEANT TO BE HER LAST?

GUILLERMO**: SHE'S A DEVIL...BUT I LOVE HER

CRISTI: I HOPE HE'LL TREAT HER WELL.

FRIDA: YOU ARE THE SUN TO MY MOON—

GUILLERMO**: REMEMBER MY SWEET FRIDA...

FRIDA: TOGETHER THE PERFECT UNIVERSE—

GUILLERMO**: I HOPE HE'LL TREAT HER WELL.

FRIDA: WHERE LOVE WILL SHINE FROM YOUR FACE ONTO MINE...

DIEGO: REMEMBER, MY SWEET FRIDA,

TOGETHER THE SUN AND MOON MAY LIGHT UP THE SKY.

BUT EACH TRAVELS ITS OWN ORBIT—

[LUPE** *makes a dramatic entrance.*]

LUPE**: [*To* FRIDA.] BEWARE ALL THAT LIGHT—

IT WILL BLIND YOUR LITTLE SOUL!

YOU'LL FEEL THE PAINFUL NIPS

THAT LOVE CUTS FROM HEAD TO TOE.

FRIDA: A MAN WHO'S A BOY, I'LL HAVE FOR MY OWN.

ALEJANDRO: HE'LL GIVE HER EVERYTHING—I CAN TELL.

GUILLERMO**: HE IS MARRYING A CHILD WHO LOVES HIM LIKE A MOTHER.

LUPE**: HOW CAN HE MARRY THAT MONSTER IN BRAIDS?

CAN'T HE SEE WHAT SHE WANTS FROM HIS SKIN?

A MINOR PAINTER ATTACHED TO A GIANT—

IT'S FAME AND FORTUNE SHE WANTS FROM HIM.

[*Spoken.*] ¡Miren!

[LUPE** *moves to* FRIDA, *grabs her, lifts her skirt to reveal her withered leg, then lifts her own skirt.*]

LUPE**: [*Cont'd.*] [*To* DIEGO] You see what you're getting and you see what you had! You're a fool!! Pinche Hombre!!

[*The orchestra plays the rhythm of a well-known Mexican curse as* LUPE** *exits in a huff. General laughter, uproar. The* WEDDING GUESTS *applaud.*]

FRIDA & DIEGO: I WANT YOU SWEET COLOSSUS!/MY LIT-TLE DOVE!

CRISTINA & WEDDING GUESTS: ¡Que vivan los novios!

[*The* GUESTS *explode into an orgy of movement,* FRIDA *dances with* GUILLERMO, *then* ALEJANDRO, *then* DIEGO, *who picks her up and carries her off as the others continue to dance and the lights slowly fade.*]

WEDDING GUESTS: FELICIDADES! FELICIDADES! QUE DIOS LOS CUIDE TODOS SUS DIAS.

FELICIDADES, FELICIDADES! QUE DIOS LOS GUARDE SIEMPRE FELIZ.

FELICIDADES, FELICIDADES! QUE DIOS LOS BENDIGA EN ESTE DIA.

VIVAN LOS NOVIOS Y LA ALEGRIA. QUE DIOS LOS GUARDE SIEMPRE FELIZ.

SCENE 5

1930. DIEGO'S MURALS ARE CRITICISED.

Lights up on DIEGO *on his scaffold, painting Zapata mural.* BUSI-NESSMEN* *enter. They pause beneath. On the other side of the stage,* FRIDA *sketches in a small notebook.*

DIEGO: [*Calling down to* FRIDA.]What do you think, niña fista?

FRIDA: [*Looking up, sizing up the problem quickly.*] No balance. Too much red. Add some green.

DIEGO: Claro.

FRIDA: [*Indicating a horse in the mural.*] And, Sapo-rana, the horse Zapata rode was black.

DIEGO: But white is more heroic. The people need heroes. And a hero needs a heroic setting.

FRIDA: [*Laughs.*] But it's not the truth!

DIEGO: I'm a revolutionary artist! I paint what I want—

[*Grotesque March: The* CHORUS *enters—five men each holding a huge three-sided rotating mask that represents the* GOVERNMENT, *the* BUSINESSMEN, *the* COMMUNIST PARTY. *All these elements in the society were highly critical of* DIEGO *and were out to destroy him.*]

MEN'S CHORUS: REVOLUTIONARY! REVOLUTIONARY! REVOLUTIONARY! REVOLUTIONARY!

DIEGO: I'M A REVOLUTIONARY ARTIST! I PAINT WHAT I WANT—

COMMUNISTS: I SPIT IN YOUR EYE!

YOU PAINT ONLY FOR THE RICH—NOT THE POOR.

WHAT THE POOR PEOPLE NEED IS BREAD—

NOT THE HOT AIR THAT FLOATS AROUND IN YOUR HEAD!

FRIDA: [*Jumping up on the scaffolding.*] IDIOTS! CAN'T YOU SEE?! THIS MAN SEES

THROUGH THE EYES OF THE POOR.

HE SHOWS TO US A BETTER WORLD—PAINTING OUR MEXICAN PEOPLE.

COMMUNISTS: IF YOU'RE A MAN DEFEND YOURSELF! COME DOWN AND FIGHT!

[DIEGO *laughs, proud and amused by* FRIDA'*s defense.*]

DIEGO: WHAT A TIGRESS! SHE'S GOT BALLS! COJONES DE ORO!

I LOVE YOU MORE THAN ANY WOMAN IS LOVED BY MAN.

FRIDA: ¡MARICÓNES! CAN'T YOU SEE THIS MAN IS A MAN WITHOUT EQUAL!?

COMMUNISTS: THIS HYPOCRITE MUST BE STOPPED—HIS IDEALS ARE SPENT.

HE PAINTS TO KISS THE ASS OF THE NEW GOVERNMENT.

THE GOVERNMENT: SHOOT HIM DEAD! STOP HIM PAINT-ING!

THIS HOTHEAD IS A COMMUNIST AGENT!

COMMUNISTS: ¡MENTIROSO! ¡MARICÓN! YOU'RE THE ONE WHO BETRAYED YOUR PEOPLE!

FRIDA: YOU IMBECILES WITH FALSE PRIDE—YOU ENVY HIS FAME—

YOU'RE CONTENT TO PLAY THE PAWNS IN A NEW FASCIST GAME!

THE GOVERNMENT: NO MORE WALLS! NO COMMISSIONS!

THIS TRASH IS INCITING THE PEASANTS!

FRIDA: Government pigs!

DIEGO: Don't waste your breath on them, Frida.

FRIDA: I FIGHT BESIDE MY MAN, MARICÓNES! JUST TRY TO FIGHT US.

ALL OF YOU! GOVERNMENT, OUR OWN PARTY, BUSINESSMEN!

BUSINESSMEN: HE DEFACES OUR ARCHITECTURE WITH HIS MONSTROUS CREATION.

IT'S NOT ART, IT'S NOT CUBISM!

IT'S COMMUNIST SYMBOLISM.

AND SINCE WHEN DOES A WORKER WEAR

A PERFECTLY PRESSED SHIRT WITHOUT A SINGLE TEAR?!

COMMUNISTS, GOV'T AGENTS & BUSINESSMEN: AND THOSE UGLY, NAKED WOMEN!

IMAGINE GOING TO BED WITH ONE OF THEM.

DIEGO: BARBARIANS! You wouldn't fuck a pyramid, but that doesn't mean it's not art!

FRIDA: ¡Cabrones! ¡Pendejos!

DIEGO: Bourgeois pigs! What do you know about art?

DIEGO: [*Cont'd.*] ART IS HAM FOR THE COMMON MAN
    TO BREATHE LIKE AIR—
    FOR ALL TO SHARE.
    NOT CAVIAR FOR THE RICH
    TO SNACK ON WHEN THEY'VE GOT THE ITCH.
    NOT BEHIND PRIVATE WALLS
    NOR IN EXCLUSIVE HALLS.
    ART IS FOR THE COMMON MAN
    TO CELEBRATE HIS DEEDS
    AND THE LABOUR OF HIS HANDS
    IN THE FIELDS AND FACTORIES.
    ART IS HAM FOR THE COMMON MAN
    FOR ALL TO SHARE!

[DIEGO *takes his gun out of the holster around his waist. He shoots his gun into the air.*]

Now get the hell out of here! I'm working!

[*Everyone* runs out.* FRIDA *&* DIEGO *laugh. Then,* DIEGO *gets serious.*]

DIEGO: [*Cont'd.*] That's it! That's enough! We're getting out of Mexico! I can't work with everyone against me!

FRIDA: I can't just go like that! Like nothing! What about my family? Our friends? Our work! The Party! Everything!

DIEGO: The Party has betrayed me! All my commissions have been cancelled! Mexico's revolution is over!
    [*Pause.*] Rockefeller and Ford have invited me. That's where we'll carry on the fight — we'll go North —

FRIDA: North! To that bloodsucking United States?!

DIEGO: Why not? After all you must know your enemy before conquering him.

FRIDA: I am not going! You'll have to kill me first!

[*Voices of returning* BUSINESSMEN** *and* COMMUNISTS** *are* *heard. Gunshots. Bullet holes appear in the mural.* FRIDA *and* DIEGO *dive to safety. Blackout.*]

SCENE 6

THE RIVERAS DRESS FOR DINNER WITH THE ROCKE-
FELLERS AND FORDS, 1933. THE MILLIONAIRE'S
BANQUET—WHERE FRIDA AND DIEGO DINE WITH
THE CAPITALISTS ON TICKER TAPE

All images of the Mexican landscape move out and are replaced with those of the United States (cf Kahlo, My Dress Hangs There, *also* Standing on the Boundary between Mexico and the USA *and* Memory) *A* CALAVERA *dressed as Uncle Sam plays American jazz on a trumpet.* FRIDA, *dressed in her Tehuana costume, moves in and stands in front of a column, as in the painting* My Dress Hangs There.

FRIDA: Pastels are a poison. Once carnation pink is in your soul, you never know who you really are. I am Mexico. And that's how they must see me. I create the story of my life with every ribbon, every ring—I wear two on each finger... This way I become my grandmother's mother and her mother before her. Or anything else I chose to be... The Tehuana is perfect, the everyday dress of the forgotten people. It's something different for these Yanquis from "down Mexico way!" It was Diego's idea—to cover the limp, but I really love these dresses...

[DIEGO *enters from behind the image of Mae West, dressed in a tuxedo.*]

FRIDA: [*Cont'd.*] [*Angrily.*] Why the hell are you wearing that? Is this a costume party we're going to?

DIEGO: [*Enjoying himself.*] It's not every day I get to dress like a capitalist.

[*Honking of a car horn. A* CALAVERA *dressed as a chauffeur drives a cut out of a new Ford onstage.* DIEGO *whistles.*]

DIEGO: [*Cont'd.*] ¡Hijo de la chingada puta! Look what Ford sent to get us! Incredible! What a machine!

FRIDA: A toy for the rich! I'm not riding in *that*!

DIEGO: C'mon, Frida.

[DIEGO *climbs in.* FRIDA *hesitates then follows him into the car.*]

FRIDA: Damn you!

[*The car drives off. The New York cityscape moves off to reveal the Rockefeller Banquet (Rivera:* The Night of the Rich.*) A table is set up by the* CALAVERAS. *Around it sit the* RICH PEOPLE* *of the United States, including* MR. AND MRS. HENRY FORD*, MR. AND MRS. NELSON ROCKEFELLER*, *and* MR. JOHN D. ROCKEFELLER, SR.*. *They dine on gold ticker tape. The* RICH PEOPLE* *are much larger than life-size. The women wear long, pastel, floor-length evening gowns. Sound of ticker tape as a long roll of it is passed from hand to hand.*]

[*A* CALAVERA *dressed like a* BANDLEADER *enters holding a megaphone.*]

CALAVERA & THE RICH*: THE PEOPLE HERE ARE HAPPY— AS HAPPY AS CAN BE.

I THINK IT'S SOMETHING IN THE AIR—THAT SMELLS LIKE BEING FREE.

THE RICH*: WE'RE SO HAPPY TO BE US—MONEY'S NICE TO HAVE AROUND.

LOVE THAT JINGLE-JANGLE SOUND.

FORD*: FREE TO CHOOSE THE WAY YOU WISH TO MAKE A BUCK.

ROCKEFELLER*: FREE TO FIND A BETTER LIFE WITH JUST A LITTLE LUCK!

THE RICH*: IN AMERICA EVERYONE CAN EAT STEAKS.

THE RICH* (WOMEN): MONEY'S NICE TO HAVE AROUND.

FORD*: ALL IT TAKES IS HARD WORK AND A FEW LUCKY BREAKS.

THE RICH*: LOVE THAT JINGLE-JANGLE SOUND.

MRS. ROCKEFELLER*: BUT WE NEED MORE THAN PRIME BEEF TO KEEP US ALIVE.

MRS. FORD*: THE KEY TO OUR SUSTENANCE IS TO OWN A PICASSO—

PERHAPS FOUR OR FIVE.

ROCKEFELLER*: [*Laughing.*] WE HAVE THE BRILLIANCE, WE HAVE THE MILLIONS

TO COMMISSION NEW PAINTINGS TO HANG ON OUR WALLS

AND LEND THEM TO MUSEUMS

SO ANYONE CAN SEE THEM IN THEIR HALLS.

THE RICH*: WE'RE SO CREATIVE WITH OUR MONEY—

WE BUY OUR OWN MILK AND HONEY!

WHEN WE BUY ART, OUR PLACE IN HISTORY IS REVEALED—

OUR SOPHISTICATION CAN'T BE CONCEALED!

[*They raise their glasses in a toast.*]

TO ART! TO ART! TO ART!

[*Fanfare.*]

CALAVERA/BANDLEADER: Here he is! The Great Diego Rivera... and wife.

[*The Riveras enter,* DIEGO *in a tuxedo and* FRIDA *in her Tehuana dress.* THE RICH *all raise their glasses in a toast.*]

ROCKEFELLER*: TO OUR NEW FRIENDS FROM LANDS AFAR!

FORD*: TO NEW IDEAS WITH CHRISTIAN OUTLOOKS.

DIEGO: TO MR. FORD'S AMAZING CARS!

FRIDA: TO NEW LOVES AND LOVERS...

[*Everyone stares at her.*]

FRIDA: [*Cont'd.*] OF ART!

THE RICH*: TO ART!

[*Goblets are clinked. They all sip elegantly except for* FRIDA, *who throws back her drink.* FRIDA *notices them watching her and laughs.*]

MRS. ROCKEFELLER*: [*To* DIEGO, *insincerely.*] Delightful, isn't she?

DIEGO: She's more than that.

FRIDA: [*Smiling sweetly.*] She's right here! She can hear you.

MRS. ROCKEFELLER*: Oh, sorry, I—I—Why yes . . . What an interesting dress!

[FRIDA *stares menacingly at her.*]

MRS. FORD*: It's very, it's . . . Mexican, isn't it?

FRIDA: Yes! Like me!

MRS. FORD*: How intriguing . . . [*Whispering in* FORD'*s ear.*]

FRIDA: Mr. Ford, is it really true? I heard you don't like Jews . . .

[*Awkward coughs from the* RICH.]

FRIDA: [*Cont'd.*] I'm just asking for my father. He's Jewish, you know . . .

[*Deathly silence.*]

MRS. FORD*: How really very interesting you are, Mrs. "Riv-i-era" . . .

DIEGO: [DIEGO *laughs, coming to the rescue by breaking the tension.*] Frida, chiquita, you're priceless!

FRIDA: [*To* DIEGO.] I can't stand women who wear pink! Just how low will you let yourself stoop??

DIEGO: Don't you see we are in Rome? We must dine with the devil.

[*The* RICH *all turn away from* FRIDA *to concentrate all their attention on* DIEGO.]

THE RICH*: [*Raising their goblets.*] To Diego! To Diego Rivera!

FRIDA: [*To* DIEGO.] WHAT THE HELL ARE WE DOING IN THIS VERY NORTH AMERICA?

IT'S MADE YOU CRAZY. YOU'RE TURNING INTO ONE OF THEM!

ROCKEFELLER*: Rivera, tell us more.

DIEGO: WELL, YOUR GAME OF FOOTBALL IS SPLENDID FOR A START—

A POWERFUL LIVING PICTURE...IT'S A NEW FORM OF ART!

FORD*: That's capital, Diego Rivera!

FRIDA: DOESN'T ANYONE NOTICE THERE ARE PEOPLE STANDING IN BREADLINES?

[*Awkward silence while* THE RICH* *all stare at* FRIDA *and then turn away, ignoring her question.*]

DIEGO: AND YOUR AMERICAN SKYSCRAPERS! EXTRAORDINARY!

LIKE PRE-COLUMBIAN ARTIFACTS—

ROCKEFELLER*: I LIKE THAT! PRE-COLUMBIAN ARTIFACTS!

FRIDA: If anyone bothered to ask me— [*Getting louder.*]

IF ANYONE BOTHERED TO ASK ME

I'D SAY YOUR SKYSCRAPERS LOOK LIKE...TOMBSTONES...

[*Awkward pause.*]

DIEGO: [*He ignores her.*] Well, Ford's the real genius—

[THE RICH* *turn towards him with a sigh of relief.*]

DIEGO: [*Cont'd.*] And his machines are the true subject of our day!

FORD*: Yes. Efficient and cheap. That's how I like it!

[*He laughs.* EVERYONE *follows his lead. They all sit and begin to consume gold-colored ticker-tape.* FRIDA *suddenly pushes her plate away.*]

FRIDA: I won't sit here eating steak, when there are people in the street who don't have a thing to eat! [*Under her breath to* DIEGO.] Let's get the hell out of here before I...

[*She starts to pull him away but he gently stops her.*]

DIEGO: Frida... Frida...

ROCKEFELLER*: Not so soon, please, not so soon... We need to know how you intend to decorate the wall of my new building—Rockefeller Center!
[*Amused with himself.*] Will your art tell the people what we want them to think?

[*Polite laughter and then* DIEGO *sings the following verse like a hymn.*]

DIEGO: INTO OLD BOTTLES I'LL POUR NEW WINE.

I'LL PAINT THE STORY OF A NEW MANKIND.

SCIENCE, FACTORIES, ASSEMBLY LINES...

THAT'S THE STORY OF OUR TIME!

ROCKEFELLER*: Sounds good enough to me! You've got a deal fella!

THE RICH*: Hurrah! Hurrah!

FRIDA: ¡Ay, que sinvergüenza! Now, we're in for it!

DIEGO: And now to celebrate—Frida let's teach them to dance a jarabe in this magnificent North America!

[*Everyone joins in a wild jarabe dance.* FRIDA *leads* FORD* *in the dance.* DIEGO *dances with* MRS. ROCKEFELLER*.]

DIEGO: [*Noticing* FRIDA.] You're flirting!

FRIDA: [*Annoyed.*] Just trying to keep it interesting...

[*Dance finishes. Blackout.*]

SCENE 7

DIEGO LOSES HIS WALL AND FRIDA LOSES HER BABY

BARKER/CALAVERA *appears on the scaffold. A drumroll.*

BARKER/CALAVERA: Tickets! Tickets! Get your tickets here to watch the great Mexican painter, the fabulous Diego Rivera at work. Diego Rivera at Rockefeller Center. Get your tickets here!

[*Lights up on* DIEGO *painting the mural* Man at the Crossroads

(including figure of Lenin), on top of scaffolding at the RCA build-
ing, Rockefeller Center. People enter to watch DIEGO *at work.*
FRIDA *stands behind the crowd, watching the proceedings. Lights*
emphasize FRIDA *who is being interviewed by a reporter.*]

FRIDA: Yes, I'm also an artist... but, not like Diego. Little things...
nothing serious... No, I didn't study with him or anyone else.
One day, I just started to paint... He paints the big outside, and
I paint the secrets inside... It makes for a very pretty marriage.
Oh...

    [*She leans forward and whispers mischievously.*] And there's
only one thing Diego likes to do almost as much as paint...

    [*Laughs.*] Make love... especially to me.

    No, it doesn't hurt. But I understand the question... me,
with my uterus pierced by a handrail—like a sword through a
bull. I'm small, but I have tough skin—It's the German in me,
I think. Or maybe the Jew. I know how to fight and what to
fight for. Love, sex, cigarettes and tequila. No, not painting...
that's just a fact, like taking a breath on a cold day—you see it
going out before it has a chance to go down—proving you're
alive... Self-portraits? Well, why not look out and see yourself
as others see you? I prefer to suffer in a Catholic way—publicly.
And I never complain... well, almost never. I simply paint...
and I want this baby.

[DIEGO *plays to the crowd. Laughter and applause.* FRIDA *moves*
downstage, isolating herself from the action around DIEGO. FRIDA
sits at her easel and begins painting. Soon she throws her brushes
down in frustration.]

FRIDA: I CANNOT DISTRACT DIEGO—

HE HAS HIS WORK THAT MUST COME FIRST.

BUT THIS ONE... BUT MAYBE THIS ONE.

I WANT TO HOLD THIS LITTLE DIEGO

GROWING INSIDE OF ME.

MY BODY BETRAYS ME, DIEGUITO...

DIEGO: Why don't you paint something? It'll help you pass the
time...

[ROCKEFELLER* *enters. He looks at the mural. There is a sense of unease amongst the crowd.*]

ROCKEFELLER: [*Suddenly suspicious.*] That head... on the wall... surely it couldn't be the head of a... a certain Russian... Could it?

DIEGO: Why not?

ROCKEFELLER: There must be some mistake here, fella.

FRIDA: DIEGUITO, MI HIJITO—

YOUR FATHER WANTS TO BE MY ONLY SON.

HE DOESN'T WANT TO BE A FATHER.

[*From this moment,* DIEGO *interacts simultaneously with both* ROCKEFELLER* *and* FRIDA]

DIEGO: [*To* FRIDA.] Maybe you should learn to drive a car.
[*To* ROCKEFELLER] You suggested the theme "Hope For the Future," didn't you?

ROCKEFELLER: Well—yes!

DIEGO: Well then, who else did you expect me to paint? [*Indicates the head of Lenin.*] Who else provides us with hope for the future? Lenin, only Lenin!

ROCKEFELLER: But... listen fella...

FRIDA: NO... I CANNOT AFFORD TO LOSE DIEGO.

I MUST NEVER LOSE HIS SCENT FROM MY PILLOW.

BUT THIS ONE... BUT THIS ONE...

THIS BABY I HAVE FELT. THIS ONE I'VE HAD TIME TO LOVE.

Diego, I'm...

DIEGO: Frida, don't make me ask you again! Have you seen the doctor?

FRIDA: Yes, yes, yes, I have! But what use is he? He says I must stay in bed—I would rather be dead!

ROCKEFELLER: You've gone and painted a communist! How can I

ROCKEFELLER: [*Cont'd.*] rent the office space now? This is a capitalistic place, Rivera. Red is not our color. Too bad you couldn't paint the stars and stripes! Here's your check. Hasta luego, Diego!

[*The mural disintegrates into pieces; newspaper headlines are shouted as the mural is destroyed: "VANDALISM" "RIVERA KNOCKOUT AT THE HANDS OF ROCKEFELLER FAMILY," New York Times, Feb. 13, 1934: "LENIN PAINTING DESTROYED AT NIGHT," "FRESH FUEL PROVIDED FOR POLITICAL ART CONTROVERSY" "RIVERA LOSES 100 POUNDS."*]

DIEGO: NO ONE HAS THE RIGHT TO ASSASSINATE HUMAN CREATION . . .

IN THIS OR ANY OTHER NATION.

[*There is a musical note of pain indicating the beginning of* FRIDA*'s miscarriage.*]

FRIDA: [*Clutching her stomach.*] Get a doctor!!

[*A piñata of a pregnant* FRIDA *is flown in. (cf. Kahlo,* Henry Ford Hospital, *1932.) The* CALAVERAS *enter, open the pregnant stomach and take out a purple orchid and other objects from the painting.*]

CALAVERA 1*: SHE LOOKS SO SMALL.

LIKE A GIRL OF TWELVE.

HER BRAIDS ARE WET WITH TEARS . . .

CALAVERA 2*: HUGE CLOTS OF BLOOD AND FRIDA

CALAVERA 1* & 2*: SCREAMING . . .

[CALAVERA 1 *hands the purple orchid to* FRIDA.]

CALAVERA 1* 2* & 3*: [*Giving* FRIDA *the orchid.*]

HERE IS AN ORCHID FROM DIEGO—

A LAVENDER FLOWER IN FULL BLOOM . . .

FRIDA: IT LOOKS LIKE MY BODY GAPING OPEN, SO EASY TO TEAR.

A LAVENDER ORCHID FROM DIEGO.

DIEGO: [*Standing on the scaffold.*] A woman is superior to a man—

CALAVERAS: [*Imitating* DIEGO.] A woman is superior to a man—

DIEGO: There's so much pain that she can stand...

CALAVERAS: [*Continuing their ridicule.*] There's so much pain that she can stand!

FRIDA: [*Empty of emotion.*] Drowned spiders... alive in alcohol... children are the days... and here is where I end.

DIEGO: FRIDA YOU'LL CREATE SOMETHING INCREDI-BLE OUT OF THIS.

FRIDA: Can I be complete without a child to call my own?

DIEGO: POURING YOUR AGONY ON CANVAS—

YOU'LL HEAL YOURSELF LIKE THIS.

FRIDA: I have a cat's luck—lucky me—I do not die so easily.

DIEGO: I CAN'T STAND TO SEE HOW YOU MAKE YOUR-SELF SUFFER,

BUT I DON'T NEED A CHILD TO PROVE I'M ALIVE.

CAN'T YOU SEE I NEED YOU, FRIDA,

NOW THEY'VE TURNED MY WORK TO DUST?

STAND BESIDE ME IN THE STRUGGLE, AGAINST ALL THAT IS UNJUST?

FRIDA, I CAN'T STAND TO SEE HOW YOU MAKE YOURSELF SUFFER.

BE MY FRIEND—MY WIFE, MY LOVER.

FRIDA: NO ONE SEES THE PAIN, THE PAIN YOU HAVE IN-SIDE YOUR HEART—

UNLESS YOU PAINT IT AS YOUR SOUL IS TORN APART!

I am hungry for home. I dream of a boat sailing back to Mexico...

DIEGO: But my work is here now! This is where I feel alive!

FRIDA: DIEGO, PLEASE, LET'S GO HOME...

[*As* FRIDA *and* DIEGO *turn to leave they are accompanied by a big sun* (DIEGO) *and a little moon* (FRIDA) *that move above a boat traveling back to Mexico.*]

ACT TWO

The structure of this act is to echo the surrealist element in FRIDA'*s painting: "Her fantasy was a product of her temperament, life and place: it was a way of coming to terms with reality . . . It is a magic of her longing for her images to have, like ex-votos, a certain efficacy." Frida said: "They thought I was a Surrealist, but I wasn't. I never painted dreams. I painted my own reality."*

SCENE 1

THE RIVERAS RETURN TO MEXICO

A large white scrim now covers the scaffolding from Act One. This backdrop will be used for shadow-puppet sequences which represent FRIDA'*s thoughts, emotional and psychological realities as expressed through the images contained in her work. Schematic renderings of* FRIDA *and* DIEGO'*s dual houses—the blue and pink houses at San Angel, stand on stage. They are sleek, modern shapes, surrounded by a wall or organ cacti and connected by a foot bridge. A Moon floats above* FRIDA'*s blue house and a Sun above* DIEGO'*s pink house.*

FRIDA *throws open the door of her blue house. She watches the sunrise, full of joy at being back in Mexico.*

FRIDA: Finally . . . Home again!

THE SUN AND THE MOON ARE HOME AGAIN, IN MEXICO

WHERE I CAN BREATHE—WHERE I BELONG, IN MEXICO.

HERE IN SAN ANGEL, WE'LL BOTH BE FREE.

HE IN HIS PINK HOUSE, THE BLUE ONE'S FOR ME.

HOME IN MEXICO, WHERE I WANT TO BE!

WE'LL PAINT OUR LIVES HERE, DIEGO AND I—

FRIDA: [*Cont'd.*] ON CANVAS AND PLASTER AND PIECES OF TIN.

FULL OF MY SEX, MY GRACE AND MY SIN.

HERE'S WHERE I'LL REST MY CHINGADA SPINE—

MEXICO...MEXICO IS MINE!

[FRIDA *knocks on* DIEGO*'s door.*]

FRIDA: Diego! Come look! Our first sunrise back home.

DIEGO: [*Entering from his pink house.*] Damn!

DAMN THE MEXICAN SUN!

MY LIFE WILL DRY UP LIKE THE CACTUS HERE!

FRIDA: MY HEART IS ROOTED IN THIS MAGENTA DUST.

DIEGO: DUST RAISED BY PEOPLE MOVING BACKWARDS!

DON'T YOU SEE, MY LIFE IS USELESS HERE?

MUJER, I CAN'T BE AT YOUR SIDE EVERY TIME YOU THINK YOU NEED ME.

AT LEAST, LET ME PAINT TO FORGET THE MISERY OF MEXICO.

Leave me alone!

[DIEGO *exits into his house, banging the door in anger.*]

FRIDA: ONLY A GREAT LOVE SURVIVES TWO DOORS BE-TWEEN.

[*A* PARADE OF WOMEN* *moves toward* DIEGO*'s Pink House and through the front door. As they enter the house, the lights go up and then down.* FRIDA *watches the parade and then says, with a shrug.*]

FRIDA: ¡Así es la vida!

I AM THE WISE AND FORGIVING WOMAN.

THE WORLD CAN GO TO HELL AS LONG AS WE ARE ONE—

THE PRIVATE MOON, THE PUBLIC SUN.

I'M THE WISE AND FORGIVING WOMAN...

FRIDA: [*Cont'd.*] IN SPITE OF WHAT YOU THINK AND DO
I KNOW YOU ALWAYS LOVE ME TOO.

TRAGEDY IS FOOLISH, LIFE IS MUCH TOO SHORT!

I'M THE WISE AND FORGIVING WOMAN ...

I'LL ALLOW YOUR LITTLE SPORT!

[*The* PARADE OF WOMEN* *moving into* DIEGO's *house continues.*
FRIDA *suddenly sees* CRISTI *as part of the* PARADE.]

FRIDA: [*Calling out innocently.*] Cristi!

[CRISTI *pulls her scarf further over her head and quickly enters*
DIEGO's *house. The lights in* DIEGO's *house go off.* FRIDA *realizes
the truth of* CRISTI *and* DIEGO's *betrayal. Silence.*]

FRIDA: Oh, Diego, not Cristi! Please, not Cristi! ...

[FRIDA *moves to a table. (ref:* The Wounded Table*). She cuts
prickly pears. (ref:* Fruits of the Earth*).*]

All the surgeon's knives never made me bleed as I am bleeding now ...

[*She slices one cleanly in half, reaches into it and with both hands,
viciously pulls out the red pulp. (ref.* Cactus Fruit, *1937) She runs
the fruit down every finger, grinding it into her skin. She takes a
pitcher of water and passes it over her hands. She sits in stunned silence for a moment.*]

SCENE 2

THE TROTSKYS** ARRIVE IN MEXICO

Russian music depicts TROTSKY's** *arrival in Mexico.* FRIDA *rises
to greet* TROTSKY** *as he enters.*

FRIDA: Querido Comrade Trotsky ...

YOUR VISIT TO MEXICO HAS BEEN DELICIOUS.

TROTSKY**: OH, YES, IT HAS ... NOT AS BIG AS RUSSIA
BUT CERTAINLY WARMER ...

FRIDA: [FRIDA *looks at him flirtatiously.*] YOU'VE HAD A GREAT INFLUENCE ON OUR LIVES.

TROTSKY**: [*Flirtatiously.*] ON YOU?

FRIDA: [*Evasively.*] ON DIEGO. HE HAS NEW ENERGY FOR HIS WORK.

HE'S SO BUSY THESE DAYS, I HARDLY SEE HIM...

TROTSKY**: A MAN SHOULD ALWAYS MAKE TIME FOR SUCH A BEAUTIFUL WOMAN.

DON'T YOU SEE IT'S YOU I WANT TO INFLUENCE?

[DIEGO *enters, having overheard the previous conversation.*]

DIEGO: TELL ME, LEON, WHY DID YOUR FELLOW RUS-SIANS THROW YOU OUT?

TROTSKY**: I CHOSE TO LEAVE, DIEGO—TO ESCAPE THEIR COWARDLY DOUBTS!

[TROTSKY** *moves downstage to a table where his wife* NATALIA** *is seated. She** is very depressed and sits tearing up* FRIDA'*s face from photographs.* DIEGO *strides up to* FRIDA *who sits at the wounded table. The two unhappy couples, each in their own houses, sing a Quartet.*]

NATALIA**: WHAT ARE YOU DOING WITH THAT WOMAN AND HER MUSTACHE?

TROTSKY**: DON'T BE RIDICULOUS.

NATALIA**: DO YOU PLAY RUSSIAN SONGS ON HER LITTLE WHITE BED?

DIEGO: THERE'S AN ANCIENT RAT IN MY HOUSE—

HE TAKES MY HOSPITALITY

AND MY WIFE, MY WIFE!

HIS WIZENED LITTLE TAIL LEAVES A TRAIL OF SE-MEN BY HER DOOR.

FRIDA: LISTEN TO "EL GRAN MACHO"—EL GRAN MA-CHO—

FRIDA: [*Cont'd.*] AFRAID YOU CAN'T COMPETE WITH HIS INTELLECTUAL CHARM?

TROTSKY**: NATALIA, SHE STIMULATES ME WITH HER MIND—

WE EXCHANGE IDEAS AND BOOKS.

NATALIA**: I'VE SEEN THE LOOKS YOU EXCHANGE!

DIEGO: HIS INTELLECT I TOO ADMIRED, UNTIL IT MOVED

FROM HIS HEAD, DOWN HIS CHEST, TO THAT WITHERED THIRD LEG.

NATALIA**: I'VE SEEN THE LOVE NOTES.

[*Lights up on* CRISTINA, *in a separate stage area, lighting candles as if at a mass.*]

CRISTINA: HIS BRUSH EXPOSED MY NAKEDNESS ON CANVAS—

HIS TOUCH EXPOSED MY HEART LIKE A LILY UNDER GLASS.

HE PAINTED HIS WIFE'S SISTER AND MADE LOVE TO HER—

I PRAY FOR FRIDA'S FORGIVENESS IN A PRIVATE MASS.

FRIDA: DIEGO, YOU DON'T UNDERSTAND—HIS SEX IS IN HIS BRAIN—

COMMITTED TO RELIEVE HIS COUNTRY'S PAIN.

DIEGO: I ADMIRED HIM... THE ANCIENT RAT.

SO COMMITTED THAT EVERY COUNTRY BUT MEXICO TURNED HIM AWAY.

FRIDA: THIS OLD MAN WHO BEFRIENDS YOUR WIFE SETS OFF ALARMS...

DIEGO: I OFFERED HIM MY HOME. I SHOULD HAVE OFFERED HIM A FIST,

DIEGO: [*Cont'd.*] INSTEAD OF GIVING HIM A HAND.

Which he bites.

FRIDA: He doesn't bite.

NATALIA**: SHE'S A DEMON, A DEMON DISGUISED AS A MEXICAN WHORE.

TROTSKY**: DON'T BE RIDICULOUS, NATALIA.

FRIDA: ¡PARA MACHO SI, PERO HEMBRA NO!

FOR THE MAN YES, WOMAN NO!

DIEGO: I'LL KILL HIM!

CRISTINA: EACH TIME HE ENTERED ME, I FELT ALIVE…
AND YET…

HOW COULD HE BETRAY HER? HOW COULD I?

MY MOTHER TAUGHT ME TO ASK FOR FORGIVE-NESS—

I'LL PRAY FOR FRIDA'S MERCY IN A PRIVATE MASS.

NATALIA** & FRIDA: DO YOU THINK I WANT TO LIVE IN THE SHADOW OF YOUR LIFE—

YOU PLAY AND I STAY HOME THE PERFECT WIFE?!

DIEGO & TROTSKY**: OTHER WOMEN ARE JUST DIVER-SIONS—YOU KNOW THAT'S THE TRUTH!

FRIDA & NATALIA**: WHY COULDN'T I BE ALL YOU NEEDED?

CRISTINA: I PRAY, DEAR FRIDA, YOU'LL FORGIVE…

ALL: WHY DO THOSE YOU LOVE THE MOST

KNOW BEST HOW TO TORMENT YOU?

WHY DO THOSE YOU LOVE THE MOST

KNOW BEST HOW TO TORMENT YOU?

[DIEGO *and* TROTSKY** *move away from their wives in exasperation and collide.*]

TROTSKY**: I heard you enjoy playing the great artist—dressed in tuxedo black.

DIEGO: I see why you surround yourself with such prison-like security. You make a man want to kill you!

TROTSKY**: How can you call yourself a Communist and rub elbows with the rich? You betrayed the Party!

DIEGO: You betrayed my trust!

I WARN YOU ONLY ONCE—STAY AWAY FROM MY DOOR!

TROTSKY**: [*Phonetically.*] Zhopa! [*Bastard.*]

DIEGO: ¡Vete al carajo! [*Go to hell.*]

TROTSKY**: Yop tvayu mat! [*Fuck off.*]

DIEGO: ¡No me jodas, hijo de tu chingada madre!! [*Don't fuck with me, you son-of-a-bitch!*]

[DIEGO *takes out his pistol and fires into the air.* TROTSKY** *&* NATALIA** *take fright and rush off.*]

I forbid him to come here anymore, Frida.

FRIDA: Hypocrite! You can't compare Trotsky to one of your sluts! He's a man of substance. A world leader! Not some cheap gringa tourist begging you to show her the pyramids and your prick! Don't throw your own shit back at me! I know what you've done!

DIEGO: Nothing you didn't know from the beginning. I've never tried to deceive you!

FRIDA: But with Cristi, Diego?! With my blood! How dare you?!

DIEGO: Stop playing games, Frida.

FRIDA: Games!?

DIEGO: Yes. Games. You set it up. You encouraged Cristi to model for me. What did you expect would happen with you sick in bed all the time? Leaving me alone to paint Cristi—Who is, after all, an irresistibly beautiful woman? And since we're talking about sex, Frida—what about you?

FRIDA: For me, it's not only a matter of sex, Diego! I don't just have sex...

I HAVE LOVE. I MAKE LOVE.

I LIKE THE URGENT FEELING OF A MAN'S HAND ON MY BACK—

THE SOFTNESS OF A WOMAN'S CHEEK AGAINST MY OWN.

NO SPACE BETWEEN US... IT'S IN THE TOUCH FOR ME.

FINGERS SWEEPING GENTLY ACROSS MY LIPS.

A TONGUE IN THE SOFT, WRINKLED FOLDS OF MY HAND.

IT'S IN THE TOUCH FOR ME.

NOT THE PENETRATION. NOT THE INVASION.

I HAVE LOVE. I MAKE LOVE.

AND I KNOW WHAT YOU HAVE DONE.

DIEGO: INSIDE YOUR LOVE I SEE WHY I'M STILL HERE.

I WILL NOT LEAVE YOU—YOU NEED TOO MUCH FROM ME.

I'M NOT A HERO TO SAVE YOU.

WILL WHAT I HAVE EVER BE ENOUGH?

YOU TAKE SO MUCH FROM ME.

A LIFE WITHOUT DOCTORS AND THE CONSTANT SMELL OF BLOOD...

YOU DESERVE BETTER AND SO DO I.

Stop draining me of my life! [*He exits.*]

FRIDA: I have a life too, Diego.

[FRIDA *moves to her own house, and enters it, slamming the door behind her.*]

SCENE 3

WHAT THE WATER GAVE HER:
FRIDA IN THE BATH

The two houses move apart to reveal FRIDA *in a bath facing the audience. The large white scrim is now illuminated to represent the painting,* What The Water Gave Me. *At first, the only elements present are her feet, the right one cracked and bleeding, the upper edge of the bathtub and grayish mass representing the water.* FRIDA's *thoughts and visions are represented on the backdrop as shadow puppets of The Dead Dimas, the child in the womb from* Moses, *and* FRIDA *holding the baby* DIEGO *from* The Love Embrace of the Universe.

FRIDA: I have visions... in the water. They're often very dark... Not wanting a child but still mourning for the children I have lost... frightened gasps from a wounded deer, drowning in my bath.

[*SILENCE to include a sense of suspension.* FRIDA *lights a cigarette.* INSECTS* *move across a tightrope suspended above the bath... also a* CALAVERA*. A* SPIDER* *reaches down and touches her neck. Slowly sounds are introduced. Sound of her breathing, water washing over her skin, tap dripping. Blood drips from her cracked foot.*]

FRIDA: NAKED, I'M REMINDED OF MY PASSION—

REMEMBERING THE WORLD I ONCE HELD IN MY HAND.

REMEMBERING THE TOUCH OF LOVE ON MY SKIN,

ROUGH SCARS RECALL THE PAIN THAT PLEA-SURES BRING.

[*Gentle laughter. Image of two women—*FRIDA* *and the* DARKER WOMAN* *(ref:* La Tierra Misma/The Earth Itself*). During the following sung sequence the foliage behind* THE WOMEN* *moves and intertwines. The* MONKEY's* *tail tightens slowly around the branch of a tree.* THE WOMEN's* *arms embrace and legs entwine.*]

LOVE IS ALL THAT BATHES ME CLEAN—

FRIDA: [*Cont'd.*] WIPES AWAY THE BROKEN FLESH.

LOVE MAKES AN ISLAND OF MY SOUL.

CHORUS: [*Offstage; Single voices.*] LOVE IS AN ISLAND SUR-
ROUNDED BY TIME—

WAITING…WAITING…

WILL SOMEONE COME AND FIND ME? OR SEE
AND PASS ME BY—

LOVE SINKING INTO ALL THAT CAME BEFORE?

[*A* NURSE/LOVER *enters and helps* FRIDA *from the bath. She sen-
sually dries her off.*]

FRIDA: [*Deliberately and slowly.*] Slow, slow. Flesh tight and smooth.
A thin splinter of pain enters me, and its warmth closes my
eyes.

MAKE LOVE, HAVE A BATH, MAKE LOVE, HAVE A
BATH.

FRIDA & LOVER: MAKE LOVE, HAVE A BATH, AND THEN
MAKE LOVE AGAIN.

[*They gently laugh.*]

FRIDA: [*To the* LOVER.] Diego has a woman's breasts. That's why I
still love him…

[FRIDA *and* LOVER *exit as the bath moves off. The shadow puppets
are replaced by multiple images of* FRIDA, *from her various self-portraits.* DIEGO *enters and stares at the screen.*]

SCENE 4

FRIDA SELLS HER FIRST PAINTINGS, FINDS INDEPEN-
DENCE AND LOSES DIEGO

Images of FRIDA *include* Self-portrait With Monkey [*1938*],
Fulang-Chang And I [*1937*] *and* Self-portrait—The Frame
[*1938*]. *These do not attempt to be full reproductions but, rather,
stress certain elements such as her eyes and her breasts.*

DIEGO: [*Checking his watch.*] Movie stars are always late.

[EDWARD G. ROBINSON* *enters with brassy "show-biz" music.* DIEGO *attempts to sell him* FRIDA's *paintings*]

DIEGO: See, Edward? Why waste your time buying my paintings? When Frida's the genius—no one paints a face as well as she does.

EDWARD*: Your pretty wife? Does she paint as good as you?

DIEGO: Not merely paints, but breathes life onto a canvas — hard as a diamond that can split your soul in two.

[EDWARD* *looks carefully at her paintings.*]

EDWARD*: THOSE EYES ARE SO STRANGELY HYP-NOTIC—

THAT FACE MAKES ME FEEL SO EROTIC!

DIEGO: THOSE EYES ARE A TRAP. THEY COULD TEAR YOUR HEART APART.

EDWARD*: Curious about her: Freda Carlo;

CURIOUS ABOUT HER: EYEBROWS THAT MEET,

EYES FRANKLY STARING. DARING NOT SWEET.

DIEGO: YOU'LL BE THE FIRST ONE TO OWN THOSE EYES.

THEY'LL ALWAYS MESMERIZE THE ONE WHO BUYS.

EDWARD*: HER PAINTINGS PULL NO PUNCHES.

THAT FACE SHOULD BE SEEN ON A BIG SILVER SCREEN.

DIEGO: THUNDER AND LIGHTNING—OVER THE SEA...

WILL YOU TAKE TWO OR THREE?

EDWARD*: She's a sexy broad!

THOSE EYEBROWS...IT'S THOSE EYEBROWS I ADORE.

I'LL TAKE FOUR!

DIEGO & EDWARD*: THE PAINTINGS OF FRIDA CREATE THEIR OWN MYTHS.

WHAT A JOY TO POSSESS!

EDWARD*: NO ANDS, BUTS OR IFS!

[*A cocky aside to audience.*] Yeah.. and what d'you know, I'm the first American to buy her work!

DIEGO & EDWARD*: FRIDA KAHLO, YOU'LL BE FAMOUS!

EDWARD*: All that blood and organs and things...I kind of like that.

DIEGO & EDWARD*: WAIT AND SEE!

[EDWARD* *hands* DIEGO *the money.* DIEGO *takes it.* EDWARD* *exits with the paintings as the wall moves out to reveal* FRIDA *sitting in a wheelchair painting at her easel.* DIEGO *moves into the scene victoriously holding the money out to her.* FRIDA *whistles astonishedly as* DIEGO *approaches and hands her the money.*]

FRIDA: [*Triumphantly counting the bills.*] Híjole! Eight hundred dollars! And all for me?

DIEGO: He loved your paintings!

FRIDA: He did? That crazy Yanqui actor—Edward Gee?

DIEGO: Robinson!

FRIDA: All right! Okay! I like this Edward G. Robinson!

[*They laugh.*]

FRIDA: [*Cont'd.*] Diego, I really wish you'd come with me to that rotten Paris.

DIEGO: It's you they've invited. Think of all those admirers waiting for you...Andre Breton, Duchamp, and Picasso in Paris, and that handsome photographer, Nickolas Muray in New York. You might have so much fun, you might not even want to come back!

FRIDA: You know I'll always come back...to Mexico.

DIEGO: Of course...

[*As* FRIDA *exits,* DIEGO *sings.*] FRIDA KAHLO, YOU'LL BE FAMOUS! WAIT AND SEE!

[*Entr'acte. French accordion music then New York style jazz depicting* FRIDA's *journeys. Lights fade. Camera flash. Lights come up on* FRIDA *seated in a New York hotel-style bedroom chair during a photographic session with her unseen lover Nickolas Muray, the famous New York photographer. The way* FRIDA *moves and poses and the camera flashes denotes his presence. She smokes a clipped joint as she speaks.*]

FRIDA: I'm so happy to be back in our New York, Nick ... I hated Paris. I used to hate it here too, but it's beautiful now because everything makes me think of you ... The "Half Moon" at Coney Island is your lips and every tree in Central Park shades only us from the sun.

[*Pause. She has lifted her blouse so her breasts show. A rectangle of light is on her torso.*]

It seems I'm always offering these to my lovers ... What do you think of my nipples, Nickolas. Too big? Unnatural? They feel unnatural sometimes, but that's why I like them. André liked them too. He liked everything about me. My paintings. My body. He liked how I stared at his wife. She has perfect breasts, like mine. Anyway ... that's why he brought me to Paris ... the Louvre bought a painting. Do you think that's good?

[*With a laugh.*] I got some dough anyway.

[*Pause; she inhales deeply.*] I'm killing myself with this—but it feels so good going down. I imagine the blue-black smoke filling out my legs, making me whole. This poison is like sex — breath that pounds my heart, parts my lips — so that pounding can get up between my thighs.

[*She takes another drag.*] I get daydreams about all the lovers I've ever slept with. I keep a hand on my hip, covering the bruises from the needles. A woman pulls it away and rests her lips there. It's always a woman who knows where I need to be kissed.

[*Pause.*] Hurry up, Nickolas ... I'm getting tired. I'm always so tired lately. Will you show everyone these pictures? At least if I'm not remembered for my paintings—someone might remember my breasts.

[*She smiles, takes a deep drag.*] I love you, darling Nick, almost as much as I love Diego.

[*Lights come up to reveal* DIEGO.]

DIEGO: I want a divorce.

FRIDA: What the hell are you talking about, Diego?

DIEGO: YOU FLAUNT YOUR LOVERS IN MY FACE—

DIEGO: YOUR LOVERS! FRIDA: AS I LEARNED FROM YOU, DIEGO!

FREEDOM YES, I'LL BE AS FREE AS YOU!

BUT NOT THIS MOCK-ERY!

YOU'RE BEGINNING TO DISCOVER YOUR OWN LIFE... WHAT A HYPOCRITE!

DAMN YOU!

YOU DON'T NEED ME... CAN'T YOU SEE, DIEGO—

YOU DON'T NEED ME ANYMORE. DON'T YOU KNOW YOU ARE MY HEART?!

IT'S OVER... I THOUGHT WE HAD LOVE...

[*Shouts.*]Then go!!

[DIEGO *exits, as the houses move offstage to denote the break in their marriage.*]

SCENE 5

FRIDA PAINTS.

The three CALAVERAS, *dressed as doctors, enter, wheeling* FRIDA *in an apparatus suggesting both an operating table and a spit.* FRIDA* *is turned around on the spit like an animal in the furnace of hell (cf* The Broken Column) FRIDA *the actor stands alongside the spit, in* *deep anguish and despair, cutting off the puppet* FRIDA*'s long hair.* CRISTI *enters with the doctors and stands outside the immediate action, observing the scene of* FRIDA's *torture with horror.*

CALAVERAS: LOOK IF HE LOVED YOU, IT WAS FOR YOUR HAIR

NOW THAT YOU'RE PELONA, HE WON'T LOVE YOU ANYMORE.

TWO FRIDAS—ONE DIEGO LOVES. ONE HE LOVES NO MORE.

FRIDA/CALAVERAS: CUT OFF THE HAIR HE LOVED—CUT OFF MY/HER WOMANLY DISGUISE.

WHOEVER NEEDS THE LOVE OF MEN IS HELPLESS AND UNWISE.

CALAVERAS: MIRA QUE SI TE QUISE, FUÉ POR EL PELO,

AHORA QUE ESTÁS PELONA, YA NO TE QUIERO.

[FRIDA *finishes the haircutting and collapses into a wheelchair.*]

CALAVERA 1: All the usual childhood diseases . . .

CALAVERA 2: Plus Polio at eleven.

CRISTINA: SHE NEVER REALLY WALKED, YOU KNOW.

SHE FLEW AND HOPPED LIKE A BRIGHT YOUNG BIRD.

[CALAVERA 2 *laughs.*]

CALAVERA 1: I loved that . . .

[CALAVERA 2 *stifles his laughter.*]

CALAVERA 2: After the accident . . .

CALAVERA 3: Three months in the Red Cross Hospital.

CALAVERA 2: Nine months in a plaster corset . . . and every now and then for the remainder of her life.

CALAVERA 1: Normal sex life.

CALAVERA 2: Really?

CALAVERA 3: Congenital malformation of the spine.

CALAVERA 2: A little trophic ulcer in the right foot.

CALAVERA 1: The cracked one...the one that always bleeds...

CALAVERA 2: Scoliosis. And a fusion of the third and fourth lumbar.

CALAVERA 3: And so many operations...thirty!

CALAVERA 1: Twenty-three.

CALAVERAS: [*Sung with a barber-shop quartet sweetness.*] SHE'S AL-MOST OURS...

[*The* CALAVERAS *exit with the spit as* NURSE *enters. She comforts* FRIDA, *then wheels* FRIDA *to her easel downstage, and then exits.*]

FRIDA: My life is painted bread—a promise of food that leaves you hungry. I'm starving so I paint...
[*Mocking herself.*] And paint and paint and paint some more.
[*Pause.*] My comforts—portraits of me. Empty space where my heart used to be.
Messages for you, Diego.

[*THE WOUNDED DEER*]

A musical interlude follows, underscoring FRIDA'*s continuing transformation of her life events into art.* FRIDA *picks up her paintbrush and begins to paint. The following sequence, created through overhead projections and puppets, appears on and in front of the scrim behind* FRIDA (*cf* The Little Deer).

A background of a stormy sea and sky is established. Against this, a branch of a tree falls as a forest is established, one tree at a time. The WOUNDED DEER*, *a bunraku puppet with* FRIDA'*s face, appears from behind a tree. The deer moves amongst the trees.*

Suddenly, a CALAVERA *wearing a* DIEGO *mask appears from behind a tree and pierces the Frida* DEER* *with an arrow. A bleeding wound appears. Out of the wound falls an object such as Diego's face, The Flower of Life, etc. This stabbing sequence is repeated nine times by other* CALAVERAS. *Each time the* DEER* *recovers, in fact, she* *seems to become stronger and more audacious. From the last blow, however, she* *takes longer to recover. She* *confronts the audience without moving as "milk tears" fall from the sky, filling the canvas (cf.* My Nurse and I). *Lights fade on the* DEER* *and come up on* FRIDA *at her easel.*

FRIDA: [*Wistfully.*] Nine antlers. Nine arrows...[*Recognizing her own joke with a laugh.*] And nine lives for Frida.

[FRIDA *continues to paint as the* CALAVERAS/MONKEYS *enter and crowd around her. They pose themselves around* FRIDA *to evoke* Self Portrait with Monkeys.]

CALAVERAS: SHE PAINTS SO MANY MONKEYS. WE WONDER WHAT IT MEANS...

CALAVERA 2: IS IT BECAUSE THEY'RE SO CUTE AND SMALL?

CALAVERA 1: OR IS IT A SEXUAL SCENE?

CALAVERA 2: THE CHILDREN THAT SHE NEVER HAD?

CALAVERA 1: THE LOVE OF SEX THAT DROVE HER MAD?

CALAVERA 2: SOMETHING SMALL TO CALL HER OWN...

SOMETHING TO KEEP HER FROM FEELING ALONE.

ALL: SHE PAINTS SO MANY MONKEYS. WE WONDER WHAT IT MEANS...

IS IT A SEXUAL SCENE.

FRIDA: MONKEYS HELP TO KEEP ME SANE.

MONKEYS HELP ME LAUGH AT THE PAIN.

WHEN A TEAR ROLLS DOWN MY CHEEK,

THEY LIFT MY SKIRTS AND TAKE A PEEK.

CALAVERAS: THEY DON'T LEAVE YOU AS LONG AS YOU FEED THEM.

[*The* CALAVERAS *make the sound of approaching footsteps.* FRIDA *looks out expectantly.*]

FRIDA: Diego?

[*The* CALAVERAS *laugh.*]

FRIDA: [*Cont'd.*] Puñeta!

[CALAVERA 3 *touches her hair.* FRIDA *enjoys his touch.*]

CALAVERA 1: He's not coming back.

[FRIDA *pulls away from* CALAVERA 3.]

FRIDA: He's a Bastard!

CALAVERA 2: A Pig!

CALAVERA 3: ¡Un mierda!

CALAVERA 1: ¡Un maricón!

[CALAVERA 1 *hands her a drink in a flask.*]

FRIDA: YES...THAT'S EASY. COGNAC Y MARIJUANA... makes me feel...half human—for almost a day...

UNTIL I LOOK IN A MIRROR, THEN I KNOW IT'S JUST A LIE.

[CALAVERAS *exit.*]

FRIDA: Don't forget me damn it, I won't let you say goodbye.

ACUÉRDATE DE MÍ, COMPAÑERO.

CUANDO MIRES A MIS CUADROS, CAIGAS EN MIS OJOS.

LOOK AT MY PAINTINGS AND FALL INTO MY DARK EYES.

I will learn to live alone in this empty world.
[*With a sense of discovery.*] THAT'S HOW I'LL KEEP FROM LYING TO MYSELF.

THAT'S HOW I'LL KEEP FROM DYING...

[*With a sense of victory.*] THAT'S HOW I'LL KEEP FROM DYING!

SCENE 6

FRIDA'S DEATH

The NURSE *enters and crosses to* FRIDA. *The* CALAVERAS *wheel on a hospital bed and sit beneath it. The* NURSE *wheels* FRIDA *to the bed and with difficulty helps the physically weakened* FRIDA *onto the bed, tucks in her bedclothes, exposing the painted corset* FRIDA *now wears. Above* FRIDA, *on the screen behind her, we see an image of*

FRIDA *as if in prison.* FRIDA *begins to writhe in bed, trying desperately to remove her corset which restricts her movement and her breathing. She is having a nightmare. She raves disjointedly over the music as a flood of haunted images appears in her head/on the screen: a sense of confusion, chaos and delirium.*

FRIDA: Stop! I can't —breathe! Breath! Let me—catch—I must— Get out!

> I have to—get out!

[*An image of* TROTSKY'*s head appears on the screen behind her. A* NURSE/CALAVERA *enters and begins to interrogate* FRIDA.]

NURSE/CALAVERA: Yellow?

[*An ice pick appears on the screen over* TROTSKY'*s head.*]

FRIDA: Madness. Sickness. Part of the Sun—Damn you Diego for running off and leaving me like this!

[*The ice pick stabs* TROTSKY'*s head, and a red gash appears. The screen turns red, depicting the murder of* TROTSKY.]

> Trotsky?! Oh my God... Diego, they think you did it!

NURSE/CALAVERA: BLACK?!

FRIDA: Black... Black is nothing! Don't you understand?!! Get out of here! Oh God, please leave me alone!
> [*In a small voice; with a laugh.*] Red... no black... nothing... really nothing. Stop!
> [*She screams.*] You're torturing me! Nurse! Some Demerol! Please! I can't take anymore! They arrested me and Cristi. Because of him—all these questions! Where the hell are you, Diego?! Ay Virgen de Guadalupe! Please get me out of here!

[FRIDA *sits bolt upright as if coming out of a nightmare as the image of* TROTSKY *fades. She sees* DIEGO *who has entered the room playing a tambourine. He proceeds to dance around her like a bear in an effort to amuse and seduce her back into loving him as he sings a funny, Mexican-style love song.*

At first, FRIDA *is too stunned to respond, then she willfully chooses not to respond and then she can't help but start laughing.*]

DIEGO: [*Gentle and playfully suggestive.*] ¡SOY EL OSO NEGRO DE LA MONTAÑA ROJA,

Y TENGO MUCHO HAMBRE POR TU MIEL SABROSA! [*Miel meaning honey with sexual connotations.*]

¡SOY EL OSO NEGRO DE LA MONTAÑA ROJA,

QUIERO BEBER UN TRAGO DE TI, HIJA!

FRIDA: Bastard! So finally, you've come back to the wife who made you sick with all her sickness...

[DIEGO *kisses* FRIDA.]

DIEGO: I need you, Frida.

FRIDA: But *I* don't need *you* anymore, Diego Rivera!!

DIEGO: MARRY ME, WE NEED EACH OTHER!

LET'S TAKE THIS LAST CHANCE...

SPEND THE REST OF YOUR LIFE IN MY ARMS.

MAKE MY LIFE DANGEROUS AGAIN, CHIQUITA.

FRIDA: Marry you? Again? What for? You're crazy, Diego!

DIEGO: Maybe. But marry me, anyway...

MY LITTLE DOVE.

FRIDA: I can live without you now—but you're an old fool and I still love you...

[DIEGO *lifts* FRIDA *gently. She pushes him away, and with difficulty manages to stand on her own. Defiantly discovering her independence, she sings.*]

FRIDA: THE FRIDA YOU SEE BEFORE YOU

ON OUR SECOND WEDDING DAY...

NOT RAPHAEL'S MADONNA,

NOR DA VINCI'S FLIRTING MONA LISA—

I AM A WOMAN AS SEEN BY A WOMAN—

FRIDA AS SEEN BY FRIDA HERSELF.

NOT AS A MAN DESIGNS ME,

NOR AS A MAN DESIRES ME—

BUT AS I CONSPIRE TO BE!

> That's all I ever wanted.
> [*Pulling off her corset.*] ¡Viva la vida!

[*The sense of* FRIDA*'s victory as a woman, the triumph of her life explodes in a carnival of life and death. The wedding guests from the first wedding, including* LUPE, *enter. Each takes his/her turn dancing with* FRIDA. *They sing as they all dance.*]

ALL: LIFE'S A GIFT SO TEAR IT OPEN!

LAUGH AT DEATH Y POR QUÉ NO?

LA PELONA LOVES A JOKE OR TWO—

TAKING SOULS NOT YET DUE.

LIFE'S A GIFT SO LET'S UNWRAP IT!

DANCE AWAY THIS LONG BLACK NIGHT!

FRIDA: LA VIDA ES PARA ROMPER!

I AM NOT SICK—I AM BROKEN!

SO WHAT IF I AM IN PAIN—

I AM HAPPY TO BE ALIVE TO PAINT AND PAINT AGAIN!

CALAVERAS: LA RAZA BAILE CON ALEGRÍA—

MAÑANA TRAERÁS MÁS TEQUILA!

> [FRIDA's dance with DIEGO is interrupted suddenly by her sense of approaching death. The CALAVERA enters silently behind her and moves slowly forward to claim her.]

FRIDA: I HEAR THE SILENCE DROPPING...

NIGHT IS FALLING IN MY LIFE.

YESTERDAY I FOUGHT FOR FREEDOM—

NOW I'M FIGHTING FOR MY LIFE.

> [DEATH/CALAVERA *enters, waiting to dance with* FRIDA.]

DEATH DANCES AROUND MY BED AGAIN TONIGHT—

FRIDA: [*Cont'd.*] THIS TIME I WON'T TURN HER AWAY.

THIS TIME I'LL LET THE MUSIC PLAY

UNTIL I'VE FOUGHT MY LAST FIGHT.

[*She moves to the* CALAVERA.]

La Pelona, my oldest Cachucha—together at last.

[FRIDA *embraces* DEATH.]

Viva la vida, la Alegría, and Diego.

[DEATH *sweeps* FRIDA *up in his/her arms and dances with her off-stage as if with a precious trophy of victory. The stage floods with color.* FRIDA's *image appears on the scrim. A halo of flames illuminates and then destroys/consumes the image. All the players enter.*]

QUARTET: DE PETATE A PETATE—FROM BIRTH TO DEATH.

MEXICO MOURNS FRIDA KAHLO—A DAUGHTER OF THE EARTH.

THE ONE WHO GAVE BIRTH TO HERSELF

WRITING THE MOST BEAUTIFUL POEM OF HER LIFE.

DE PETATE A PETATE—FROM BIRTH TO DEATH.

HER COLORS GO OUT INTO THE WORLD

TO THE WORLD, FOREVER.

END OF PLAY

Claire Chafee

WHY WE HAVE A BODY

Why We Have a Body was produced by the Women's Project &
Productions under the artistic directorship of Julia Miles at the
Judith Anderson Theatre, New York City, November 1-27, 1994.
It was directed by Evan Yionoulis with the following cast:

LILI	Jayne Atkinson
ELEANOR	Trish Hawkins
RENEE	Deborah Hedwall
MARY	Nancy Hower

Set Design by Peter B. Harrison
Lighting Design by Donald Holder
Costume Design by Teresa Snyder-Stein
Production Stage Manager: Renee Lutz

CHARACTERS

MARY

LILI

ELEANOR

RENEE

ACT 1

SETTING: MARY, *in an orange mechanic's overall, stands center stage in very dim light, pointing a semi-automatic hand gun with both hands, at the audience, her feet spread apart. Music: Lyle Lovett's "North Dakota," just the intro, fade. Lights increase to full brightness.*

MARY: FREEZE! O.K. FREEZE! [*Pause.*]

Yes this is a hold-up. Now. Listen: I will only say this once.

I am the way things go.

I've been called, The Lark, La Pucelle, deceiver of the people, sinner, murderess, saint, invoker of devils, an idolatrous, cruel, dissolute heretic, so I think this gives me some ground to talk. And I can tell you this:

I am tired of putting my mood at the mercy of strangers.

[*Cocks gun.*]

Take all the money out of the drawer . . . [*Points.*] *that* drawer . . .

. . . and put it in a to-go container. [*Watches him.*]

Any size.

[*Really noticing him for the first time.*]

Is this your first time, you're very nervous.

Are you kidding? This is my fifteenth Seven-Eleven. So you can trust me here.

Now I want you to put the cup on the counter and slowly

MARY: [*Cont'd.*] turn to face the wall.

I am *not* going to shoot you. *You are a very negative person.*
Since I came in here, it's been worst-case scenario in your
mind, boom boom boom.

The world is going to get to you if you keep on like that
... and let me tell you —

there is very little Prozac can do for you, when push comes
to shove, as it did in my case.

[MARY *motions for him to throw to-go container. One is thrown
from the audience, which she catches one-handed.*]

Now I'm gonna back out of here and I want you to close
your eyes. Close ... your ... eyes.

If you think that you can love me unconditionally, press 1,
NOW. If you love me a lot but you just can't take my moods,
press 2, NOW.

If you're calling from a rotary phone, wake up.

Go and get yourself a touch tone — something to lean against.

It's important that you pay attention.

You cannot return to the main menu at any time.

There will be no pitons on which to hook your rope, no
themes, no easy contradictions.

You are skidding sideways on the ice and there's nothing
you can do about it. It's not your fault that you don't listen
to your unconscious mind. That's why it's there.

[*Music: Scarlatti, Pastoral in C major.* LILI, *in a white slip, is lying on a white bed propped up by pillows. She is asleep. An alarm
clock goes off: digital.*]

LILI: [*Turns off clock, hears music.*]

LILI: [*Cont'd.*] When I was in the womb, my mother
listened to nothing but Scarlatti.
Scarlatti. Over and over.
[*Music out.*]
All day long she would rock by the window ... in the dead
heat of morning ... in a lemon colored dress. She would look
out at the desert and picture different forms of transportation.
[*She finds her silk bathrobe and puts it on.*]
She'd tilt her head to one side and
I was the thought that she was having.
She thought me up.
[*She finds her slippers.*]
She wanted something different.
That is why she called me "Lili," thinking it was French.
That is why, when she got mad, she'd say,
"Mais, qu'est-ce que c'est que ça?"
[*Pronounced: may kess kuh seh kuh sa? hand on hip.*]
The voice of my grandmother was all around me; told me
details I would not remember but nevertheless just know.
"A pound of butter equals four sticks."
Things like that.

When my mother put her hand against her belly, I could feel
her pat me on the head.
She was working on a promise, the details of which she
would not remember but nevertheless
just know.

LILI: [*Cont'd.*] I can hear her heartbeat going "thud, thwat, thud, thwat." I can hear the saltines that she is chewing aimlessly. I can see the pictures play against the inside of her rib-cage . . . those home movies of the heart . . . I become the shape of things my mother never tried. Things my mother gave up on to have me. I can see that there's a highway, I can see that there's a suitcase. And I start to get a restless feeling like I want to get born but I don't know how.

[LILI *closes eyes. Lights up on* ELEANOR.]

Before I attached myself to the womb,

in that tiny fall, when

I was both,

when I was anything, and could be anything, before the loss

of becoming *specific* . . . when I was single.

Before I became this shape of wanting you.

[*Lights up on* ELEANOR, *pointer in hand.*]

ELEANOR: Compare the brain of a perfectly normal woman, with that of a Lesbian.

The Lesbian Brain is divided into *three* sections,

as opposed to the sub-division into two sections of the normal brain.

MEMORY . . . LUST . . . and HAMMERING DOUBT.

[*Points to small circle below Lust.*]

Because the Lesbian is born without a future,

the Lesbian Brain is born with more past

to remember

ELEANOR: [*Cont'd.*] and has developed a larger location
in the pre-frontal cortex, specifically for this function.
It is still not clear however
whether this area develops in utero, therefore
forming a certain predilection to be a lesbian,
or whether
this extended capacity for memory develops later, simply as
a by-product of years of living
without a future and more past than one can possibly
manage.

It is confusing.
I sincerely try to pierce that question.
At one time I did blame myself that Lili was a lesbian...
but she just told me: "Why should you take all the credit"
so I guess that finally just sunk in.
Now I live by the great words of Ophelia: "Lord we know
what we are, but know not what we may be."

And as you know with science, once you start to *ask*
there are just more questions than there are answers.
However, it is safe to say that...since the dawn of time, we
have been mostly sleeping.
[*Lights out on* ELEANOR. *Music: Ella sings "Honeysuckle Rose."*]
[*Lights up on* MARY *in the desert, putting on make up. She has
propped up a little mirror on her travel make-up case. She has on
hand cuffs. A slide of the desert is behind her.*]
MARY: I swear to God you are my only friend.
[*Putting on lip stick very carefully.*]

MARY: [*Cont'd.*] When I talk to you
I want to be glamorous.
Now . . . I can hear you tell me . . . : "You don't have to be
glamorous when you talk to me." But . . . if you sat by the
highway and hallucinated for days at a time, you would
want to at least be good looking. [*Looking into mirror.*] People
ask me when did Joan of Arc surrender . . .
the truth is
[*Blots lips with a Kleenex.*]
there were many surrenders.
[*To audience.*]
What's the definition of insanity . . . say it . . . say it!
[*Says as if it's common knowledge . . .*]
Doing the same thing over and over and expecting different
results.

I've got my session on tape. Travel therapist, for the patient
on the move.
[*Presses play on boom box . . . hears lines.*]
MARY'S VOICE: "How do you feel?
What's come up for you this week?
How does this relate to your mother?
And how does *that* make you feel?
Have you expressed any of this to her?
And what do you feel about me?
Do you see a pattern here?
Can you forgive that in yourself?
Is there a way to integrate the two?

MARY'S VOICE: [*Cont'd.*] Well I guess that's all the time we
have this week."

[*Puts box down.*]

MARY: [*Cont'd.*] Usually I actually answer the questions on the tape.
It helps you more than it looks like it would...

[*Continues to make herself up.*]

I just love that they call this "making yourself up."

LILI: [*Walking to her office, everything is fancy. Computer, fax, printer, fancy swivel chair. She starts up computer, taps on a few keys, turns on desk lamp.*]

When I was growing up,

they taught you very young to tell them right away

if you were a boy or if you were a girl.

And from then on you were sent to live in

two different worlds.

Even before you were born, you hear

this question over and over,

and from in there you can't imagine what

the problem is.

[*She starts to look through a file.*]

Girls did crewelwork, boys had shop.

They got to bring home breakfast trays made out of

plywood: things you had a use for.

We sewed those pictures with the poked out holes. A picture

of a rabbit done in yarn. We all did the same picture of a

rabbit, or else you could choose a baby chick, but that was it.

The good part about living in the world of the girl

[*Starts up printer.*]

is it prepares you for absurdity.

LILI: [*Cont'd.*] Centuries from now, they are going to dig up those things and wonder: "What culture, what form of life, what pattern too intricate to discern created the need for these?" [*Opens a FILE in her computer.*]

[*Lights up on* MARY, *who looks in make-up case and takes out a bent hairpin, starts to pick the lock of one of her handcuffs.*]

MARY: The thing about leading an army, any army, is they don't just *follow*

out of duty . . . it's the back of your head they watch. And if you haven't made that *adjustment* . . . inside . . .

they can tell.

[*The handcuff opens easily, slips off. She leaves the other one on as a bracelet and returns the hairpin to her make-up case.*]

I was a soldier for her. I love battle.

But I don't have a saviour thing — I have a *hero* thing.

Because: she is a regal person.

Let's face it, who can actually stand to be saved? It feels disgusting.

Rescue is a different matter: heroes rescue . . . rescue's not your fault. It's an emergency.

And it was my particular crusade, to rescue my mother.

Because she is a regal person.

May not be France, but she was just as difficult in her own small way.

But, of course, I was thwarted in my attempts.

She just . . . wouldn't . . . budge.

I kept misplacing myself in her mood swings.

MARY: [*Cont'd.*] I was out collecting firewood when I first
heard my Voices.
I was thirteen years old.
A shepherd girl, with nothing but the sheep to watch, gets
ideas in her head.

"Don't get nervous," I told myself. "Miracles happen." I told
myself.
"You're out collecting firewood, you hear your voices — there
they are."
Who was I to judge their motives?

LILI: The first lesbian I ever met was
Harriet the Spy. The second was Margaret Mead.
I fell in love 4 times before the age of 8 . . . and each time it
was with a girl . . . and no: I did not want to be like them.
I did not want to write romantic letters from camp.
I did not want to share their skates.

What I wanted was to take them on the rug.
Of their parents bedroom.
Exactly.
So, I had no other choice than to be a spy.
[MARY *stands in front of pay phone and concentrates.* LILI's *fax
starts to print.*]
This must be Mary.
[*She watches it. Waits.*]
I still can't figure out how she does that.
Every time she hits another Seven-Eleven,
she faxes a confession. *Telepathic* fax . . .

LILI: *(Cont'd.) (Reading.*] "Pulled another job. Some complications: cashier a novice. Was chased and apprehended.

But... lept out back of van: angels

slipped inside the car lock... Ran into a crowded

mall... Lost authorities in a gourmet jellybean store...

I love you and you know that, Mary."

[*The telephone rings.* LILI *looks at it.* MARY *picks up phone.*]

OPERATOR'S VOICE: Will you accept a collect call to anyone from Mary?

LILI: [*Staring straight ahead, pause.*] Yes.

MARY: Lili? Lili hi. Hi. Listen... would you get me out of here? I need you to get me outa here. [*Pause.*]

My roommate's got a walkman and she plays that thing so loud I can hear it coming outa her eyes... she's got that knob on *ten*, you know, and you wanna know what she listens to Lili? [*No answer.*] Willie Nelson. Willie Nelson day and night and night and fucking day, and I told her, "If I had the authority and the money right now I would *go* to Willie Nelson, to his house or mansion whatever and ask him, "How much money will it take for you to stop singing altogether? I'm talking permanent retirement, no comebacks. What's it gonna take for you to never sing another note?" And I bet you he'd do it too. You live in a lousy city for an operator call.

[*Long pause. She lights a cigarette.*] If you love me anywhere at all in your being, you will pay someone to get me out of here. I don't care what it takes.

MARY: [*Cont'd.*] Where's our mother?

I'm just trying to reach my mother.

LILI: She's in Palenque. In the Yucatan.

Paddling up remote jungle tributaries.

[*Pause.*] Where are you?

MARY: I just feel like I have to get in touch with my family. I just feel like I have to make contact.

LILI: What's it mean, the part, "was chased and apprehended," Mary?

[*Silence.*] Where are you anyway? You sound like you're by the highway, in the desert and distinctly NOT in a group home.

MARY: You are so good at what you do. What was it, the background sound?

[*She looks around her.*]

LILI: I don't hear upholstery, Mary. I don't hear wall-to-wall.

What I get so far is pay phone, desert, with a hot dry wind.

MARY: [*Almost excited.*] Where am I?

LILI: I'm not sure , but I hear handcuffs.

MARY: [*Smiling.*] You're an artist, Lili, never fucking let anyone tell you otherwise.

[*Silence.*] I love you, Lili. I love you and Mom. You know that. You shouldn't have to ask yourself over and over if you are great. That can be dangerous.

You *are* great. You have the emotional calcium for that somehow . . . you know what I mean?

LILI: Mary, I may not be able to get you out of trouble this time.

MARY: I'm going to order some clothes from this catalogue.

Do you want me to order you anything?

LILI: What catalogue?

MARY: [*Pulls it out from back pocket.*] L. L. Bean.

LILI: That's O.K.

MARY: Are you sure?

I'm getting myself some lightweight hiking boots. Are you sure you don't need anything? A canvas tote bag? Some turtlenecks?

LILI: No. I don't need anything.

MARY: But what do you *WANT*? I want to send you something! A present or something. You're my sister. I love you and you know that.

LILI: Send me a letter.

MARY: I don't know you well enough.

Look, I'm just taking a wild guess here, but...do you want me to pick you up a parrot or a fish tank or something? It would be simple.

How about a surf board? Do you surf?

LILI: No, I don't think so.

MARY: Well...when you look out at the water, does it look like you would *want* to ?

[MARY *spreads out hand indicating distance.* LILI *stares out at audience for a long time.*]

MARY [*Cont'd.*] O.K. let's not drag this out, let's not deface the moment. Do you want to take my case?

LILI: Mary.

You hold up Seven-Elevens with a semi-auto-matic in broad daylight.

There aren't a lot of blanks to fill in.

MARY: Do not be so sure...

MARY: [*Cont'd.*] *What's my motive?*

LILI: Look, I'm in the middle of something here.

Can I get back to you?

MARY: You have work to do.

LILI: Yes.

MARY: I'll call you later. I'll call you in an hour. [*Starts to hang up.*]

LILI: [*Loudly.*] Mary? Call me later on than that, O.K.? A while from now. O.K.?

MARY: I keep thinking over and over about

that they burned her, Lili.

LILI: Ya? [*Pause.*] I know. It's hard to imagine.

MARY: They tied her to the stake. The flames crackled and rose.

LILI: You're still reading that book?

MARY: Ya.

LILI: Well. It was a horrible way to die.

MARY: It wasn't the flames.

It wasn't the smoke.

It was the shame of being naked in front of so many men.

LILI: That's probably right.

[*They hold still, facing forward. They both put the phone down.*]

LILI: [*Cont'd.*] Well I might as well start with her hair:

it was short in a long kind of way.

She had kept a sense of flowing.

She had held on to the memory of when it was long.

We had a flashback relationship:

everything took place in memory.

Making everything seem strangely familiar.

[*A spot up on* RENEE, *in a lab coat pointing to a slide of a dinosaur ... with a metal pointer.*]

RENEE: [*Points to slide.*] Brontosaur. Any of a genus of sauropods of the Cretaceous period, weighing about 30 tons.

They lived ... they died ... they left their bones. Part of a lost and restless generation.

Most species, in fact some 99% of all species that have ever lived, are now extinct.

When a species disappears, it cannot easily be discerned whether it is through extinction or evolution.

Without extinction, evolution would be impossible.

Extinction, therefore, is not a failure. [*Clicks slide.*]

This is a picture of Gloria. Hence, the "Gloria Project" ...

Gloria being the name given an immature female whose incomplete neckbone fragments I had virtually tripped over in a parking lot in the Kalahari Desert ... [*Takes off glasses.*] that just did not belong that far from Montana.

[*Clicks to a slide of the galaxies.*]

... But ... during the Mesazoic period ... what with meteors, slamming into the earth ... at a variable speed of 4000 miles per minute ... [*Clicks to slide.*]

And with Triceratops, the vicious vegetarian, always on your tail,

if I had been a baby duck-billed dinosaur,

well I would want to migrate too.

LILI: She was an ardent fan of free association.

The "wild guess" would always be more accurate to her.

LILI: [*Cont'd.*] Here was

> her genius and her disguise
>
> so inextricably bound that
>
> you couldn't tease them apart.
>
> She kept the rhythm up.

RENEE: The whole notion of going to remote places to look for

> dinosaur bones captivated my childhood so much, I just
>
> never questioned that was how I'd spend my life...
>
> and... it's on my knees, at work, with that
>
> hydraulic air-brush
>
> in my hands, that I just think... "We're ancient beings —
>
> we're pretty spectacular
>
> and could be anything."

LILI: I have no way of knowing this is true, but

> somehow, I felt so sure
>
> that she would never have the courage to keep loving me,
>
> and there was nothing I could do about it
>
> ... and that the memory of how she *had* loved me, once,
>
> was the only thing that was still keeping her here,
>
> fascinated.
>
> We are taught we are an absence and mistake this for a
>
> longing to be found.
>
> [*Cross-fade to* ELEANOR.]

ELEANOR: Any woman has within her a profound hatred for sex.

> Even if, by some fluke, she herself escaped some direct
>
> violation through any number of assaults on her dignity, her
>
> desire and her view of these two things...

ELEANOR: [*Cont'd.*] then surely she will have experienced an
   indirect assault on her dignity, her desire and her view of these
   two things, while playing jacks with her friends in the school
   courtyard.

INHERITED, at the very least, in the tissues of her sex,
   a collective shame passed down through tiny chinks in her
   mother . . . happening in imperceptible increments every night
   as the mother wipes up crumbs from dinner with a damp
   sponge.

The daughter watches.
The sound of the fork against the mixing bowl, the sinking
   feeling the shine on the kitchen floor can summon . . . these
   are things that pass through her mind while having sex. Or
   trying on a bathing suit.

Every woman has a day when she hates the form that she
   has taken on so much that she makes plans to have it
   destroyed.
The will to change is somehow hindered by her body. The
   doubt of God exists behind her ear. Her unmet strength
   collects around her hips and makes them sore
   for no apparent reason.
She feeds herself too much . . . she feeds herself too little.

She steals, she flirts, conceals the truth.
She counts the beans on her plate. She adds up

ELEANOR: *(Cont'd.)* numbers with phenomenal speed,
the approximate number of calories in the plate
that's put before her. The speed of her equations impresses
astronomers. She is calculating just how much she can expect
from things . . . and at what speed. This is the New Math.
Her own world asks her to undress.
The father's glance, the brother's trap, the mother's
disbelief.
Every woman is an incest survivor, if you count the thoughts
of the world . . . if those count.

[*In darkness, sound of a plane taking off. Music: tabla duet. Lights
up dimly in a plane at night.* LILI *sits by a window, the seat next to
her is empty. The reading light is on over-head, a blanket is across*
LILI's *lap, one hand is clutching the armrest. In her other hand is a
mini-tape recorder. She is looking out the window.*]

LILI: [*Softly, into recorder.*] Dear Renee. [*Looks out window.*]
I miss you. [*Presses PAUSE button. Unpresses it.*] I can't stop
thinking of you night and day and crave your body
always.
[*Presses STOP. Rewinds tape. Begins again less intimately.*]
Renee: I'm airborne, above a vast landscape of . . . snow.
Either that or the moon is making the ocean look white.
There are no lights and still the ground looks
surprisingly close.
I've been practicing my takeoffs and my landings:
breathing, like you showed me, but it hasn't made that much
difference. [*Pause.*] It's almost impossible to hope for this
but I picture that you leave your husband. I play

LILI: *(Cont'd.)* that movie again and again.

I've scored the soundtrack...

[*Presses STOP. Rewinds that much and listens to it. Erases it all. Starts again, looking at the recorder like Renee's inside.*]

Renee? Renee. I feel kinda like Dick Tracy here. I feel...very private. There is no one next to me. No one can overhear.

I am kissing you. Can you feel me? Renee? I want to wear lingerie. *(Smiles.)* I want you down around me.

And I want to fuck you...and I mean that in the nicest possible way. [*Clicks off tape.*]

[*To audience.*] I had written letters like that to her for a long, long time before we met.

I was thinking her up.

[RENEE *enters, walks down aisle and finds her seat next to* LILI.]

LILI: [*Cont'd.*](*To audience.*) I met her on a plane. She was sitting next to me...and...

I could tell immediately that she was a good conversationalist from the way she crossed her legs, took out her novel and sent out the message, "Please don't talk to me."

[RENEE *does this. Pause. Weird airplane sound.*]

But after takeoff,

this sound kept happening, like they were...

pressing a button over and over, like they were trying to retract the landing gear and couldn't...and it was the niggling fear of death

LILI: [*Cont'd.*] that made us start to talk..

RENEE: [*Still looking out the window.*] What's your line of work?

LILI: I'm a private investigator.

[*They both nod.*]

You?

RENEE: Paleontologist.

[*They both nod.*]

LILI: [*To audience.*] And that was that. We started talking. There was a lot of turbulence as we climbed up to our cruising altitude.

RENEE: [*Looking into* LILI's *eyes.*] So. It is your job to notice little, imperceptible things that most of us would overlook, that tell the story of a person's curse...or shadow...that which they can't help but be attracted to — yet that which they cannot permit in themselves and therefore strive to conceal. And, in doing so, of course, reveal it all the more.

LILI: [*To audience.*] I mean I knew just what she meant but I would never think to say it all at once like that.

RENEE: Are you in crime or insurance?

LILI: Well, both. But I prefer the intricacies of adultery.

RENEE: Oh I see.

LILI: I work for women who want evidence. I track down husbands.

RENEE: That must be exhausting work.

LILI: I actually find it quite relaxing.

I'm a lesbian.

[RENEE *pauses, like she doesn't get it. Then, as if she's piecing it together.*]

RENEE: So...you don't get...over-involved...

LILI: I travel blind.

Being an outcast helps.

LILI: *(Cont'd.)* In my work, a pre-conceived notion
is a flat tire.

RENEE: Do you carry a gun?

LILI: Yes I do.

RENEE: Well. For what it's worth, just seeing you at the gate, I would
never take you for an outcast.

LILI: [*To audience.*] Was she flirting with me?

[*To* RENEE.] Well, nobody looks much like an outcast
anymore. These days, we take great pride in looking not at
all the way you would expect us to. At least in the business
world.

[RENEE *nods*]

How long have you been separated from your
husband?

RENEE: Four months. That's pretty good. That's sharp.

LILI: [*Picking up her hand.*] You've got a faded tan line on your
ring finger, your luggage tag says, "MRS." and you're reading
Sylvia Plath: The Complete Works. Something's going on . . .
[*Pause.*]

RENEE: When I'm with men they all complain I always lead.

[*LILI looks at her.*]

I always lead. Out . . . dancing.

LILI: Well, I know why you do. You can't just go all limp and
let a man drag you across the dance floor.

[*Pause.*] You have to hold a bit back from a man.

RENEE: Does your mother know?

LILI: [*Not sure what she means at first.*] Oh yeah.

LILI: It threw her for a loop at first.

For some reason she had a hard time imagining what
we do in bed. [*Pause.*]

RENEE: I don't have trouble with that part.

LILI: [*To audience.*] She was flirting with me. She had to know
that she was definitely flirting with me.

RENEE: I'd be scared I wouldn't want to get up. The next morning.
That it would bring out some strange-victim-love-haze thing
in me.

[LILI *looks at her.*]

...sleeping with a woman... [LILI *nods.*]

Did you know you were gay? I mean early on?

LILI: Three years old....in playgroup... I was inexplicably
drawn to the Superman cape, and ran around at nap time
rescuing all the girls... who didn't seem to mind, they were
already kinda lying down... but it set the boys on edge. They
would start to cry, and Miss Appleyard finally had to call up
my mother to get me to share.

RENEE: And did you?

LILI: I sort of back-paddled.

I never wore it again.

RENEE: While the other girls were guessing each other's favorite
color and putting little plastic barettes in each other's hair,
I was constructing a geodesic dome out of
my brother's Lego set.

LILI: Well, — that's unusual...

A geodesic dome out of Lego.

LILI: [*Cont'd.*] That sounds impossible.

RENEE: It was.

[*Lights bump down. Up again. It's later, there's a blanket across their laps. Nightime.*]

[*Looking out the window —pulling away.*]

RENEE: [*Cont'd.*] — I've always wanted to try parachuting.

[LILI *looks out window.*]

As a *sport.*

LILI: As a *sport.* Oh.

RENEE: Have you ever wanted to?

LILI: Try parachuting? No. Me? No. I'm a little phobic. No, I might try...maybe...ballooning. I would maybe try ballooning.

RENEE: Maybe ballooning. Maybe. *Maybe* ballooning.

[*She leans over to check if* LILI'S *smiling. BLACKOUT.*]

[*Lights up on* ELEANOR, *downstage, in a pith helmet, in the bow of a canoe, paddling up a remote river. Shadows fall across her face. She paddles. Music fades out. Sound of water.*]

ELEANOR: I am convinced there is something in the female psyche that gets stuck and it just circles in and circles in like a 747 over Chicago, trying to land and can't. We just don't think it's our turn.

For five decades, I have struggled to say something more than, "Where could I have put my pocketbook?" which is the central thing I remember my mother saying. "Where could I have put my pocketbook?" She would say it like it meant... Like she meant to say, "Now where could I have put my ...mind?"

ELEANOR: [*Cont'd.*] We haven't thought big enough.

Our thoughts are small. We retrace our steps constantly.

[*Resting paddle, taking off helmet.*]

Once you come to ... you have no place to start from.

Nothing here will make any sense to you.

Nothing here will make any sense.

Including becoming a student of history.

Including becoming a student of the female brain.

Including becoming a feminist

archeologist/historian/bilingual

student of the female brain.

You will be stuck without a ride.

[*She starts to paddle again.*]

At this point your only recourse is to choose between the

following methods of transportation:

falling into madness, falling in love,

committing suicide or burning at the stake.

Which is by far the trickiest one to engineer. You have to

get somebody else to do it to you.

But ... that's also what makes it the elegant choice ... Leaving

you free to signal through the flames.

[*A huge, blow-up slide of a photograph of the "AIRPORT
HILTON" sign. Music: Duke Ellington's, "Stompy Jones." RENEE
sits in a chair facing LILI, who sits on the still-made bed. RENEE has
her head in her hands.*]

RENEE: I can't believe I'm here with you.

RENEE: [*Cont'd.*] I cannot believe I'm here.

LILI: [*Pause . . . looks at* RENEE.]

Why don't you take off your coat?

RENEE: I think I'm not going to stay.

LILI: Oh. [*Pause.*]

Do you wish I were a man?

RENEE: Don't be ridiculous. I'm *married* to a man.

Do *you* wish you were a man? [*No response.*]

LILI: [*Looking around room.*] Did the bellboy make you nervous?

RENEE: [*Leaning forward.*] I don't want to disappoint you.

Did you think I was gay? . . . When you saw me on the plane?

LILI: [*This is a lie.*] I didn't think about it.

RENEE: But would you think that I was? If you saw me . . . just . . .

on a bus?

LILI: Probably not. Maybe a little.

Around the mouth.

RENEE: The mouth?

That's really odd.

LILI: Maybe it's more the walk.

RENEE: The walk. You're saying you could tell . . . you would think

I liked women if you saw me walking . . . toward a bus?

LILI: It's possible. I could tell there was a possibility.

RENEE: [*Matter-of-factly takes off coat. She is wearing a slip.*]

A possibility I liked women.

[*They smile.*]

That's really odd.

Maybe I'm a man. Is that a possibility? I *feel* like a man . . .

LILI: Feeling like a man means: wanting it direct, to the point

LILI: [*Cont'd.*] and now. Is that at all how you feel?

RENEE: Yes. A *lot* of the time.

LILI: Then maybe... you are... a man.

And maybe *I'm* a man too... and that is why... you can't tell we are gay.

RENEE: If we were both men we'd still be gay.

LILI: True.

Why don't you just let it out Renee.

[RENEE *gets up, goes to her purse, takes out a changer, points it to the wall, a slide comes up.*]

RENEE: These are my parents, just after they married.

[*Click.*] This is my mother with her best friend Zelda.

[*Click.*] This is my mother as a girl.

[*Click.*] This is my mother with me.

[*Click.*] This is me.

I am not a child, but a nuclear physicist trapped in the body of an infant.

This is not just my mother, but an orchestra... swelling to the night's crescendo...

[*Clicks off slides.*]

I am my father.

Brave, close-shaven... my arm around your waist.

Dipping every now and then.

A bit too often...

You are soft, unsure. The color of your powder's called "sand dune"... the shade of your lipstick's called "coral."

RENEE: [*Cont'd.*] You're a lot like your mother, though you don't want to be. Your lips are dry as you try to feel light in my arms, as you try to dip. As you try to let me lead.

[*They look at each other. They are about to kiss.*]

That is what I started with. I just think that you should know.

LILI: I know.

[*They kiss. It takes awhile because it is the first time. They kiss again, harder. Lights fade. Music: Aretha Franklin's "I Never Loved a Man." Lights up on* MARY *in an orange coat with a small hard suitcase on the floor next to her, sitting at a table in the Airport Bar. She lip synchs to Aretha. Music fades. She looks for* LILI. *She arranges herself. She angles the empty chair away from the table to make it seem more welcoming. She waits.She switches chairs. She hails cocktail waitress.*]

MARY: WATER WATER EVERYWHERE AND NOT A DROP TO DRINK.

Yes. Let's see. [*Examines a huge drink menu.*] Why don't you bring me . . . I'll have two grasshoppers, please.

I'm expecting somebody.

(*She looks at her watch.* LILI *walks in.*)

Lili.

LILI: Hi Mary.

[*BLACKOUT. Lights up again. They are both seated, drinks half empty. We hear constant ambient airport noise. The lights are cocktail lounge red. They are mid-conversation.*]

LILI: The thing is . . . sometimes life is very strange. Very strange.

[*She takes a handful of peanuts.*]

MARY: I'm not exactly sure what it is I want to ask. The thing is hard to pinpoint. The idea. The feeling. It's hard to pinpoint.

LILI: Take my collection of love affairs, for example.

[MARY *nods.*]

Each situation, completely unique...all totally different people, yet...uncannily alike.

[*They both sip from tall drinks through straws.*]

MARY: Are you an Aquarius, or a Virgo?

LILI: Virgo.

MARY: [*Annoyed at herself.*] Right.

LILI: I mean, how do we spot each other from across a crowded room . . . and *infallibly* [*Strikes her palm with the back of her hand.*]

find the one who's going to make us crazy.

[*She looks at* MARY.]

Not *literally* . . . but . . .

[MARY *nods gracefully.*]

There were signs, little tip-off points about them
that could have clued me in. Some of them had the
same last name, or identical family structures, or a freckle
in the same place. I coulda spotted it.
But, instead of being like *warnings*, or *signals* . . .
and this is what I'm getting at,
those signs became like little arrows
pointing to something familiar . . . to something . . . erotic.

MARY: [*Sends hand through air.*] ...looking for a place to happen . . .

[*They take another sip from straws.*]

LILI: The repetition compulsion is by far the most . . .

evolutionarily *cruel* phenomenon we've ever had, don't you

LILI: [*Cont'd.*] think?

MARY: Yes, I do.

LILI: I mean the desire to do it over and over again, in the vain
hope of getting it right is ... well, it's
pathetic. Especially considering we take such pains to
accurately reproduce, in loving detail,
the original situation which brought us to our knees in the
first place.
Seeking some sort of deliverance from the same fucked thing.
[*Pause. Looks at* MARY.]
Where did you fly in from?

MARY: Nowhere. Took the bus here from downtown.

LILI: So why'd you have me meet you at the airport?

MARY: It's my favorite bar. I love the atmosphere.
The mix of terror and boredom. It's what
drinking's all about ...

LILI: Are you going to be coming home with me?

MARY: [*Reaching into her bag.*] I did order you something ... small.
[*Brings out a badly wrapped parcel.*] I know you told me not to.
[*Puts it in front of* LILI]
Just a token. A little nothing that caught my eye.
Just a little something that reminded me of you.

LILI: [*Not touching it.*] I guess there's nowhere else. Hmmm? At
least until we contact Mom.

MARY: [*Joining in.*] And figure out what's next.

LILI: That's right.
And as usual our agreement is: it cannot be a long term
thing here, Mary.

[MARY *takes out inhaler.*]

MARY: Granny used to breathe like this: ">>>>>>>>>>".

[*Uses inhaler.*]

LILI: Are you O.K. ?

[MARY *nods.*]

Are you agitated or anything?

[*Pulls out a prescription bottle.*]

I still have extras from before. If you feel, and I quote "disoriented and/or violent toward yourself and/or others."

MARY: No, I actually feel quite well.

Have you ever listened to Don Cherry?
When I was in the 10th grade everybody listened to this
album by Don Cherry, trumpet player,
and there was a lot of pressure then to live that way...like
you were bumping into things...like you were free...

LILI: Mmm-hm.

MARY: ...and a lot of people faked it...
and now are living in apartments, and
holding down jobs, and *I*, who hated this music,
I, who was made nauseous by it, somehow,
inadvertently...I don't know.
Somehow this became the way my life went.

[*Long pause.*]

LILI: Life does separate out, eventually, the ones who have real
trouble from the ones who are looking for it.

[*They smile.*]

MARY: Which is something else entirely.

[*They both smile.* MARY *points to present.*]

MARY: [*Cont'd.*] I got Mom a harmonica and a luggage lock. And I got you this and some shampoo. I don't know what happened to the shampoo . . . but . . . [*Gestures.*] open it.

[LILI *starts to unwrap the present. It is a toaster-oven. Lights fade. End ACT 1.*]

INTERMISSION

ACT II

Lights up on RENEE, *somewhere in Mexico, in a bathing suit and shirt.*

RENEE: The other day I went into the supermarket . . . and all I could see were women. Now, I go into the supermarket all the time . . . but I never noticed women. There are women everywhere . . . picking out heads of lettuce, picking out cans . . . standing behind their metal carts they stare at the frozen foods in their own little world.

And I wanted to go up to them . . . any one of them and say: "Excuse me, but I made love to a woman, and I could probably make love to you too, if you would like me to." I could barely control myself not to do that.

I made eye contact with every woman in there. I would stand beside them, wait till I got their attention and look them straight in the eye. I think they thought I was psychotic.

I especially made eye contact with the check out girl who I swear imbued the question, "Do you want paper or plastic?" with the vague feel of sex. I would have never noticed this before . . . but now I do. There is a subterranean life that runs just beneath and below the normal life, and you only see it

RENEE: [*Cont'd.*] if you fall in there ... and you either fall in there or you get pushed in, but you really don't go there for just a little excursion ... because there really is no way back ... to not noticing once you start. So I really don't know why they call it sexual preference.

[RENEE *exits, cross-fade* ...]

[*Lights of* LILI'S *apartment come up.* MARY, *in white gloves and orange crossing-guard straps, sits with a small STOP sign on her lap.* LILI *goes to desk and starts looking for a set of keys.*]

MARY: At the time of her trial ... Joan of Arc was expected to be, a terrified, humble girl.

Her first words revealed a different disposition: when asked to swear upon the Gospels that she would answer nothing but the truth, she said, "Perhaps you'll ask me things I will not tell you." [*Pause.*]

There's a girl who trusts her voices.

LILI: ... Hmm-mm.

MARY: The only modern version of this I know of, is bulimia. [*Pause.*]

LILI: [*Throwing her keys.*] Here's an extra set, top and bottom lock front door, top and bottom lock back door. The Medeco is the downstairs front door. The police lock's only used at night, from the inside. I do that.

I expect you to come right back here after work, at 3:15. I expect you to report to me about your whereabouts at all times. And I assume it is clear without my even *specifying* this: convenience stores are out of bounds.

When are you due at work?

MARY: Not for another hour.

[*Looks at her equipment.*]

I just wanted to be ready...

LILI: You were always like that. Remember when Mom'd drive us to the pool and you'd already have your bathing cap and goggles on in the car? That was very embarrassing.

MARY: ...but that way, you're already on vacation. That way it starts before you get there.

LILI: You are just so literal.

You are incapable of metaphor.

MARY: Remember when you begged Mom to send you back to that camp, because you were so moved by the candlelight closing ceremony at the end of the summer that it completely wiped out the memory of how much you hated that place?

LILI: What's your point?

MARY: ...just that all you're capable of *is* metaphor. Deep down everything always reminds you of something else...

[*Looks at her.*]

What's her name? [*Looks at* LILI.]

LILI: Renee. [MARY *looks at her.*]

She's straight.

MARY: Of course she is.

What's she do?

LILI: Paleontologist.

MARY: [*Shaking her head.*] You have my sympathy.

That is a very sexy thing for a woman to do.

LILI: She's married.

MARY: Of course she is.

LILI: She's with her husband now in Mexico, trying to patch things up.

MARY: [*Smiles at* LILI.]

I bet it's going badly.

I bet she's hitting the rum.

She misses you.

LILI: It's in this place . . . [*Draws a square in the air.*] over here.

It's what it is.

MARY: Well, that's O.K. then.

LILI: Yeah but I'm just tired of compartmentalizing.

MARY: Be grateful you *can* compartmentalize.

To me emotions are like a big wind. A tornado with people and garbage and furniture whirling around....

[LILI *takes out wallet, pulls out a photo of* RENEE *and gives it to* MARY, *who studies it.*]

MARY: [*Cont'd.*] [*Looking at photo.*] Looks like she's got fruit in her hair.

Is that fruit?

LILI: [*Looking on.*] No . . . I don't think so. That's just her hair.

MARY: It looks as if she's turning half away from you . . .

LILI: She's at a dinner party . . .

MARY: But, see how her face is pointed at you but her shoulders are sort of tilted away to one side? Like she's about to get up and get herself a snack? [*Pointing to photo, does pose.*] See that?

[*Hands back photo.*] Looks like she's gonna bolt.

LILI: Well, I'm don't know how you get that from a snapshot of a

LILI: [*Cont'd.*] person eating paella.

MARY: You always pick somebody busy not noticing you.

[*Spot up on* RENEE *in a robe, the phone in her hand. The phone rings.* LILI *looks at it. She goes over and answers it.* RENEE *hangs up. Dial tone.* RENEE'S *light goes* out. LILI *hangs up. Sits staring at phone.*]

MARY: [*Cont'd.*] [*Looking at* LILI.] Last night I had another in my series of Celebrity Nightmares.

LILI: Like the one where you were supposed to give Jeremy Irons a neck-massage?

MARY: Right right. Or, I'm driving Richard Gere and Cindy Crawford to the airport? No . . . this time, I'm with . . . Omar Sharif, only sometimes I *am* him too, just a different version of Omar Sharif . . . and I'm supposed to help him choose a wardrobe . . . only we can't decide if he should go Arab or Western.

LILI: And . . . ?

MARY: Well, that's about the end of it. Those dreams just have that snapshot-feeling. It's nice though. It makes me wake up feeling like I touched something magic. That's what the famous do: they make you feel half-famous for a split of an instant. That's their job. It's hard work.

LILI: I think it's depressing. The whole thing.

MARY: Well, that's because you don't enjoy yourself.

You gotta just enjoy the human dilemma, Lili.

That's why it's there.

[*BLACKOUT. Music up immediately: Jane Siberry's "Are We Dancing Now?" Lights up on* RENEE *in a poolside chaise lounge, in a bathing suit, holding a sun-reflector under her chin. Next to her*

is another chaise, with a man's robe and towel and a copy of ES-
QUIRE on it.]

[*On a little table beside her is a man's watch and a wallet. She suns*
awhile, then shields her eyes and watches a figure swim laps, left to
right, in the first row of the audience.]

[*Music fades.*]

RENEE: What, sweetheart? [*Speaking up.*]

No. I don't want to come in right now,

I'm reading my book.

[*She leans back. She picks up* ESQUIRE *and flips through it.*]

[*Very loudly.*]

Do you want me to order you another Tecate?

[*She picks up his watch and looks at the time. She looks out at him*
again.]

[*Shielding her eyes, nodding.*] I can *see*. You going for half a

mile? Great.

[*Shakes her head.*]

No, I don't want to come in again . . . the sun's starting to go

down.

[*Puts on her flip-flops.*]

I'm going to go order another drink.

[*Puts on robe.*]

Do you have any cash?

[*He can't hear.*]

Cash. [*He can't hear.*]

Never mind, honey. You keep swimming.

See you up in the room.

[*She gives a tiny wave. Picks up his wallet, and she picks up his watch and puts it on. She feels its weight on her wrist . . . feels what it's like to wear a man's watch. She stares out.*]

[*Cross fade.* MARY *in white gloves and crossing-guard straps, stopping traffic at an intersection. We still see* RENEE'S *fade out as scene begins. Sound of city traffic mixed with sound of planes taking off.*]

MARY: [*As she unfreezes.*] Hold up, hold up, hold up. *You.* Hold up.

Stop!

[*Points to other group.*]

You. Come on.

Go. Go!

[*Points to someone else.*]

Hurry up here, keep it moving.

O.K., O.K., if you're going to make the turn, make

it, but blend. Blend with this guy.

Are you blending?

And you. Yield. He has the right of way.

[*Back to other group.*]

O.K., you guys go.

Move up into the intersection . . . you're blocking

this whole lane.

YOU — IN THE TOYOTA . . . MOVE!!

Go around him. Go.

Make a choice! This is the 90s . . . choose a lane

and fill it . . . pull out and be hopeful.

Yeah, alright . . . that's it. We got a flow going now.

Very good.

Don't worry about the traffic lights —

MARY: [*Cont'd.*] I'm superseding
the traffic lights.
I'm the way things go.
[*Motions for new lane to pull forward.*]
Lady, why are you stopping?

You see me standing here. Would they
put a traffic engineer out here if
they wanted you to pay attention to the lights?
[*Honk-honk.*] What's *your* problem?
You see me talking to her.
[*Shakes her head.*] It's not your turn.
[*Sound of cars swooshing by her.*]
[*Points.*] YOU. STOP.
Oh, jeez... what, I don't exist now? Is that it?
(*Pulls out gun.*]
Which part of "hold up" did you not understand?
[*Puts it back.*]
It's amazing how they listen to that.
[ELEANOR, *in her own spot, is staring into a pool of water . . . which
casts a blue light on her face.*]

ELEANOR: There was a lot of ice in my background. Ice skating,
iceberg lettuce, the sound of ice in a highball glass...
When I think of my childhood, I am skating an awful lot of
the time.
I lace my skates up on the bench.
I try to be safe. I try to push off. I take little trips, little
half-circles on the ice. Like the marks left on
cocktail napkins by our mothers' Martinis: half-circles

ELEANOR: [*Cont'd.*] on the ice — over frozen lakes with
Indian names.

Little trips.

[*Dangles hand in water, sound of splashing.*]

Try to make it look like you're practicing: never ever let it
seem like you are actually doing this.

[*Pulls hand out.*]

I can feel them pulling, but I won't go back.

(*Cross-fade to* LILI *and* MARY. *Back in her apartment,* LILI *is working on her computer, compiling evidence.* MARY *enters, taking off her uniform.*]

LILI: [*Not looking up.*] How was work?

MARY: [*Cheerful.*] Fine.

LILI: I'm working on your case.

MARY: [*Drinking a YooHoo.*] You seen my *Sylvia Plath:
The Complete Works* anywhere?

LILI: You're reading that book?

MARY: Yeah. Why not.

LILI: Well, it's just I wouldn't recommend her for people with a
tendency toward depression.

MARY: I find her hysterically funny myself. [*Looks for book.*]

LILI: Sylvia Plath?

MARY: She is one of the great comic writers of the 20th Century.

LILI: Prove it.

MARY: [*Finding book, she walks to the center of room, and 'delivers' the section, loudly and as one sentence.*]

"You who have blown your tubes like a bad radio

Clear of voices and history, the staticky

Noise of the new.

MARY: [*Cont'd.*] You say I should drown the kittens. Their smell!

You say I should drown my girl.

The baby smiles, fat snail,

From the polished lozenges of orange linoleum.

You have one baby, I have two.

I should sit on a rock off Cornwall and comb my hair.

I should wear tiger pants, I should have an affair.

We should meet in another life, we should meet in air,

Me and you."

[*Pause, sits down, closes book.*]

LILI: That's not funny.

MARY: To each his own. [*Pulls out another book.*]

When I'm done with her I'm starting on, "The Encyclopedia of Amazons."

LILI: [*Taking book, reading cover.*] "Women Warriors from Antiquity to the Modern era." "Absorbing . . . a fresh, sometimes surprising look at the role of women in the world's long history of combat."

MARY: After they burned her, they also tried to burn her heart . . . because there were these rumors that her spirit would escape . . . but they *couldn't* set it on fire no matter how much lighter fluid they used . . . and they ended up having to throw it in the river.

. . . and that is when the executioner went mad . . . because he knew he burned a saint. That is a fact. If you watch the Ingrid Bergman movie, you can see him get upset and beat his fist against his head, but they don't explain why or anything. I guess they didn't think it was integral to

MARY: [*Cont'd.*] the plot . . .

LILI: They shoulda gotten you to play her.

MARY: [*Looks at* LILI.] Yeah well.

I know I'm not really her.

LILI: I know you do.

Come here. I'll show you what I'm working on.

I'm working on your past. [*Points to a pile on the floor.*]

Baptisms, report cards, early poems . . .

MARY: There were just so few examples of a woman I would want to be when I grew up.

LILI: [*Typing on the keyboard.*] There was Harriet the Spy. There was Margaret Mead.

MARY: Those were yours. Besides . . . I mean they were nice, but you couldn't qualify them as warriors.

TinTin and Go Speed Racer were the only two I liked and they were boys.

LILI: *And* both cartoons.

MARY: *And* both cartoons.

[*The phone starts to ring. Spot up on* RENEE, *at a pay phone in an overcoat.* LILI *looks at the phone. She goes over and answers it.* RE-NEE *hangs up. Dial tone.* RENEE's *light goes out.* LILI *hangs up. Long pause.*]

MARY: [*Looks at* LILI *who is frozen.*]

The thing you want to say is:

"I am not a thought you're having."

MARY: "I am not a thought of yours."

Am I right?

What ever happened to that U.P.S. delivery woman ?

LILI: I sent her her stuff

LILI: [*Cont'd.*] in a cardboard box. There wasn't much:

her toothbrush, perfume, an extra T-shirt,

photographs of her naked, photographs of me naked, a pair

of dangly earrings and a map.

MARY: Did you send it U.P.S.?

LILI: [*Breaking into a smile.*] I certainly did.

MARY: Why do you live like this?

LILI: Why do you commit crimes?

MARY: [*Nods, as if to say, "good point."*]

I think we need to bring Mom back here.

LILI: No offense, Mary but since you've come to stay I have been

searching for our mother's whereabouts with something

approaching desperation.

The Palenque police have got her photo, I put an A.P.B. out

in Peru and I've contacted the Smithsonian, the State

Department and Kundalini Tours.

MARY: (*Sits down at computer, taps out message.*] "Come home."

"We need you for verification. Huge chunks missing.

Make haste, your daughter Mary, and your daughter Lili."

Have you got that printer on?

LILI: Where are you going to send it?

MARY: Telepathic fax: just print it out, and it goes to where she is.

Angels ... slip inside the lock.

LILI: [*With her.*] ... slip inside the lock.

[*Blackout.*]

[*Lights up on* ELEANOR.]

ELEANOR: I suppose my girls are mad at me.

ELEANOR: [*Cont'd.*] I imagine I did a number of horrible

things to them growing up.

Whole entire lapses of concern . . .

In fact I spent the whole time

that they would describe as their childhood

in a sort of fog.

I was in a light trance at the time. And now I honestly do

not remember when I said, for instance, : ",,,,,,,,,,,,,,," which

turned Mary into a criminal. Or the time I asked the

salesgirl for help in Bloomingdale's and completely mortified

Lili, to the point where she *still* hates being naked. I take

their word for it but I don't remember.

If it's true that we replace each cell entirely every seven

years, and if the soul does

progress across the sky, like the planets . . .

then it's fair to say I was a different person.

Someone I no longer am. The person you have come for is

no longer here.

And the little girls they were, are no longer here.

So . . . it is just a memory talking to a memory.

There maybe should be a statute of limitations on this kind

of thing, but there isn't.

[*Lights up on* RENEE *on a plane, a pineapple in the seat next to her.
She is reading a magazine. Lights also up on* LILI *alone, in a robe
on her bed, a mini-recorder in her hand.*]

LILI: [*Into mini-recorder.*] Dear Renee. I have to tell you

something right now.

I may be a first for you . . . but you are my one-too-many

LILI: [*Cont'd.*] times. You are the thing that keeps coming back at different intervals. What's missing is the same. It's the same ache. You want to play missing persons? You pretend you're missing and I search for your whereabouts?
So I can trail you, do surveillance?...dust for prints?...stake out your home?...run a credit-check ?...figure out if you're gay? So that you could be my subject...and I could deliver you back explained.

I have stared in people's eyes until they bloom their secrets...took their private puzzles on and solved them.
I have cracked the hard ones, Renee.
But secretely, I became a private investigator because I wanted, with something approaching despair, for someone to figure *me* out. That I could just for once be the subject...of an investigation.
That it would be my turn to be the mystery.
It is my turn to be the fucking mystery.

RENEE: [*Reading from* ESQUIRE.]
HOW TO MAKE LOVE TO A WOMAN:
start with the throat. Start there. Look at this place. Is it open? Is it closed? Notice the adam's apple. Place of the great fall. The face may be the road-map, but the throat will show you all your short cuts.
Look at her lips. Now kiss them.
Here the rules of the road apply:
If you go into a skid, steer right into it...and for god sakes keep your foot off the brake.

RENEE: [*Cont'd.*] Take all the hard right hand turns you want, but always, always signal.

Pass a hand across her belly, travel South. Slow down on the entrance ramp.

Cross the isthmus of her down-below ... as lost and as convinced as any Columbus.

[*Lights up on* MARY *awake late at night. She has a sleeping bag, her boom box and a camping lantern. She drinks hot chocolate from a tin cup.*]

MARY: I can't believe I'm here again. I cannot believe I'm here.

I am trying to remember **childhood**:

I remember the brown sand road and me alone on it.

I remember the cove, and the swimming pool but noboody touched me.

I would dive beneath the waves all day, touch bottom, push off ... climb back up, feel the blue rush past me like a slow embrace.

Repeat. All afternoon. Every afternoon.

Diving under in a one-piece: lunatic daughter called in from lunch ... sitting on a lawn chair ... in a bathrobe ... eating tuna-fish sandwiches but nobody talked to me, nobody touched.

[RENEE *appears beside* LILI *in bed asleep. She carries the pineapple.*]

RENEE: I am watching her for signs.

Something crucial. Something slow.

There are places she'll remember when you touch her.

RENEE: [*Cont'd.*] The body holds grudges. The body is old.

[*She sits beside her.*]

Maybe that's why we have one:

It's the only thing we take everywhere.

Tells us what we can't remember.

In dreams the fathers still are stalking us in the woods,

daggers at their sides like tiny flames.

The past.

The unremembered memories . . . of fierce assaults and slow

betrayals . . .

place of all places, soft tongue pressing on it . . . pressing till it

hurts.

Something crucial . . . something slow begins.

[LILI *wakes up.*]

RENEE: [*Cont'd.*] When I was in Mexico . . .

All I could think of was your hipbone against my cheek.

LILI: When you were in Mexico [*Sitting up.*]

all I could think of was:

which aftershave does that guy use?

Mennen? Old Spice?

RENEE: I'm leaving him.

LILI: Brut? Fabergé?

RENEE: I've left him.

LILI: Eternity for Men?

RENEE: It *is* your turn to be the mystery.

That's why you're so pissed off.

[*They kiss.*]

RENEE: [*Cont'd.*] I always wondered why
   I wanted to be
   a paleontologist
   so badly.

   But I think now having kissed you I might have made that
   my career.
   [*Cross fade back to* MARY *looking through her own file.*]
MARY: My two favorite subjects growing up were slavery and the
   Holocaust.
   I wanted to find out about a thing I had something in
   common with.
   Every day I practiced leaving in some
   form or another.
   Sometimes I would practice getting out of the car, and
   slamming the door.
   Sometimes I'd practice stepping out of the school bus onto
   the curb.
   I'd picture I was somewhere else . . . somewhere in Europe.
   Or I'd get in an elevator, and watch the door close behind
   me and focus on the sound it made "ssshhhhhhtt . . . " And
   then I'd press any floor other than the one I was going to . . .
   little things like that. Little trips.
   All my life I've had these two consuming fears, that
   1) I would *never* make something of myself, and
   2) that I would one day *make* something of
   myself.

MARY: [*Cont'd.*] It is unlikely you can actually learn

anything from success, anyway.

Failure:

It's like the desert, it's like Windex, it makes everything

clear.

LILI: How long have you been up?

MARY: A while.

I just keep drinking hot chocolate. [*Shrugs like there's no explaining it.*]

I don't think she's coming. I don't think she's coming back.

LILI: Ya. This time I think you're right.

I think she's gone.

MARY: Are we talking about our mother?

LILI: Yeah.

MARY: So. I guess this is pretty much it then. I guess we are the next

generation.

LILI: Yeah.

MARY: Well all I can say is: this is a small world.

LILI: You know what's stuck in my head? The music to that show,

"Mission Impossible." Remember?

LILI: I used to pretend that music was playing when I'd walk

around the house late at night. I pretended I was breaking

in to spy on Mom.

MARY: I did the same thing. Only I pretended I was gonna hold her

up.

LILI: There you go.

MARY: I just want to be part of this family.

This family is the schrapnel flying out in a million directions.

This is life after The Blast.

MARY: [*Cont'd.*] I just kept telling myself:

> I chose these parents.
>
> I slipped between their grief. I parachuted into their neglect.
>
> I came back to work on this, I told myself.
>
> There's too much energy in my hands. There's no where for it to go.
>
> I feel like they're gonna clench up on me . . .

LILI: What helps?

MARY: It feels like they're gonna fly off the ends of my arms.

> Like they're separate.

LILI: *What helps*?

MARY: I guess if you could hold them down . . . hold on to them . . .

> [LILI *holds* MARY's *hands.*]
>
> Tighter.
>
> [LILI *does that.*]
>
> Tighter.
>
> [LILI *squeezes them tight.*]

LILI: Like that?

> [MARY *nods.*]

MARY: I've been trying to remember my childhood.

> I think I need a better past.

LILI: You just have to know what it is, apart from everything else.

MARY: I wouldn't know my own life if it walked right up to me.

> We split, you and me. We divided, like one cell.
>
> It's limiting enough to be a human being, it's fucked enough without having to split the traits with someone else.
>
> Why couldn't I be fierce for example? Is it your opinion

MARY: [*Cont'd.*] that I was never capable of being fierce??

Wasn't it in my column?

Life is hard enough without having to lop off an entire column of human attributes in order to survive.

LILI: I think you're fierce. I think of you as fierce all the time.

MARY: [*Furious.*] What I'm lacking is an achievement.

Of any kind.

LILI: *You are not.* [*Pause.*]

You have sailed through practically an *armada* of therapists ... completely unchanged. That has got to count for something.

MARY: [*Stopping in her tracks.*] ... didn't touch me did they?

LILI: [*Shakes her head.*] They shoulda paid *you.*

MARY: ... for the privilege.

LILI: ... of your company.

MARY: Is there someone in your bedroom? I think I heard some Spanish music ...

LILI: [*Leaving.*] She's back. Early. She came back early.

MARY: Well if she tries an escape ... you know what the King of Spain once said, on how to put down a coup d'etat ...

LILI: [*Getting up to go.*] No — what'd the King of Spain say?

[LILI *starts to leave.*]

MARY: 1) Stay in the palace.

2) Hold your ground, whatever the cost.

3) Do not leave under any circumstances, whatever they promise, whatever they threaten.

[LILI *goes. Comes right back.*]

LILI: Well. It's different.

[LILI *exits.*]

MARY: [*To herself.*] It's going to have to be.

[*Starting to collect her stuff to leave.*]

I thought I couldn't be the first to go, cause someone beat me to it. But I knew one day it would be my turn.

I'm gonna serve my time.

I'm gonna turn myself in.

[MARY *clicks on her own handcuffs. Collects all her stuff. Starts to go.*]

LILI: I'll get you out.

MARY: This is where the science comes up empty. We are at that place.

LILI: You can't go. Mom's gone. And I'm here.

Without some disaster to cope with.

MARY: You have your own disaster. God gives us each our own disaster. Believe me, you'll be fine.

[MARY *goes. Lights stay on* LILI, *who looks at* RENEE, *sleeping beside her.*]

[*Lights up on* ELEANOR, *fly-fishing in waders. She is knee-deep in water.*]

ELEANOR: I wish I knew the basics of voodoo.

The subtle realm.

Something happens here, and something over there gives way. The otherworld.

For me it's never been a two-way street.

It's always seemed to me like

"this is all there is."

I was never told. [*Upset at this.*]

That you have to look for your life.

ELEANOR: [*Cont'd.*] That some of us aren't born into our lives:
we have to go and look for them . . .
as if they're taking place somewhere
without us.

I wish that I had known that.

And now, the thought [*She looks at her watch.*]
of catching up to it . . .
[*She sits on the bank.*]
It's quite a moving target.

When my girls were in the womb, I listened to nothing
but Scarlatti.
Over and over. That was my plan.
I would sit by the window, stare out at the desert
and picture different forms of transportation.
I was hoping I could throw them far enough.
Something to lift them up and out.
[*Lights up on* MARY, *in prison orange, by a pay phone. Sound of coins dropping.*]

VOICE OF OPERATOR: "Will you accept a collect call to anyone
from Mary?

LILI: [*In her office, in different clothes, into speaker phone.*] Yes, I will.

MARY: Hey, Lili. Hi. Hi, It's me. How's it going?

LILI: Holding down the fort.

MARY: Good work. Remember what the King of Spain said, on how
to put down a coup d'etat . . .

LILI: [*Interrupting.*] I remember.

MARY: Listen, I just wanted to tell you . . . I think my
roommate . . . whatever you call 'em in here . . . I think she's
a multiple. [*Pause.*] Personality.

LILI: What's she in for?

MARY: Credit card fraud.
She's really touchy that you use the plural.
You don't say, "She's nice," you say, "They're nice." Or, "Do
they want to sit down?" Like that. So I wanted you to know.
In case you come to visit. I just wanted to warn you.

LILI: I'm coming Tuesday. I told you. [*Pause.*]
You sound good.

MARY: You sound: [*Thinks awhile.*] spectacular. [*Long pause.*]
At first I was really afraid to be locked up.
I thought:
I'm too individually directed for this. "I can't take the
organization." I told myself. But I found out it is a big relief.

LILI: Listen. I'm going to order myself something from this
catalogue. Do you want me to order you something?

MARY: What catalogue?

LILI: Smith and Hawkins.

MARY: Gardens! I love garden equipment. Listen —
you know me better than I do myself. You pick it out.

LILI: They have some trowels here from Sweden that are very nice.

MARY: What about those plastic clogs? Do they have any of those
yellow plastic clogs?

LILI: They have them but they come in wine, periwinkle blue or
ochre.

MARY: . . . no . . .

LILI: How about an outdoor grill specifically for salmon that's shaped like a salmon?

MARY: That reminds me why I called you. That reminds me why I called you up. Last night I had another in my series of Feminist Nightmares.

LILI: Like the one where you're in a big circle and you have to come to an unanimous decision?

MARY: Right right . . . only in this dream we were fishing, Lili. The two of us. We were back in Minnesota. We had cut a hole in the ice and made a fire right there to stay warm. On the ice. And we were fishing.

All of a sudden you caught something big. It felt really big. You reeled it in. It was Virginia Woolf. And she was angry, Lili . . . She was furious. She told you to throw her back in and you said are you sure? And she said, "Yes" so you did. And we just sat there and looked up at the stars . . . the monogamous stars . . . until I felt a tug, a tiny tug, it felt like *I* had caught something big, and so I reeled it in . . . And it was . . . you gotta believe me here, it was Ophelia. In the dream I caught Ophelia.

And she was nicer about it but still, she said to throw her back. And I said, "Are you sure?" and she just said: "Goodnight . . . goodnight goodnight goodnight" and started singing. And so I threw *her* back. We could hear her singing as she sank back under. And we both thought, this is some mother fucking river here we picked.

[*Listens to* LILI's *silence.*]

MARY: [*Cont'd.*] It really creeped us out. So we turned to the fire to stay warm, but pretty soon we heard something pulling my pole across the ice, so I picked it up and reeled it in and out of the ice came this bright red blob. It was a heart, Lili. Joan of Arc's ... and it was frozen solid.

I held it in my hand until it got warm and started beating again. It got all red and then it spoke. It spoke to me, and what it said was really simple.
It told us, "Fish somewhere else."

[*Silence.*] Is that amazing. Huh?
Is that a message?

LILI: That is a bonfire. That is a sentence in the sky.
[*Makes an arc with her hand.*]

MARY: [*In a tiny voice.*] "Surrender Dorothy,"
Listen ... do they *have* any outdoor lights in that catalogue?
Any like ... torches ... like the Tonga Room?

LILI: Well ... let's see they have some patio bonfire holders. They have a luau kit, "Complete supplies and instructions for a traditional luau."

MARY: What I'm thinking of are lights. A string of lights.

LILI: I can get those anywhere. Those are easy.

MARY: Why don't you send me those.
I'll have to ask my roommate, if it's alright with her ...
[*Hits her forehead.*] if it's alright with "them" ... if I hang them in our cell. On the ceiling. That way I'll have some stars.

MARY: [Cont'd.] That's what I need in here, some stars.

You won't forget to send them, will you?

LILI: No I won't.

MARY: I like a bonfire. I like a good bonfire...you know
that...

LILI: I know you do.

MARY: But I think I'd like those little lights. You know?

Those small fires...everywhere...are harder to put out.

[*Lights up brighter on* LILI *and* MARY, *then up on all, to include*
ELEANOR *and* RENEE. *BLACKOUT.*]

END OF PLAY

Heather McDonald

DREAM OF A COMMON LANGUAGE

Special thanks to Sharon Ott, Liz Diamond, and Julia Miles. *Dream of a Common Language* was commissioned by the Women's Project & Productions. The play was first presented in 1992 at the Berkeley Repertory Theatre and subsequently produced by The Women's Project & Productions under the artistic directorship of Julia Miles in association with AT&T Onstage© at The Judith Anderson Theatre, New York City, May 13-June 7, 1992. It was directed by Liz Diamond with the following cast:

MYLO	J. R. Nutt
CLOVIS	Mary Mara
VICTOR	Joseph Siravo
MARC	Rocco Sisto
POLA	Caris Corfman
DOLORES	Mia Katigbak

Set Design by Anita Stewart
Lighting Design by Michael Chybowski
Costume Design by Sally J. Lesser
Composer and Sound Design by Daniel Moses Schreier
Production Stage Manager: Jill Cordle

CHARACTERS

VICTOR   A painter. Thick-haired and full-bearded. A large, burly man with a powerful male energy. Vigor. A bouncing gregariousness as though he is anxious for people to think well of him.

CLOVIS   Victor's wife. A painter who hasn't painted in some time. Beautiful and sad. She has lost something about herself. Someone who was vibrant, passionate, curious. A strong woman who has been knocked over. Not someone easily given to depression. She is actively trying to understand something.

POLA   Their friend who makes pilgrimages. A painter. A not conventionally beautiful woman. Odd looking at times with a taste for colorful, exotic clothes.

MARC   A painter a few years younger than the others. He wears fine clothes well. There is a bit of the dandy about him but not silly. A walrus moustache waxed and twisted up at the ends. Fingernails buffed to a fine polish. A fastidious man, he has a horror of being out of control.

MYLO   Clovis and Victor's son. A thin, 9-year-old boy with yellow hair and pale gray eyes. Something sad and lost about him.

DOLORES   A nurse/companion to Clovis and governess to Mylo. Of another place and culture suggesting magic, mystery, secrets. Dresses simply, plainly. Catholic. A comforting presence but not grandmotherly.

TIME: *1874*

PLACE: a garden behind a country house outside Paris and a graveyard/sanctuary near the house

Origins and History of Consciousness
No one lives in this room
without confronting the whiteness of the wall
behind the poems, planks of books,
photographs of dead heroines.
Without contemplating last and late
the true nature of poetry. The drive
to connect. The dream of a common language.
— Adrienne Rich

"... wherever one looks twice there is some mystery."
— Elizabeth Bowen
A World of Love

"However much we may go to the work of male artists for
pleasure, it is difficult to go to them for finding a voice."
— Virginia Woolf

ACT I

SCENE 1

Dark. Just before dawn. The air is still. A garden behind a French country house. At the back of the house are three large windows where people can look out over the garden.

A nightmare. Framed in one of the windows is a small boy, MYLO, *bouncing a ball.*

MYLO: [*A whisper.*] It's dark, Maman.

[*Fire. A burning window. Framed in another of the windows, Clovis appears almost as an apparition in her white nightdress.*

There are other figures with CLOVIS. *They pull on her arms, pressing against her, yanking hard.* CLOVIS *struggles.*]

MYLO: It's dark, Maman.

[CLOVIS *waves around wildly trying to free herself. The tussle and the lines grow frenetic.* MYLO *repeats his line until the scream on the next page.*]

[*There are other voices now.*]

CLOVIS: Get away from me.

VICTOR: I have had enough.

CLOVIS: Let go of me.

MARC: I don't understand you.

[*Laughter mixes with the echoes of voices.*]

CLOVIS: Ugly?

DOLORES: You're going to hurt someone.

CLOVIS: Ugly?

POLA: Give it to me.

CLOVIS: Something happened.

MARC: You're crazy.

POLA: Give it to me.

CLOVIS: Stop.

MARC: I just don't like the mess you're making.

VICTOR: I have had enough.

CLOVIS: Please.

DOLORES: You're only hurting yourself.

CLOVIS: What you're doing to me. Stop. Please. Stop.

MYLO: [*Screams.*] Maman!

[*Suddenly, there is the terrible sound of shredding material and* CLOVIS' *arms are ripped off. She is torn apart.*

MYLO *stops bouncing his ball. Blackout.*]

[*Lights come up softly in the garden.*

DOLORES *lays out a deck of tarot cards.* MYLO *covers his ears with his hands.* MYLO *is a thin, nine-year-old boy in a white nightshirt. Yellow hair, pale gray eyes, something sad and lost about him.* DO-LORES *gently removes his hands from his ears.*]

DOLORES: She's awake now.

[CLOVIS *drifts past the windows and we glimpse a dreamlike, fleeting image.*]

VICTOR: Is she gone already? [*Exiting.*]

DOLORES: When I was young, I went with any man who wanted me and I stayed with them until they didn't want me anymore. I kept thinking that if I had someone, someone of my very own, it would be more than happiness. It would be like discovering the reason for my existence, the very reason for being the person I am.

Then I came here. Because of a woman. The first place I'd ever come not because of a man. I'd worked at the hospital eight years when your mother was carried in bald and screaming. When I met her, she asked me who I was, and I said, all I know of myself, where I come from, who I am, is that my name is Dolores.

MYLO: Which means sorrow.

DOLORES: [*She laughs.*] Well, it is funny because I've always thought of myself as a rather contented person. Clovis said, I like your name. So I came here.

VICTOR: [*Returning.*] Is she gone already?

DOLORES: Not yet. But soon. She's up.

VICTOR: [*An ache.*] I can't much longer.

DOLORES: [*Exiting.*] I know.

[VICTOR *strides off carrying a box of paints, an easel and a gun. He stops for a moment, turns back to the house, and then moves purposefully forward. The ghostly figure of* CLOVIS *passes by the three windows again and drifts out to the garden. She's barefoot, in her nightgown. Her face is pale, her hair messy, her eyes shadowy, and there is a dark privacy to her grief.*]

CLOVIS: Look at that. My god, I envy his vigor. His purpose.

MYLO: Maman. Maman, don't leave.

[CLOVIS *turns away. She sees something shiny in the garden and picks it up.*]

CLOVIS: A clear stone. Look how you can see the light coming through.

MYLO: Don't leave me.

[CLOVIS *goes into the woods.*]

DOLORES: Mylo, Dolores is coming.

MYLO: Maman?

DOLORES: It's morning. You're safe now. We're all safe.

MYLO: Where's Maman going?

DOLORES: Dolores is bringing you steamed milk.

MYLO: With cinnamon?

DOLORES: With cinnamon.

CLOVIS: [*Away.*] I think my very favorite smell in all of the world is cinnamon.

MYLO: Maman, where are you?

DOLORES: Mylo, I'm here. We'll have steamed milk.

MYLO: With cinnamon.

DOLORES: Yes, and will you remember to sip it slowly?

MYLO: I'll remember.

DOLORES: Don't want to burn your tongue.

MYLO: Don't want to burn my tongue.

[*Lights fade on* DOLORES *and* MYLO *and come up slowly, illuminating* CLOVIS *in the graveyard.* CLOVIS *kneels at the altar she has built around one of the grave markers. (Her creation is something similar to altar boxes or to Joseph Cornell's shadow boxes and assemblages.)* CLOVIS *faces a small headstone. Glued to the surface of the headstone are shards of different colored broken glass. The altar piece is filled with shiny things that catch and refract light. Colored glass jars, a string of glass beads, a ladies' hand mirror, half-filled bottles of perfume, silver earrings, shiny stones, a ruby ring, a piece of Venetian carnival glass, glittering pieces, reflective surfaces.*]

[*This place is* CLOVIS' *sanctuary. She holds out the shiny stone. She fixes the bottles working on her sanctuary. She talks to someone she senses is there. We glimpse a vision of a little girl. A mirage. A flutter of a skirt, a wisp of hair, a whisper*].

CLOVIS: I like this place at dawn. I breathe easier out here away from the house. The party is tonight. I hope I'll be fine. Victor says it's time. A year and a half. I should be able to manage a dinner.

I keep having this dream where I'm eleven and my father and I run through a field up a hill. We're out of breath and laughing. It's a beautiful sunny day and we're surrounded by light. I lean back my head, close my eyes, and smell the most extraordinary fragrance. Cinnamon. My father says to me, you can take this moment with you for the rest of your life.

That day with my father I felt that I could run and laugh forever and would always be surrounded by the most extraordinary smell.

[CLOVIS *looks around her sanctuary.*] This is now my field of cinnamon.

[*A train whistle blows.* CLOVIS *jumps up on the bench to watch the train. A vibrant young woman carrying a satchel dashes across the stage. Out of breath from running, she hikes up her skirt and rushes headlong after the train, laughing. (Or we only hear the young woman's voice, full of verve.)*]

A YOUNG WOMAN'S VOICE: [*From off.*] OH GOD, WAIT. WAIT FOR ME.

CLOVIS: Astonishing. That used to be me. That girl was me.

[*A gunshot from off.*]

VICTOR: [*Shouts, from off.*] Got her!

[*The train whistle recedes.* MYLO *bounces his ball.*]

SCENE 2

[DOLORES *and* MYLO *sit in the garden drinking steamed milk.*]

MYLO: Maman's in the woods again.

DOLORES: She'll come back soon.

MYLO: Maman likes to be alone in the woods. She told me.

DOLORES: Don't you like to be alone sometimes?

MYLO: Maman loves the woods more than she loves me.

DOLORES: That's not true, Mylo.

MYLO: It is true. She takes presents to the woods. I've seen her.

DOLORES: Well, it doesn't mean she loves the woods more than she loves you.

MYLO: What does it mean?

DOLORES: Drink your milk.

MYLO: Why doesn't Maman paint anymore?

DOLORES: I don't know.

MYLO: I thought I would like it better if Maman didn't paint anymore, but I don't.

[MYLO *looks for something in the garden.*]

DOLORES: Mylo?

MYLO: It's gone.

DOLORES: What?

MYLO: My magic stone. It's gone. I've lost it.

DOLORES: I've lost lots of things, Mylo, it's not so bad.

MYLO: Dolores, tell me again the story and the poem.

DOLORES: All I know is that my name is Dolores—

MYLO: —Which means sorrow.

DOLORES: Yes. And where I come from—

MYLO: —You do not know.

DOLORES: I do not know.

MYLO: The horses.

DOLORES: I remember my mother and father riding standing atop two beautiful white bare-backed horses. My mother and father wearing white and gold costumes with bits of ribbon that fly behind them. And they're laughing.

MYLO: The Hundreds and Thousands candies.

DOLORES: On special days, Papa would take the big fat bottle of Hundreds and Thousands candies off the shelf and say,

MYLO: Hold out your hands, Dolores.

DOLORES: Hundreds and Thousands of round sweetnesses, all colors. These candies came from far away in England and they were so small that separately they weren't worth eating. But to eat them by the handfuls as a little girl was wonderful. Papa tipped the bottle and poured and down the candies bobbed into my hands and out came my tongue and licked the Hundreds and Thousands.

MYLO: Now say the poem.

DOLORES: Gypsy wagons roll into the town,

Girls selling marbles and balloons,

A man and a woman dance by the river,

DOLORES: [*Cont'd.*] The man and the woman kiss,

    They find a bowl of apples in the river,

    And give them to the little girls,

    Candles and butterflies, little girls waving,

    Gypsy wagons roll out of the town.

    [CLOVIS *returns from the woods. She is beautiful with loose hair.*]

CLOVIS: I saw this girl in the woods. I saw her hike up her skirt and run headlong after the train. She grabbed a handle on one of the doors and pulled herself up. And when she stood in the car moving away from me, she had a huge grin on her face.

MYLO: Who was she?

CLOVIS: That used to be me. That girl was me.

MYLO: What was she running from?

CLOVIS: Where was she running to?

DOLORES: I don't know, Clovis.

CLOVIS: When she stood in the moving car with her hands on her hips and breathing hard, she looked radiant.

DOLORES: Do you know that it is one year today? Our anniversary.

CLOVIS: [*Touching* DOLORES' *hand.*] I'm glad you came to live with me. I've thought a great deal about my life this year. In the hospital I hallucinated much of the time. I worry that I've given away all these pieces of myself, that my things are scattered all over the place. I've lost so many things. I want to go and gather them all together.

MYLO: We've all lost lots of things. It's not so bad.

CLOVIS: Why did I give all those pieces of myself away?

DOLORES: You must not really need those things or you wouldn't have given them away.

CLOVIS: But sometimes I miss them.

DOLORES: You must've known that you could do without them.

    [VICTOR *returns carrying his box of paints, easel, the gun and a dead rabbit wrapped in burlap.* VICTOR *is a large, burly man. There is a bouncing gregariousness about him as though he's anxious for people to think well of him.*]

VICTOR: [*Shouting as he enters.*] Hello! Hello! I'm back. Someone come and greet me. Someone come and welcome me home.

[MYLO *rushes over and hugs his father around his legs.*]

MYLO: Papa! Papa!

VICTOR: Good morning, good morning my little monkey.

MYLO: Good morning, Papa.

VICTOR: Good morning to one and all.

[VICTOR *hands* MYLO *the sack.*]

VICTOR: [*Cont'd.*] Here, take this to the kitchen.

DOLORES: What is it?

VICTOR: Dinner.

[MYLO *leaves the garden but stands watching from one of the windows. He holds the sack with the dead rabbit.*]

CLOVIS: I thought we were having chicken.

VICTOR: Now we can have rabbit, too.

DOLORES: You're back early.

VICTOR: It's clouding over. Besides there's a lot to do to prepare for tonight. I've made a list.

DOLORES: Oh, Victor, you and your lists. Everything's in order.

VICTOR: I want to make sure everything goes smoothly. It's an important evening.

CLOVIS: Do you know that today it is one year since Dolores came to live with us?

VICTOR: There are many things to celebrate today. Dolores. Tonight's dinner. Pola returning from one of her trips. Where was she this time?

CLOVIS: Ceylon.

VICTOR: Pola and her pilgrimages. And Marc is back. So many things to celebrate.

CLOVIS: Marc is coming?

VICTOR: Of course. It's been months since I've seen him.

CLOVIS: Yes. Months.

DOLORES: Let's see this list of yours. Hmm...hmm...yes...all taken care of. One thing we could talk about, Victor, is the seating.

VICTOR: The seating will take care of itself.

DOLORES: We can't really do it boy and girl because I imagine there won't be enough women at the table.

VICTOR: There won't be any women.

CLOVIS: No women?

VICTOR: Dolores will be there, Pola will be there, and you will be there.

CLOVIS: Will be where?

VICTOR: At the dinner.

CLOVIS: But not at the table.

VICTOR: This is a meeting for painters, Clovis. We're planning an exhibit.

CLOVIS: I only have red wine.

VICTOR: What?

CLOVIS: I only have red wine and we're having chicken and rabbit.

VICTOR: We've had red wine with rabbit before. No one seemed to mind.

CLOVIS: I only have three chickens.

VICTOR: So?

CLOVIS: That's only six legs.

VICTOR: So?

CLOVIS: A chicken only has two legs, but the way they behave, you'd think they expected them to have more.

VICTOR: The way who behaves? The chickens?

CLOVIS: No. Everyone. The way everyone behaves.

VICTOR: Who?

CLOVIS: Everyone. They all expect a leg. Haven't you ever noticed? Especially Thomas.

VICTOR: Who?

CLOVIS: It never fails. He always grabs a chicken leg.

VICTOR: Thomas who?

CLOVIS: Well, I don't want him to have a leg this time. Let him see he can't always have exactly what he wants. Like we owed it to him or something. Why should he always be the lucky one?

VICTOR: Oh, for godsakes, give them all chicken legs. Get extra legs. Let everyone have as many chicken legs as they want. But above all, get chicken legs for Thomas because he wants them so goddam badly.

MYLO: Thomas can have mine.

[MYLO *exits.* CLOVIS *turns to leave.*]

VICTOR: Where are you going?

CLOVIS: To skin the rabbit.

VICTOR: I'll do that.

CLOVIS: Fine.

[*She's leaving again.*]

VICTOR: Where are you going now?

CLOVIS: To bed. I'm very tired.

VICTOR: You just got up. [*Pause. More softly.*] Can you sit for me this afternoon after you rest? I'd like to get far enough along so I can show it tonight. See what they all think. I'm a bit nervous.

CLOVIS: What time?

VICTOR: About two. The light will be right then.

CLOVIS: Fine, and now if you'll excuse me, I'm very tired.

[*She exits.*]

VICTOR: [*Embarrassed, he looks at* DOLORES.] She sleeps all the time yet she's always tired.

MYLO: Papa, Papa, come and help me pick out what to wear to your dinner.

DOLORES: Mylo will be at this dinner?

VICTOR: [*Wry.*] Is he a boy or a girl?

DOLORES: A boy.

VICTOR: Then I suppose he can come. [*Beat.*] Don't think too badly of me, Dolores.

DOLORES: I don't, Victor.

[*From off, we hear* MYLO.]

MYLO: Gypsy wagons roll into the town,

Girls selling marbles and balloons,

A man and a woman dance by the river,

The man and the woman kiss,

They find a bowl of apples in the river,

And give them to the little girls,

Candles and butterflies, little girls waving,

Gypsy wagons roll out of the town.

SCENE 3

[VICTOR *stands in the garden bewildered.* DOLORES *is busy.*]

VICTOR: She's gone again.

DOLORES: Yes.

VICTOR: She's always leaving.

DOLORES: Victor, I don't think badly of you.

VICTOR: Dolores?

DOLORES: Yes?

VICTOR: Are you busy this morning?

DOLORES: I have this list.

VICTOR: I know and it's not Tuesday, but would you like to do a letter?

DOLORES: With "The Centaur in the Garden?"

VICTOR: Yes.

DOLORES: I have been thinking of a letter.

VICTOR: And this would be a good time for you?

DOLORES: Shall I get the paper and pens?

VICTOR: Yes.

[DOLORES *exits.*]

[*We glimpse something moving in the garden, the head and shoulders of a man with the body and legs of a horse, a centaur. The image is reminiscent of the vision of* CLOVIS' *little girl. Almost a mirage. The centaur is hidden in shadows. A kick of the hind legs, a toss of the head, a whisper as the mythic creature disappears through the leaves.*]

[DOLORES *returns bringing* VICTOR *his special Florentine papers and quill pens.*]

DOLORES: How shall we begin my letter?

VICTOR: The same as usual?

DOLORES: My Dearest One.

VICTOR: Why don't you ever use his name?

DOLORES: I like it this way.

VICTOR: So much mystery. I imagine him to be all sorts of people. I fantasize about who this dearest one might be.

DOLORES: So do I.

[*There is a ritual in the way the table is arranged and they sit as if on cue.*]

VICTOR: What do you want to say first?

DOLORES: I want to talk about a memory of one of our first times together.

VICTOR: What about the memory?

DOLORES: That it stirs something deeply inside of me.

VICTOR: I like the phrase "stirs something deeply inside."

DOLORES: It was the day we went to the Italian mind reader in the back of that cafe off the Piazza Navona.

VICTOR: What kind of a day was it?

DOLORES: Rainy.

VICTOR: Cold?

DOLORES: Yes.

VICTOR: [*Scribbling away.*] All right, go on. The mind reader.

DOLORES: I think we went to this mind reader to allow us to say certain things that were on our hearts.

VICTOR: Oh, yes, that's good, "to say the things that were on our hearts."

DOLORES: Then we walked through the city together.

VICTOR: What do you remember about that?

DOLORES: He was very tall.

VICTOR: So you had to take big steps to keep up?

DOLORES: Yes.

VICTOR: But you didn't mind.

DOLORES: I didn't mind.

VICTOR: Now, let's connect this memory to this stirring deeply of something inside.

DOLORES: The minute I heard my first love story, I started looking.

VICTOR: Started looking.

DOLORES: I'd always known a great love makes a woman's life worthwhile.

VICTOR: Who told you that?

DOLORES: My mother.

VICTOR: What else could we add to that?

DOLORES: When he came into my life, everything opened.

VICTOR: In what way?

DOLORES: It was like discovering the reason for my existence, the entire reason for being the person I am.

VICTOR: We'll need something to round that out. Maybe something of joy.

DOLORES: Then something about how I think of him.

VICTOR: How do you think of him?

DOLORES: I think of him all the time. In the morning, I am sad because he has to go away, but in the evening, I am happy because he returns.

VICTOR: I can do something with that. Where to now?

DOLORES: Why have you abandoned me?

VICTOR: Why are you so far away?

DOLORES: Yes, I ache for him.

VICTOR: You must tell me what you want.

DOLORES: Yes.

VICTOR: Clovis has a look when she seems to let go of everything around her. I'm afraid she's dying.

DOLORES: You want to comfort her.

VICTOR: Why is it so hard for us to comfort one another?

DOLORES: I don't know.

VICTOR: I'm sorry, a digression, forgive me.

DOLORES: There's nothing to forgive.

VICTOR: Where were we?

DOLORES: Abandonment. Each time we were together nourished me, yet when he went away I was so quickly hungry again.

VICTOR: You want him to return to you.

DOLORES: It's night, my love, and it's time for you to return home.

VICTOR: It's night, my love.

DOLORES: Return to me.

VICTOR: Return to me.

DOLORES: Return to me.

VICTOR: I think I have most of it, the ideas you want. Is there anything else?

DOLORES: I'm not sure. I have a recurring dream.

VICTOR: A good or a bad dream?

DOLORES: It might not mean anything.

VICTOR: Go ahead.

DOLORES: I'm in a train station. I seem to be lost. I recognize no one. Then, suddenly, the Italian mind reader runs down the platform to me. He takes me by the arm. The next thing I know it's dark outside and I'm driving the train up a mountain and I'm scared. I cry out but I can't tell what I'm saying.

[VICTOR *thinks a moment and then writes* DOLORES' *letter.* DOLORES *moves through the garden cutting flowers for the dinner.* MYLO *stands in the window eating the Hundreds and Thousands candies.* CLOVIS *passes another window. She stops while the letter is read and then leaves.*]

VICTOR: Signed, The Centaur in the Garden. Read it aloud to see if it sounds all right to you. After all, it is your letter.

DOLORES: [*Reads.*] My Dearest One. Do you remember the day we went to the Italian mind reader? What causes each of us to live so hidden that we need a mind reader to allow us to breathe the things that are on our hearts but are too frightening to say out loud?

Later, we walked through the city arm-in-arm. I was delighted to walk with you even though I had to take giant steps, for you are much taller and take longer steps. But I didn't mind. It was gray and rainy and cold, but I didn't mind that either.

My mother told me that a great love makes a woman's life worthwhile, and that day I knew it was true. I had discovered the entire reason for being the woman I am. In the morning, I'd see you walking by, I'd almost cry. In the evening, again, I'd see you walking by, it would make me fly.

DOLORES: [*Cont'd.*] Why have you withdrawn your tenderness? Why have you gone so far away? After our first time together when we were still touching, I looked over and saw a radiant third body between us, a radiant third body that we had created. I thought that I would always know what you wanted, but I don't. I know what I want. I want to be the woman who will love you when your hair is white.

It's dark and cold tonight and I am lost. Sometimes in dreams, the Italian mind reader comes to me and I find myself at the controls of a train I have no memory of boarding. I am the driver of this lost train hurtling through the dark who keeps repeating her cry.

VICTOR: Is it all right?

DOLORES: Yes.

VICTOR: I embellished a bit, here and there. I hope that's all right.

DOLORES: Yes, Victor. It is the letter I imagined. Thank you.

VICTOR: And your name goes here. [DOLORES *signs her name.*] You won't tell me who the letters are to?

[*She opens a cigar box with many letters tied up in colored ribbons.*]

DOLORES: They're to no one. The letters are to my cigar box.

VICTOR: A cigar box?

DOLORES: It's the one place where I don't have to hold back. Where I'm allowed to love somebody as much as I want.

[CLOVIS *passes by the three windows.*]

VICTOR: Now I have to go back to my problem of making her less unhappy.

[*He moves to leave.* DOLORES *folds her letter.*]

VICTOR: Dolores, did someone really leave you in a train station?

DOLORES: It was a long time ago.

SCENE 4

[CLOVIS *enters the garden wearing a loose white gauzy cotton shift that opens down the front. It should be easy to slip the shift off her shoulders. She sits in a chair, loosens her garment and lets it drop into the chair in soft folds around her. She finds the right pose, holds it and is still. She has modelled often.* VICTOR *arranges her in the pose.*]

[VICTOR *sets up his materials and begins to work painting* CLOVIS.]

[*A stretch of stillness and silence.*]

CLOVIS: Do you know that I've never painted a nude?

VICTOR: Can you turn your head a bit more to the side?

CLOVIS: Like this?

VICTOR: Yes. Are you comfortable?

CLOVIS: [*Smiles.*] Yes.

VICTOR: You're not cold?

CLOVIS: I like feeling the sun on my skin.

VICTOR: I like looking at the sun on your skin.

   [*Silence.*]

CLOVIS: Tell me about the light in the morning. What you see.

VICTOR: I can't paint and talk at the same time.

CLOVIS: Why not?

VICTOR: I don't know. I just can't.

CLOVIS: We used to paint and talk all the time.

VICTOR: I'm working, Clovis. I want to know what they'll think tonight.

   [*Silence.*]

CLOVIS: When I was eleven, my father took me to a wonderful exhibition and showed me a room made of light. It was a complete sphere of the world made of glass. And you could walk through this sphere on a glass bridge that was the equator, bisecting the room. I remember standing at the center of that glass bridge surrounded by light. When I looked up, I saw a hemisphere of multi-colored continents and seas lit from outside so that it glowed like a cathedral. Below me was another

CLOVIS: [*Cont'd.*] hemisphere. And there I was at the center of the world standing on a glass bridge.

Oh, tell me about the light, Victor. What you see on the river.

VICTOR: It's still dark when I get there. I set up my easel and paints and I wait. Then the light starts to come so quickly that there's barely enough time to take it in. I wish it would come more slowly or that I could freeze moments. Everything is changing now. There's a faint pink in the sky that turns to crimson. Then the sky grows paler with the sun coming through and the trees can no longer hold the light back and it's silver all over the river blinding me. So bright. So bright, and then it's lost. It comes so quickly and then it's lost. I try to catch it but sometimes I can't look at my canvas because of what is happening on the river.

CLOVIS: I envy you.

VICTOR: Envy me?

CLOVIS: Each day you awaken with a purpose and hike out to a spot and paint. What is my life?

[*She holds her hands to her forehead.*]

VICTOR: What is it, Clovis?

CLOVIS: The familiar throbbing.

VICTOR: Should we rest a moment?

CLOVIS: No, I want to go on. It'll pass. [*Pause.*] What gives you the vigor to charge off at dawn with so much energy, so much purpose? Oh, if only I could sleep.

VICTOR: But you sleep all the time.

CLOVIS: While you become more in the past ten years, I seem to become less and less.

VICTOR: That's not true.

CLOVIS: It feels true.

VICTOR: You're having one of your sad days.

CLOVIS: No, it's more than that. Why is it that so many women who were vibrant, interesting people seem to become less and less in marriage? Why, Victor?

VICTOR: I don't know. Can we talk about this another time? Right now, I would like to paint but my model is fidgeting about. Can you please be still?

CLOVIS: Do you remember me when we met? That girl in a tree in her bloomers picking an apple and yodelling. That was the very best part of me.

VICTOR: Look, you're having one of your sad days.

CLOVIS: No, that's not it.

VICTOR: And you're wanting to make yourself sadder by thinking about sad things.

CLOVIS: No, I'm not trying to be sadder. I'm trying to understand something.

VICTOR: I miss that girl in a tree, too.

CLOVIS: I delighted you.

VICTOR: You still do.

CLOVIS: Sometimes.

VICTOR: Sometimes. [*Pause.*] Think about something happy. Think about Pola. She'll be here soon.

[*Silence while* VICTOR *paints.* CLOVIS *holds the pose.*]

CLOVIS: Do you remember that woman—

VICTOR: —Clovis—

CLOVIS: —who lived with the sculptor? Madeleine? She went around saying, I did the hands and feet.

VICTOR: Claude Tissot's mistress.

CLOVIS: Some people think she did a lot of Tissot's work.

VICTOR: Maybe she did.

CLOVIS: But no one ever took her seriously.

VICTOR: No one knew to take her seriously.

CLOVIS: Why didn't they?

VICTOR: I don't know.

[CLOVIS *pulls up the shift wrapping it round herself. (This is where it happened in the first production, but it could happen later and has in subsequent productions. The actors and director should find the place that feels right for them.)]*

CLOVIS: If you *had* known, would you have taken her seriously?

VICTOR: I don't know. I don't answer hypotheticals.

CLOVIS: But if you had known, would you have taken her seriously?

VICTOR: I didn't know. I don't know now.

CLOVIS: But if you had.

VICTOR: You're being silly, Clovis.

CLOVIS: No, I'm being serious. What would we call Madeleine if we had known to take her seriously?

VICTOR: I know what you're doing. You're trying to pick a fight.

CLOVIS: What would you call her, Victor?

VICTOR: Stop it.

CLOVIS: Come on, you're in a conversation with someone who says, Victor, I've never heard of this person. Who is this Madeleine?

VICTOR: She's a woman sculptor.

CLOVIS: How could she ever be taken seriously if the word "woman" always preceded her?

VICTOR: What is it that you want here?

CLOVIS: want to be taken seriously.

VICTOR: Well, right now you're being silly and difficult.

CLOVIS: I don't want to be silly and difficult.

VICTOR: You want to be taken seriously.

CLOVIS: Yes.

VICTOR: What does that mean?

CLOVIS: I don't know, but I think I would know when it happened.

VICTOR: If you want to be taken seriously, then you have to do serious things.

CLOVIS: Like what?

VICTOR: You have to be serious about something.

CLOVIS: I am serious about a great many things.

VICTOR: Like what?

CLOVIS: I'm serious about my garden and my friendship with Pola and —

VICTOR: — Yes, and?

CLOVIS: And being with Dolores and the soup I am making for dinner. [VICTOR *doesn't say anything.*] Those things don't count?

VICTOR: I didn't say that.

CLOVIS: Those aren't really serious things, are they? Are they?

VICTOR: People don't normally think of those as serious things.

CLOVIS: People take you seriously. What sorts of things do you do that are serious?

VICTOR: I am a serious painter.

CLOVIS: I *was* a serious painter.

VICTOR: But you stopped.

CLOVIS: [*A blurt.*] Yes, but . . . I had a son and a husband and a house and a garden and a sick mother and large dinners. Aren't those serious things?

VICTOR: They're different.

CLOVIS: Don't lie to me.

VICTOR: All right, those aren't serious things.

CLOVIS: But you have all those same things. You have a son and a house and a garden and large dinners.

VICTOR: And I'm a painter.

CLOVIS: I helped you. I washed your brushes. I made your food. I talked with you about paintings. I modeled for you. *I* helped you become a painter.

VICTOR: That's true.

CLOVIS: Doesn't that count?

VICTOR: Yes, it counts.

CLOVIS: Doesn't it mean something that we did those things together?

VICTOR: Yes, but I could've done those things myself, Clovis.

CLOVIS: [*As though she's been slapped. A blow.*] But I was your model.

VICTOR: I could've gotten another model.

CLOVIS: Oh. [*Pause.*] That's it then. Because you're a painter, you're taken more seriously than I am.

VICTOR: You don't take yourself seriously. You never stick to any one thing long enough to be serious. You go from playing the oboe, to dancing lessons, to reading Tarot cards, to painting, to having a child, to having a garden, to disappearing into the woods for hours. You never finish anything. Why don't you stick to one thing?

CLOVIS: I DON'T STICK TO ONE THING BECAUSE NO ONE EVER TAKES IT SERIOUSLY.

VICTOR: OH, STOP IT. STOP IT, CLOVIS.

CLOVIS: ALL I WANTED TO KNOW WAS HOW I COULD BE TAKEN SERIOUSLY.

VICTOR: STOP BEING A WOMAN.

CLOVIS: That's serious.

VICTOR: I didn't do this to you.

CLOVIS: I painted, Victor. I made paintings.

VICTOR: What made you stop?

CLOVIS: I already explained that.

VICTOR: No, what really made you stop?

CLOVIS: Were my paintings good?

VICTOR: In their own way.

CLOVIS: But they weren't the right sorts of paintings, were they? Not really the sorts of paintings to be taken seriously.

[*He moves nearer to her. He wants to touch her.*]

CLOVIS: [*Cont'd.*] Nothing about me is very fertile. I have managed one small pale boy, a few paintings, that is all.

VICTOR: [*Softly.*] Clovis? It's getting cold. Why don't you cover up. We can stop for today. I don't want you catching cold. Don't you need to fix your hair before dinner?

CLOVIS: Shall I leave it down or put it up?

VICTOR: Why are you crying?

CLOVIS: I'm having one of my sad days.

VICTOR: I want so badly to be able to comfort you.

[CLOVIS *stands facing* VICTOR. *She drops her hands to her side and lets the gauzy white wrap fall softly open.* VICTOR *and* CLOVIS *are in silhouette.*]

CLOVIS: Victor. Touch me. Now. Touch. Me. Touch. Me. Now.

VICTOR: It's cold.

CLOVIS: No

VICTOR: It's—

CLOVIS: No.

VICTOR: Clovis.

CLOVIS: When I first met you, I felt a rush of relief and something in me moved forward, pushed all the rest away.

VICTOR: And then what happened?

CLOVIS: Touch me.

VICTOR: Where?

CLOVIS: Here.

VICTOR: Where?

CLOVIS: Here. And here. And here. And here.

[*He touches her. A soft moan. She touches him. They touch each other everywhere.*]

SCENE 5

[*A transition. A lull in the late afternoon. The soft sounds of a rain shower. Everyone is off alone.* CLOVIS *napping.* VICTOR *dressing in his evening clothes. From off, we hear* MYLO *bouncing his ball.*]

[*We hear laughter.* POLA *arrives on a bicycle ringing a bell.*]

POLA: Hey! Hey, where the hell is everybody? [*She exits.*] Hey!

[*Blackout.*]

SCENE 6

VICTOR *and* MYLO *are in the garden just past dusk.* VICTOR *holds something cupped in his hands.*

VICTOR: Look.

[MYLO *comes over.* VICTOR *carefully opens his hands. He's holding something luminous.*]

MYLO: What is it?

VICTOR: A luminous golden night butterfly.

[MYLO *gazes in awe.*]

MYLO: It's a very still butterfly.

[MYLO *reaches out.*]

VICTOR: Careful not to touch their wings, they die.

MYLO: They die?

VICTOR: They could.

MYLO: Its wings are twitching.

VICTOR: Tell it a story.

MYLO: Gypsy wagons roll into the town,

Girls selling marbles and balloons,

A man and a woman dance by the river,

The man and the woman kiss.

[*The luminous night butterfly flutters away. A bit of light floating out into the night.* VICTOR *and* MYLO *look up watching the light.*]

VICTOR: It liked your story. It's dancing.

MYLO: Look.

[*He points up at a tree. At the top are many golden bits of light. A dancing halo of light hovers over the tree*].

VICTOR: [*Whispers.*] They'll be there all night.

MYLO: [*Whispers.*] Where do they come from?

VICTOR: [*Whispers.*] From the moon.

[*They look at the moon.*]

VICTOR: [*Cont'd.*] At least, that's what I've always been told.

MYLO: [*Still looking at the moon.*] Does Maman know about the night butterflies?

VICTOR: I don't think so.

MYLO: Could I tell her?

VICTOR: If you like.

MYLO: It could make her smile.

VICTOR: It could.

[*Pause. They stand looking at the night butterflies and the moon.* MYLO *holds his father's hand.*]

MYLO: They're from the moon?

VICTOR: Yes, from the moon.

SCENE 7

[CLOVIS *and* POLA *enter the garden arm-in-arm laughing. They are dressed in their evening dinner clothes.* POLA *wears something foreign and exotic in flamboyant colors.*]

CLOVIS: So you arrived at the Royal Horticultural Society on your bicycle wearing a turban.

POLA: With all these gentleman naturalists and botanists and biologists staring at me.

CLOVIS: Was it your aqua and purple turban?

POLA: With the gold threads running through the fabric.

CLOVIS: I like that turban.

POLA: I think it brings out the violet in my eyes, don't you?

CLOVIS: Yes, I do.

POLA: The ride over had been a bit bumpy — I think my bicycle needs repairing again — anyway, the turban kept falling off to the side of my head and I kept shoving it back up on top but it wouldn't stay.

CLOVIS: So you entered the hall with your aqua and purple turban perched precariously on the side of your head.

POLA: I suppose I did look a bit odd.

CLOVIS: So what.

POLA: Piss on them if they can't take a joke.

CLOVIS: Absolutely. Piss on them.

POLA: This naturalist who was lecturing had recently returned from South America where he'd repeated Darwin's journey. One thousand miles up the Amazon to the city of Manaus where the Amazon is joined by the Rio Negro. God, I would love to go there next. The whole glory of the Amazonian jungle. I would like to float over it in a balloon.

CLOVIS: Sounds wonderful.

POLA: This naturalist was cataloging species in the Amazon and, in particular, birds. He made reference to a passage in Darwin's work. In *The Descent of Man*, Darwin notes that in certain birds, the migratory impulse is stronger than the maternal. A mother will abandon her fledglings in the nest rather than miss her appointment for the long journey south.

CLOVIS: Really?

POLA: That's what Darwin found. Well, all around me I hear these gentleman botanists and gentleman naturalists clucking their

POLA: [*Cont'd.*] tongues and murmuring their tut-tuts of disapproval and disgust about these grotesque and abnormal mother birds who abandoned their babies. So, I stood up to ask a question. Of course, my turban once again slipped off to the side, so I'm not sure if it was the turban or the question that threw the lecturer the most.

CLOVIS: What was your question?

POLA: What do the father birds do?

CLOVIS: The father birds?

POLA: Yes. The father birds of those baby birds abandoned by their mothers flying south. What do the father birds do?

CLOVIS: What did he say?

POLA: He said, in this very serious tone and after clearing his throat repeatedly, uh well, the father birds lead the way south. So I said, then could you say that in certain birds the migratory impulse is stronger than the paternal impulse? Long pause. He said, it's never really come up before. I said, it's come up now, so could you say that in certain birds the migratory impulse is stronger than the paternal impulse? And he said, well, yes, I suppose you could. And then my turban fell of my head and landed on the floor with a whump. It was most dramatic.

[*They laugh together.*]

CLOVIS: Oh, Pola, you bring me such joy.

VICTOR: [*Entering.*] Pola, you're always laughing. You're such a cheerful person.

POLA: I'm not a cheerful person, Victor, I just laugh a lot.

[*They embrace.*]

VICTOR: What were you discussing?

POLA: Father birds.

CLOVIS: Pola gave a lecture at the Royal Horticultural Society.

POLA: And showed my paintings.

VICTOR: I thought you did illustrations.

POLA: They're paintings.

VICTOR: A lecture on what?

POLA: "Insect Generations and Metamorphosis in Surinam."

CLOVIS: Isn't that brilliant?

VICTOR: Yes, it's brilliant. Shouldn't you check on dinner. [*He's nervous.*] Dolores might need help.

CLOVIS: Yes, of course. Excuse me.

[*Her eye is caught by a bit of light. She picks up a shard of glass, holds it up, and drops it into her pocket.*]

VICTOR: And how about you, Pola, how are you?

POLA: When I was eleven years old, I asked my Great Aunt Elise, am I pretty? And Aunt Elise said, my dear, develop your brain and an interesting character. And that is what I have done.

VICTOR: Are you happy, Pola?

POLA: No one ever said we were supposed to be happy. At least no one ever said it to me.

VICTOR: I think someone said it to me once.

POLA: [*She laughs.*] Who?

VICTOR: I can't remember.

POLA: And are you happy?

VICTOR: Sometimes.

POLA: What does she do all day long?

VICTOR: I don't know. Sleep, drift from room to room, picking up an object, putting it down. She disappears into the woods for hours.

POLA: What does she do there?

VICTOR: I don't know.

POLA: It was months before I received your letters about the accident.

VICTOR: It won't go away. This image of her in my mind. Standing in the fire, bald and screaming.

POLA: I came as soon as I could.

VICTOR: She burned her paintings. All of them. It was a windy night and the fire blew out of control. Her hair, her nightgown, her paintings. Sometimes I wish it had killed her. Maybe she'd be happier.

POLA: No. It's just a bad spell, Victor. She'll get better. [*She reaches toward him.*] My good and dear friend.

VICTOR: You bring Clovis joy; you bring all of us joy.

POLA: Your letters brought me joy when I was stuck in Africa during the rainy season. I looked forward to those letters.

VICTOR: I have always liked writing letters. I am the author of a hundred romances in the few villages nearby. Right now, I'm carrying on a feverish correspondence between the cook next door and a girl in Vincennes.

POLA: Who is this Centaur in the Garden?

VICTOR: Someone I made up.

POLA: Why?

VICTOR: I thought it seemed more romantic, mysterious. It was how I wooed Clovis and captured her. I've always been better in letters than in person. In person I always blunder and say something wrong.

POLA: So you invented this alias.

VICTOR: Yes.

POLA: A rather sexual sounding alias.

VICTOR: I hoped so.

POLA: And she responded.

VICTOR: Eventually. We had a secret place where we left letters for each other in the garden behind the Academy.

POLA: Ahh, yes, the Academy. So, you were distracting Clovis from her studies. Wooing her. Undermining her concentration.

VICTOR: No. I mean, yes. I mean, I was distracted too.

POLA: For how long?

VICTOR: What?

POLA: How long were you distracted?

VICTOR: I don't know what you're getting at.

POLA: I remember when we were all at the Academy. You, me, Marc and Clovis. Do you remember?

VICTOR: Of course.

POLA: Do you remember the Third Year Show?

VICTOR: Vaguely.

POLA: I remember it vividly.

VICTOR: Why?

POLA: Because my paintings were not included.

VICTOR: Many people's weren't.

POLA: I remember walking down the hallway to the bulletin board and looking for my name on the exhibition list. I remember the precise way the light came through the window and the feeling of whiteness all around me. I remember the moment of not seeing my name on that list. Something profound happened to me there. I knew very clearly what I was up against. I recognized it even though I did not choose to think about it. The fact is, when I walked down the stairs and out into the sunlight, I was changed.

VICTOR: It was only a student show. You shouldn't have let it bother you so much.

POLA: You voted against me, didn't you?

VICTOR: There was a committee.

POLA: But yours was a powerful voice.

VICTOR: A voice among many.

POLA: Clovis had no paintings in that show either.

VICTOR: Why dredge this up after all these years?

POLA: How did you decide which paintings were acceptable? Which paintings were good?

VICTOR: I don't know. That's always difficult. Sometimes you don't know. I suppose the painting speaks to you in some way.

POLA: When you voted against including my paintings in the show, do you remember why?

VICTOR: Well . . . there was something not right about them.

POLA: Can you be more specific? It would help me to understand.

VICTOR: Your grasp of line seemed flawed.

POLA: What lines?

VICTOR: The human form, for one.

POLA: We weren't allowed in the life study class except, of course, if we were naked.

VICTOR: It wasn't done. I didn't make the rules.

POLA: Not proper to be a student in the class but all right to stand naked on a table.

VICTOR: It was what was accepted.

POLA: Did you know that I wanted to do portraits? That's what I wanted to do. How could I do that without studying the human body closely, both female and male?

VICTOR: It would be difficult.

POLA: It would be impossible. I don't paint people now. I paint flowers like all good girl painters. Perhaps I'll soon graduate to painting china teacups.

VICTOR: I didn't know you were so angry with me. Why didn't you tell me before?

POLA: I didn't know I was so angry before.

VICTOR: This kind of bitterness is unbecoming to you, Pola.

POLA: I know. Luckily I've developed my brain and don't have to rely solely upon having a becoming character.

VICTOR: If I hurt you sometime a long time ago, I'm sorry. I wasn't thinking. It was certainly unintentional.

POLA: But those things still hurt. They still do damage even if they're not intended.

VICTOR: But why are you angry with me? I thought we were friends, good friends.

POLA: We are friends, but that doesn't mean I like everything about you. Surely you don't like everything about me.

VICTOR: No.

POLA: I hate what's happened to Clovis.

VICTOR: No more than I do.

POLA: My clearest memory of her is from a picnic on a hill and she'd climbed to the top of a tree in her bloomers and was swaying back and forth tossing apples and yodelling.

VICTOR: I remember her laughing. Oh, Pola, what do I do about Clovis?

POLA: Listen to her.

VICTOR: I try to do that.

POLA: She needs to be heard.

VICTOR: I want to be her husband. That's what I want to be. How can I learn to be a husband? No one tells you anything.

POLA: Be careful of the little things. The insignificant moments. Like calling my paintings illustrations. Oh, it's not just you, Victor, it's lots of little failures, little humiliations, little moments of being told you're wrong, little comments about how your paintings, well, aren't quite right. These things add up and they're crippling. They diminish me. They diminish Clovis.

VICTOR: You've been very strange tonight.

POLA: I'm all on edge. My skin feels too tight. I want to make a change. I want something different.

VICTOR: I've always envied your life.

POLA: Envied me?

VICTOR: You go off, have adventures. Sometimes I want to climb on your bicycle and ride off.

POLA: You can have my bicycle. I'm very tired of riding it.

VICTOR: What's happened to you, Pola?

POLA: I've lost someone this year.

VICTOR: Someone who died?

POLA: No. Someone who left.

VICTOR: I'm sorry, Pola.

POLA: He whispered things.

VICTOR: What do you mean?

POLA: In bed. He whispered things to me.

VICTOR: What kinds of things?

POLA: Things about me. Where to move. Don't move. Things about my hair. The hollow place in my throat. The skin on my shoulders. It's what I miss the most. The whispering.

VICTOR: I'm sorry.

POLA: Do you know how rare it is to find a man who talks to you softly in bed?

VICTOR: No, I didn't know.

POLA: I'm getting too old to have a child. I thought he was the one. I won't have many more chances.

VICTOR: You will. You'll have lots of chances if you take them.

POLA: I like you, Victor, I've always liked you. And I know that you love Clovis. You still love her, anyone can see that.

VICTOR: I know that for a time Clovis was giving a piece of her love to someone else. I know this because she was buying and wearing brightly colored scarves and she was singing in the kitchen. But mostly I know this because for a time she was no longer sad. Someone was bringing her joy, and I know it wasn't me.

POLA: How do you know, Victor?

VICTOR: I know. And I have never been so scared in all my life. [*Jollies himself up.*] Stay with us awhile this time. It would be good for Clovis. Ride your bicycle around the village, read your Tarot cards in the garden, and tell her stories. You're the only one who makes her laugh.

POLA: All right, I will.

[MARC *stumbles in from the woods carrying a painting wrapped in a white sheet. He's tangled one of his feet in some brambles and drags a branch in.*]

VICTOR: [*Surprised.*] Marc.

MARC: [*Shaking loose from the branch.*] Hello.

VICTOR: You've come from the woods.

POLA: [*Teasing.*] That's not like you, Marc.

MARC: I took a shortcut. It got dark. I got lost.

POLA: Two scarves, Marc?

MARC: I have a cold.

[*Hugs and handshakes all around.* VICTOR *slaps* MARC *on the back.*]

VICTOR: I wanted you at this dinner. I think it's going to be an event.

MARC: It's good to see you, Victor.

POLA: [*Picking a twig from his hair.*] So, here we have the star graduate of the Academy.

VICTOR: The child prodigy.

POLA: You look good, Marc. You always look so ... tidy. Even with twigs in your hair. I remember you were the only student at the Academy who painted without a smock. You never splashed paint around like the rest of us. Imagine coming to painting class in a freshly pressed suit, starched white shirt, a knotted bow and the tips of your moustache waxed.

MARC: Sometimes I think I should shave this moustache. It's so silly.

POLA: Oh, no, I wouldn't recognize you without it.

MARC: I probably wouldn't recognize myself either.

VICTOR: We're glad you're back. I've missed you. You seem different, Marc. Have you lost weight?

MARC: Maybe a little.

VICTOR: [*Indicating the painting.*] Let's see what you've brought for us.

[MARC *unwraps his painting. His latest paintings are pre-Cubist, like Cezanne. He's breaking things into lines and planes. It's orderly.* POLA *steps closer to look.*]

POLA: Is that in Aix-en-Provence?

MARC: Yes.

[VICTOR *studies the painting closely. He coughs uncomfortably.*]

VICTOR: Well, that's interesting, Marc.

[POLA *points a finger at the painting following the lines, tracing planes.*]

POLA: I like the lines here and how you've repeated these planes on the houses in the hills.

VICTOR: Yes, it is interesting. Nothing like what I've been doing.

MARC: I was trying to get at the structure of things. I've been breaking things down.

POLA: Well, I like it.

VICTOR: Always one step ahead, eh, Marc?

MARC: I'm just trying something new. It's probably nothing. [*He covers the painting up again.*]

POLA: I think it's grand. Really daring, Marc. Really.

MARC: Thank you.

VICTOR: Tell us about Provence. Where did you live? What did you do?

MARC: I rented a house for the year and I painted.

POLA: Were you lonely?

MARC: No. Yes.

VICTOR: Wasn't that expensive, renting a house for a year?

MARC: Actually, I got it rather cheap because the previous owner shot himself and his wife drank poison, so people in the village thought the place was haunted.

POLA: I wonder why they both didn't shoot themselves or both drink poison?

MARC: Oh, men and women commit suicide in very different ways. Drinking poison is really a female method. Women swallow poisonous overdoses of pills or liquid medications. They inhale poisonous fumes.

POLA: What about slitting her wrists?

MARC: That happens less frequently than you'd think. And rarely does a woman use a gun. Men favor guns.

POLA: Clearly.

VICTOR: Men also leap from high places or hang themselves.

MARC: These forms of suicide are not common among women.

POLA: I wonder why?

VICTOR: Women don't like messes.

POLA: After all, who's going to clean it up?

MARC: And women cannot tolerate the idea of mutilation and disfigurement.

VICTOR: They do worry a lot about how they look.

POLA: I could cut my throat right now.

[CLOVIS *pushes open one of the French doors with her back and enters the garden carrying a tray of glasses and a carafe of wine.*]

MARC: Clovis.

[*Startled by* MARC'*s presence, she stumbles and the glasses clink together.*]

CLOVIS: Hello, Marc.

POLA: Let me help you with that. [POLA *takes the tray.*]

CLOVIS: I didn't know you were back.

MARC: I've just returned.

CLOVIS: Oh. How was Provence?

MARC: It was warm.

CLOVIS: Yes. It can be warm there.

MARC: Not too warm.

CLOVIS: Oh. That's good then. I had heard it was warm.

MARC: You've changed your hair. It's shorter.

CLOVIS: Have I? I hadn't noticed.

[*Awkward pause.*]

POLA: Shall I pour?

VICTOR: Yes. Why don't you.

[POLA *pours the wine.*]

POLA: Someone should make a toast.

VICTOR: Why don't we each make a toast.

CLOVIS: To Pola's return to us.

[*They lift glasses and drink. Salut. Cheers.*]

VICTOR: To Marc's return.

Cheers, Salut ...

POLA: To the Academy.

[*Cheers.*]

POLA: [*Cont'd.*] Go on, Marc, it's your turn.

[*Pause.*]

MARC: [*Uncomfortable. Turns to* CLOVIS.] To Clovis' hair.

[*Awkward moment.*]

POLA: To Clovis' hair.

[*Cheers.*]

MARC: So, Pola, what have you been up to? Every time I hear of you, you're in some other exotic locale.

POLA: Well, I expected the world to end in 1869 according to a prophecy I received at Fatima. That's what I was prepared for. So when the world didn't end...well...I hadn't made plans beyond 1869 so I have had to improvise for the rest of my life.

[POLA, MARC *and* VICTOR *laugh together.* CLOVIS *is distracted and has wandered off slightly from the group. She's collecting things, pebbles, a seashell, twigs with colorful garlands tangled in them.*]

MARC: And you, Clovis, how have you been?

VICTOR: Clovis?

CLOVIS: Do you know the number of things going on in this garden right now? My god, there are hundreds. Wind, insects, water seeping through earth. Literally everything. The whole world is right here.

POLA: I spend a lot of my time in gardens looking at flowers, plants, painting. I never paint just one thing, though. A flower. An insect alone. I paint the insect on a leaf with a butterfly hovering nearby. To see the web, the connections.

MARC: Your paintings aren't pure.

POLA: What does that mean?

MARC: Your paintings aren't pure but contextual.

POLA: Somehow that doesn't sound like a compliment.

MARC: It's only an observation.

POLA: An observation about women.

MARC: An observation about painting.

VICTOR: You have to admit, Pola, that women are more contextual.

POLA: And men aren't?

VICTOR: It's different.

POLA: Different how?

VICTOR: I don't know exactly, but we are different.

POLA: I don't believe that.

CLOVIS: There is a difference in our response to light.

POLA: I don't believe that.

MARC: Neither do I.

POLA: I simply don't believe that a woman enters a studio any differently than a man does.

CLOVIS: Perhaps, it's just not conscious.

POLA: You don't go into a studio and say, Oh, here I am about to make a painting by a woman. I mean, there you are alone in this

POLA: [*Cont'd.*] huge space and you're not thinking about your breasts and your vagina.

MARC: [*Flinches at words like vagina, penis.*] Pola.

POLA: Well, you're not thinking about your vagina. You are inside yourself, looking at some object lying on a table, a velvet petal of a rose, a half-filled bottle of perfume, and this is what you are supposed to make a world out of. That is all you are conscious of. I don't believe that a man feels any differently. Does a man go striding into his studio thinking, well, here I am this marvelous man with this marvelous power of the male and this marvelous penis to inspire me? I don't believe it. When you are painting, you are inside yourself. You are looking at this terrifying unknown, and trying to feel something, trying to pull everything you can out of all your experience and make something new.

[*Beat.*]

CLOVIS: Pola, why did you stop painting for a year?

[*Beat.*]

POLA: I stopped hearing my own voice.

VICTOR: We all go through that, Pola.

MARC: Being an artist of any sex is difficult.

CLOVIS: Pola stopped painting. I stopped painting. Did you, Victor? [*She turns to* MARC.] Did you?

MARC: You didn't stop because you're a woman. You stopped because painting is difficult.

CLOVIS: What's difficult about it?

MARC: As I said, being an artist of any sex is difficult.

CLOVIS: What would you say is the most difficult part of becoming an artist?

POLA: Becoming a self.

MARC: Surely you don't think that women have greater problems than men in becoming a self?

POLA: Isn't an artist someone who takes orders from an inner voice? What if she can't believe her own voice? What if she has no inner voice or none she can distinguish? Or what if she has three inner voices all saying conflicting things?

VICTOR: Surely men have similar problems hearing their inner voice.

POLA: Or what if the only voice she can conjure up is male because she can't really conceive of authority as a soprano?

VICTOR: You stopped painting because you're a soprano? That's crazy, Pola.

POLA: I bet a lot of women stop painting because they're sopranos.

VICTOR: And that is all the fault of the tenors and the basses?

POLA: No, not all. Some of it is the sopranos'. But look at Madeleine, what happened to her.

MARC: Tissot's mistress?

POLA: She was more than just his mistress.

MARC: The crazy one.

CLOVIS: Marc, you're so pure. You're taking her craziness out of context.

MARC: To be honest, I don't know much about the story.

POLA: Then let me tell you, her craziness was completely contextual.

MARC: You realize, of course, I'm speaking in metaphor.

VICTOR: Let's be honest, Pola, she was crazy. Going around all the time saying, I did the hands and feet, I did the hands and feet.

CLOVIS: [*Steady, direct.*] That's an awful lot of crazy women, Victor. Every woman that's come up today, crazy. Dolores, Pola, Madeleine, and me. That's an awful lot of crazy women.

[DOLORES *enters.*]

DOLORES: [*To* VICTOR.] Your dinner guests are arriving.

[POLA *stands and straightens her clothing.*]

POLA: Do I need to fix my hair, or is it all right?

VICTOR: Your hair is fine.

POLA: I don't want that pompous ass Clive Riviere laughing at my hair like he always does.

[*An uncomfortable silence.*]

POLA: [*Cont'd.*] What? What? [*She pats her hair.*] Oh, has it got that funny hump in the back it gets sometimes?

CLOVIS: No.

POLA: Well, what then?

CLOVIS: Pola, we will be eating in the garden.

POLA: What?

CLOVIS: We will be eating in the garden.

POLA: I don't understand.

CLOVIS: We are not included at this dinner.

POLA: Who is not included?

CLOVIS: We aren't.

POLA: There are no women at this dinner?

CLOVIS: No women at the table.

POLA: What about Berthe or Mary—

VICTOR: — They're not coming.

CLOVIS: You mean, they weren't invited.

POLA: [*To* VICTOR.] You're serious.

VICTOR: It's really more of a business dinner than a social event.

POLA: I have business.

VICTOR: We're planning an exhibit.

POLA: I have exhibits.

VICTOR: It's for a different sort of painting.

POLA: Victor, I want to be at the table.

VICTOR: This is for people whose work has not been accepted at the official salons.

POLA: Then I certainly qualify.

VICTOR: Yes, but—

POLA: —Marc?

MARC: I think you're making too much of it.

POLA: Clovis?

[CLOVIS *has moved away and is looking off into the distance. She is still.*]

POLA: [*Cont'd.*] Clovis!

MARC: You shouldn't let it bother you so much. It's only a business dinner.

POLA: [*She turns to* VICTOR.] I remember walking down the hallway to the bulletin board. I remember the precise way the light came through the window and the feeling of whiteness all around me. [POLA *finishes her glass of wine.*]

VICTOR: [*Uncomfortable. Relief.*] It's not that important. I'm sure it will be much more pleasant to spend the evening in the garden. I would rather be out here than at the table arguing with Daniel and Claude.

[MARC *nods agreeing.* VICTOR *picks up the wine bottle preparing to leave.*]

POLA: Do leave the bottle, Victor. We get so thirsty in the garden.

VICTOR: Well, here I go, this marvelous man with this marvelous power of the penis off to eat my dinner.

[*The men exit. Pause.* THE WOMEN *are quiet in the garden. Twilight.* DOLORES *pours herself a glass of wine.*]

DOLORES: In the beginning, Genesis tells us that God created man in order to give him dominion over fish and fowl and all creatures. Of course, Genesis was written by a man, not a horse.

POLA: A doctor I know in Paris was completing a study on female nervous disorders. A woman who had had a mysterious array of ailments went to see this doctor to offer herself as a subject for his study. "Madame," he asked, "are you depressed enough to qualify?" She answered, "Isn't everyone?"

VICTOR: [*Shouts from off.*] Daniel, how good to see you again. I must show you my latest work. I'm trying something new. Clovis, will you bring my painting in from the shed?

CLOVIS: No.

VICTOR: Dolores, we need more wine.

DOLORES: Shall I go serve?

CLOVIS: No.

[CLOVIS *looks into the distance.* MYLO *comes to stand at one of the windows.*]

MYLO: Maman?

CLOVIS: She's not here.

"What remains is the last of human freedoms, one that cannot be taken from you; it is the ability to choose one's attitude in a given set of circumstances."

—Jean Harris

ACT II

SCENE 1

[*It is quiet in the garden. The three* WOMEN *can hear the sounds from the men's dinner. The clinking of glasses, boisterous laughter, forks clattering against dishes. Each woman is feeling what it is like not to be at the table.* POLA *finishes her glass of wine and pours another, emptying the bottle.* MYLO *quietly watches from one of the windows.*]

POLA: What are they doing in there?

DOLORES: Arguing over what to call themselves. Deciding whose paintings should be hung where.

POLA: What is that ass Clive Riviere up to? I keep hearing his raised voice.

[*From off, we hear a banging on a table.*]

MAN'S VOICE #1: My paintings always get stuck in dark corners where no one ever sees them.

POLA: I dislike bitter men. They are nothing but a drain.

MAN'S VOICE #2: Dammit, Clive, the reason your paintings are hung in corners is that they are small. My paintings are big so I need a big space to hang them in.

MAN'S VOICE #1: Big and ugly.

MAN'S VOICE #2: Better than small and ugly.

POLA: Hang them upside down. Stupid asses. [*To* THE WOMEN.] They're doing something in there.

CLOVIS: They're only arguing.

POLA: I want to be part of the argument. I want to be in there.

CLOVIS: I don't.

POLA: You don't want to be at the table?

CLOVIS: No.

POLA: I would at least like to be asked.

CLOVIS: I definitely do not want to be *asked.*

POLA: Dolores?

DOLORES: When I was young, I went with any man who asked me to and I stayed with them until they asked me to leave.

POLA: So. What is that supposed to mean?

DOLORES: I don't do that anymore.

POLA: It pisses me off.

CLOVIS: Go in there then.

POLA: I don't want to go in there. I don't want to have to wait to be asked. I don't want to have to shove my way in. I just wanted to be there. But what I want most of all is not to care.

DOLORES: What are you going to do?

VICTOR: [*From off.*] Dolores, we need more wine.

[*She does not go.* POLA *holds up the empty bottle.*]

POLA: And so do we.

CLOVIS: If they want to be heard, the sopranos must sing louder.

POLA: What?

CLOVIS: We should have our own dinner.

POLA: Our own dinner?

CLOVIS: Yes. A Sopranos' Dinner.

POLA: Oooh, I like that.

DOLORES: The Sopranos' Dinner.

POLA: That's very good, Clovis.

CLOVIS: Our dinner.

POLA: Our dinner.

DOLORES: We'll need food.

POLA: And wine.

CLOVIS: And a centerpiece for the table.

DOLORES: And dessert.

POLA: And hors d'oeuvres.

VICTOR: [*From off.*] Dolores.

ALL THREE WOMEN: [*Vibrato.*] The Sopranos' Dinner.

[*The women run off in different directions.* VICTOR *comes out.*]

VICTOR: Clovis, the soup is getting cold. Clovis?

MAN'S VOICE #1: I'm not having my painting hung next to Daniel's.

VICTOR: Oh, shut up.

[VICTOR *returns to the men's dinner.*]

[POLA *drags in a log and some branches. She plops them on the table as an odd centerpiece. She arranges the chairs and converses with the group of empty chairs.*]

[MYLO *watches.*]

POLA: I'm collecting small statues, figurines. So, yesterday, I went to buy a small Aphrodite from that shop that deals in antiquities. You know the one, next to the Cafe D'Orsay on Place Pigalle. The large dusty shop with the fat proprietor. Yes, that one. I arrived late in the afternoon and there the proprietor sits in a fan-backed rattan chair pricing a large shipment of Aphrodites just arrived from Greece. So, I waited, watching to see which Aphrodite would be mine. As the Aphrodites were unloaded, this fat proprietor jabs a plump finger at each one pronouncing prices anywhere from a few francs to a few hundred thousand. I know. That's exactly what I thought. So I asked him, how can you price these Aphrodites so quickly and without knowing the age or the origin of the pieces? He said, I price them by the degree of energy they generate. A great work of art gives off more of a hum than a lesser one. And I thought, that's not a bad way to judge.

MYLO: Who are you talking to?

POLA: My mother taught me to be a good hostess by making me talk to empty chairs.

MYLO: Why did you want to be a hostess?

POLA: I didn't.

MYLO: Why doesn't Maman paint anymore?

POLA: I don't know, Mylo.

MYLO: I thought I would like it better if Maman didn't paint anymore, but I don't.

POLA: I don't either.

MYLO: One day Maman was painting and I knocked on the door and asked if I could come in and she said she was painting. And I said, I love you, Maman. And she said, I love you, too. And she went on painting. So I said, I love your painting, Maman. And she said, thank you. Then I said, I love your painting more than Papa's and she opened the door.

[DOLORES *runs in with a bowl of whipped cream.*]

DOLORES: Ta dah! Whipped cream!

POLA: Whipped cream! Oh, Dolores, you are a goddess. The Goddess of Delight.

DOLORES: I like that. I am Dolores, the Goddess of Delight.

POLA: And this is our centerpiece.

DOLORES: Perfect.

POLA: And now I'm off for the berries.

MYLO: Did you get your Aphrodite?

POLA: Yes. Yes, I did.

[POLA *runs into the woods again.*]

MYLO: What's a hostess?

DOLORES: What are you doing up, you little monkey?

MYLO: I couldn't sleep.

DOLORES: So you came out to look at the stars?

MYLO: Yes, and the night butterfly.

DOLORES: The night butterfly?

MYLO: It comes from the moon.

DOLORES: Oh, I see. [*She points at the sky.*] What's that?

MYLO: Sirius.

DOLORES: And that?

MYLO: [*Mispronouncing.*] Cassiopeia.

DOLORES: Cassiopeia.

MYLO: [*Correctly.*] Cassiopeia.

[CLOVIS *rushes in, plops the rabbit on the table, and grabs the tray to carry out.*]

CLOVIS: The Rabbit!

POLA: And this is our centerpiece.

DOLORES: Whipped cream and the rabbit.

CLOVIS: Wonderful.

MYLO: Dolores and I were looking at the stars.

CLOVIS: Wonderful. [*Kisses him on the head.*]

DOLORES: It's time for bed, Mylo.

MYLO: [*Playful.*] Will you tuck me in, Maman? Will you hold my hand?

CLOVIS: My hands are full.

[CLOVIS *exits.* DOLORES *takes* MYLO'*s hand.*]

MYLO: If you see a falling star, make a wish for me.

CLOVIS: I will. I'll make wishes for us all.

[DOLORES *and* MYLO *exit.*]

[POLA *comes from the woods laughing, her skirt full of berries. She spills the berries across the table.* MARC *comes to stand at one of the windows.* POLA *talks to the group of empty chairs again.*]

POLA: Something cataclysmic is about to happen. Pieces of the Sphinx are falling off, crumbling into the Egyptian desert.

POLA: [*Cont'd.*] The nose of a statue in the park fell off last week. Smashed to the ground.

MARC: Something is happening.

POLA: Oh, one of the chairs answers. My mother's training didn't go to waste. I can make empty chairs speak.

MARC: Something is in the air. I can smell it. Some of my artist friends are beginning to work small.

POLA: Small?

MARC: They are making small things out of bronze.

POLA: Bronze is heavy.

MARC: Small things that are portable.

POLA: Like Aphrodites.

MARC: Votive figures that can be left as markers or could be kept and carried along with their owners.

POLA: Carried along to where?

MARC: Do you know the Apollo Marcellus gem?

POLA: In the Medici collection.

MARC: It dates back to the time of Nero. Small objects from antiquity were the channels of influence into the Renaissance because they could easily travel along with migrant populations.

POLA: Are we going somewhere?

MARC: Sending messengers out ahead who will carry these small objects with them?

POLA: I like to travel.

MARC: Something is in the air.

POLA: I must repair my bicycle.

MARC: Are my friends working small because they sense some imminent destruction and change?

POLA: Will we be migrating soon? On the move, so to speak?

MARC: Oh, I don't know, Pola, but I lie awake at night and worry about such things.

[*Beat.*]

POLA: Marc, what are you doing out here?

MARC: What are you doing out here?

POLA: Occupying the garden. Why aren't you at the table?

MARC: I've been sent to keep the peace. [*He holds out a bottle of wine.*] I've brought an offering.

POLA: I accept. Temporarily.

CLOVIS: [*Entering.*] Fresh pecans, plates, candles, silverware, and three Mandarin oranges. [*Exiting.*]

[*Beat.*]

MARC: Smell the lavender.

POLA: Yes, I've missed that smell.

[*Beat.*]

MARC: Have you ever been in love?

POLA: The minute I heard my first love story, I started looking. Yes, I have been in love.

MARC: How did you know?

POLA: You know.

MARC: How?

POLA: One time when I was with him, afterwards, I went into the bathroom to wash the smell of sex from me, and I saw this bar of soap in the basin, his soap, soap that had touched his face, his hands, and I wrapped the bar of soap in a handkerchief and carried it around in my bag for months.

MARC: Maybe it's different for a woman.

POLA: Maybe. [*Pause.*] Marc?

MARC: I want to tell you about something that happened to me. I want to tell you something.

POLA: Tell me.

MARC: I was behind the house in Aix-en-Provence cleaning paint-brushes when the air all around me suddenly hushed. A baby

MARC: [*Cont'd.*] stopped crying. The wind ceased rustling through the leaves. All birds were silent.

I looked up and what I saw was time passing. Time rushing forward while I stood cleaning paintbrushes. Passing me by like water swirling round a big rock. And I was that rock. But am I rock? Am I made of stone? I am not so lasting nor so resistant to water. Already I was being smoothed away by the water. I could see it happening. I touched my face and there was less of me. Less muscle, less bone, less hair, less of me. And what had I squeezed from the time?

POLA: [*Almost a whisper.*] Clovis' hair.

MARC: It was then that I began to think about Clovis. Clovis swaying in the tree in her bloomers, Clovis eating blackberry jam on toast, Clovis and me rolling about the floor of my studio wrapped in a canvas and laughing. Clovis. The truth is, I had not gotten over her. I have not gotten over her. A baby cried and the moment of stillness was over. But the fact is that when I returned to cleaning my paintbrushes, I was changed.

[MARC *exits.*]

DOLORES: [*Entering.*] More wine, a bowl for the berries, and glazed carrots.

POLA: Bravo, Dolores. Brava.

[CLOVIS *enters.*]

CLOVIS: Chicken legs! I've got chicken legs!

POLA: Oh, this is wonderful.

DOLORES: Candles and berries and Mandarin oranges. It is a many-colored dinner.

[*The women finish arranging their dinner and sit round the table.*]

CLOVIS: [*A toast.*] I officially announce the beginning of the Soprano's Dinner.

POLA & DOLORES: The Sopranos' Dinner.

[*They drink a toast.*]

DOLORES: And for hors d'oeuvres.

[DOLORES *pulls out her bag of candies.*]

POLA: Hundreds and Thousands Candies!

DOLORES: It is the Hundreds and Thousands that teach me how to live. Tiny things that add up. Too insignificant to be considered individually, but a handful of these candies lapped up and sticking to my tongue make me feel very full. And like these candies, the little scraps of my life have added up and made a definite pattern. Thank you tiny Hundreds and Thousands.

POLA & CLOVIS: Thank you, tiny Hundreds and Thousands.

[*THE WOMEN dig in.*]

CLOVIS: I used to lie awake at night waiting for the dawn to come so that I could start working. I used to sing while I worked, and people would ask, are you really that happy?

POLA: And were you?

CLOVIS: I was. I really was that happy.

DOLORES: I am happy eating chicken legs with whipped cream.

POLA: So am I.

CLOVIS: One day I was painting. It was late afternoon. I was alone, completely alone, and there was this moment when I knew I was finished and I stepped back and drank a glass of water, and I looked at what I had done and it was good. And there I was all alone, no one to share the moment with, but I didn't care because I knew that I had made something good. Then Victor came in and said, when are you going to finish it?

POLA: Why did you marry Victor straight out of the Academy?

CLOVIS: The minute I heard my first love story, I started looking.

[DOLORES *smiles.*]

POLA: Why didn't you test other possibilities?

DOLORES: Women have always made bargains to avoid aloneness.

POLA: At least you have that, a marriage. Always, after leaving somebody, a group, a party, any situation where I have been included in the lives of others, my singleness impinges on me and I think, here we are, Pola, alone again.

CLOVIS: Marriage can be lonelier than solitude.

POLA: Yes, I suppose it can.

CLOVIS: It is a cushion, but you are still alone. You still have to make your life.

DOLORES: I know how you felt when you finished that painting. Many years ago I lived in a village called Medjugorge. In late February all the women go into the church to celebrate the rites of spring. We sing. We dance. We run naked through the woods to a stream, jump in the freezing water and run back through the woods, wet, naked, holding hands and laughing. Oh, the laughter of those women ringing through the woods.

CLOVIS: Let's make a list of all the women we know who are doing well.

[*Long pause.*]

POLA: There's Elise.

CLOVIS: Elise pushed her husband down a flight of stairs.

POLA: Oh. [*Small giggle.*] Is he all right?

DOLORES: [*A giggle.*] No, he's not.

CLOVIS: What about Clothilde?

POLA: She has to wear a brace for her spine.

[*More giggles.*]

DOLORES: What about that woman Lucille?

CLOVIS: She abandoned her husband and children and went to live in a nunnery.

[THE WOMEN *are laughing by now.*]

POLA: All right, all right, I've got one. Marie-Louise.

CLOVIS: Have you seen Marie-Louise in the last year?

POLA: No.

CLOVIS: She has developed an odd facial tic.

[CLOVIS *demonstrates the tic. Howls.*]

POLA: There has to be someone.

CLOVIS: There's you, Pola.

POLA: Me?

CLOVIS: We could write your name on our list of women who are doing well.

POLA: I don't think so.

DOLORES: You travel.

CLOVIS: You know interesting people.

DOLORES: You have adventures.

CLOVIS: You have a rich life, Pola.

POLA: I have a bicycle and I roam from place to place.

CLOVIS: Why did you start travelling?

POLA: Because of Madeleine.

CLOVIS: She was so beautiful.

POLA: And so much more than Tissot's mistress.

DOLORES: If I ever have a daughter, I will wish for one who is beautiful and stupid.

POLA: She was lover, cook, bookkeeper, student, model, muse, assistant. He chucked her out, so she went around scratching her name into his pieces right next to his. She hadn't come from much so had nothing to return to. She roamed the streets stopping people to tell them, I did the hands and feet. They kept denying her. You see, they could not believe she was so good. And Tissot is known especially for his hands and feet. So in the end, he had her put away, and her name was rubbed off the statues.

I went to visit her in the sanitorium. We sat in the sun eating biscuits and I said to her, Madeleine, we're close friends, tell me the truth about those hands and feet. I have never forgiven myself for that.

Shortly after that afternoon of eating biscuits in the sun, she hung herself from a hook in her closet.

DOLORES: You can't blame yourself.

POLA: There was a nun at the sanitorium who had secretly been supplying Madeleine with clay and wet cloths, and when they found her hanging in the closet, they also found dozens of the most beautifully moulded clay hands and feet wrapped in white sheets. Every one was signed and dated. [*Beat.*] Not long after that I went away.

CLOVIS: But why did you stop painting?

POLA: Because secretly, somewhere deep down inside of me, I realized that I honestly didn't believe we were as good as they were. That we could ever be as good. Remember how I was always the one shouting the loudest about being allowed into the art schools, being able to come to life class. In those days, I was always shouting. But part of me believed that I would never be as good as Victor, as good as Marc. And when I saw work that was good, really good, I couldn't believe that a woman had done it.

CLOVIS: So you stopped painting.

POLA: For a year.

DOLORES: But you started again.

CLOVIS: Whatever it was that happened to you, you eventually did start painting again.

POLA: Something beautiful fooled me into it. I was in the jungle looking for the night moonflower. They're rare and only open at night when the moon is full. I wanted to see one, so night after night I sat in the jungle waiting. One night the moonflower opened. Without thinking, I took out a scrap of paper and a pencil and I drew. I began drawing again. For me. I went into town the next day and bought a crude set of children's watercolors and began painting flowers and plants and insects. For me.

CLOVIS: Dolores, do you remember a time when you were doing well?

DOLORES: All of my most intense memories go back to childhood.

CLOVIS: Mine, too.

POLA: Mine, too.

CLOVIS: In childhood, then, do you remember a time when you felt clear about who you were and your place in the world?

DOLORES: When I was eleven.

CLOVIS: What happened then?

DOLORES: I remember that when people would tell me things that didn't seem right or true, I was very clear about saying, no, that's not right, that's not true.

POLA: When I was eleven, I remember seeing everything with such particular clarity. Colors were brighter. Lines were sharper. I remember thinking, I need to notice this because a lot is going to be expected of me.

CLOVIS: When I was eleven, my father showed me a room made of glass, and I was surrounded by light.

POLA: When I was eleven, I asked my great Aunt Elise, am I pretty? She said, develop your brain and an interesting character.

DOLORES: When I was eleven, my father left me with Challah Borovsky who taught me to tell fortunes.

CLOVIS: Papa?

DOLORES: My mother was beautiful.

CLOVIS: My mother was beautiful.

POLA: I can't remember my mother.

DOLORES: I wasn't beautiful.

POLA: Oh, I was never pretty.

CLOVIS: I was always pretty.

DOLORES: I couldn't do tricks, ride bareback, walk on my hands, or juggle.

CLOVIS: Right, Papa?

POLA: I developed my brain.

DOLORES: How could they take me with them?

POLA: How could he take me with him?

DOLORES: I couldn't even juggle.

POLA: So off I went.

DOLORES: So off I went to Challah Borovsky's.

CLOVIS: The Revolution was awful, wasn't it, Papa? I like this scarf, don't you, Papa?

DOLORES: I remember my mother and father riding two beautiful white bare-backed horses.

CLOVIS: Red wine is better than white, isn't it, Papa?

POLA: I won't apologize for who I am.

DOLORES: Gold ribbons fly behind them.

POLA: So off I went to Java to see a shadow play and to climb the Borobodur. I wore saffron colored trousers, a purple turban, and carried a walking stick.

DOLORES: And they were laughing.

CLOVIS: This is beautiful.

POLA: They'd never seen a woman in saffron-colored trousers atop the Borobodur.

CLOVIS: I was surrounded by the most extraordinary smell. Cinnamon.

POLA: What lengths to go for a chance at joy.

CLOVIS: Astonishing.

POLA: And oh how marvelous.

CLOVIS: That girl was me. Oh, let's go back, let's go back to being eleven year old girls.

POLA: God, yes, let's be eleven again. Eleven year old girls with clear blue eyes.

DOLORES: Mine are brown.

POLA: Dolores, when you were eleven, did you have a favorite game?

DOLORES: King Dido Died.

CLOVIS: King Dido Died?

DOLORES: You don't know King Dido Died?

POLA: We don't know King Dido Died.

DOLORES: You poor deprived children. First you march around in a circle.

[THE WOMEN *march in a circle.*]

DOLORES: [*Cont'd.*] Then you chant.

[POLA *and* CLOVIS *follow* DOLORES.]

DOLORES: [*Cont'd.*] King Dido, King Dido, King Dido died, [*Clap, clap.*] King Dido died, [*Clap, clap.*] King Dido died doing this.

[*And* DOLORES *flaps one arm and shakes her hips back and forth in a wild fashion.*]

DOLORES: [*Cont'd.*] King Dido, King Dido. Pola.

[*And* POLA *leads the chant.*]

POLA: King Dido, King Dido, King Dido died, [*Clap, clap.*] King Dido died, [*Clap, clap.*] King Dido died doing this.

[*And she imitates* DOLORES, *one arm flapping and hips shaking and she adds something of her own.*]

POLA: [*Cont'd.*] King Dido, King Dido. Clovis.

CLOVIS: King Dido, King Dido, King Dido died, [*Clap, clap.*] King Dido died, [*Clap, clap.*] King Dido died doing this.

[CLOVIS *imitates* DOLORES' *actions and then* POLA'*s and then adds her own movements.* THE WOMEN *continue the game, repeating the chant and growing wilder and freer. King Dido builds and builds as* THE WOMEN *create a kind of pagan dance. Finally, the game peaks and they collapse breathless.*]

DOLORES: A falling star.

POLA: Oh, god, make a wish.

CLOVIS: Make wishes for us all.

[THE WOMEN *stop and look up and each silently makes a wish.*]

CLOVIS: I want to tell you about something that happened to me a long time ago.

[*Light comes up and remains on the graveyard illuminating the altar piece* CLOVIS *has built. It dazzles with all her shiny things catching and refracting light.*]

DOLORES: Clovis?

CLOVIS: I want to tell you something.

[*We glimpse a vision of a little girl. A mirage. A flutter of a skirt, a wisp of hair, a whisper, and she is gone.*]

CLOVIS: [*Cont'd.*] A long time ago I made a painting. I wanted to capture the color of glass and the changes in light that occur in a half-filled bottle. I was fascinated with the way light touches on reflective surfaces. So I gathered together a ladies' hand mirror, shards of a broken vase, silver earrings, a string of glass beads, half-filled bottles of perfume, a piece of Venetian carnival glass, a ruby ring, my mother's porcelain bracelet. I chose the objects I loved. But it wasn't the objects I was painting; it was the light.

POLA: You made that painting?

CLOVIS: I called it "Salon Jolie."

POLA: You painted "Salon Jolie?"

CLOVIS: I submitted it anonymously. On the opening day of the exhibition, I went to the gallery and watched unnoticed. People laughed at the painting. It was called frivolous. I was described as a greedy person because of all the jewellry. One critic called it the ugliest painting of the year. Another said, the silliest painting he'd ever seen.

What did this mean? I was baffled. My motive was beauty not ugliness, and greed played no part. What is frivolous about trying to paint the way light touches on different surfaces? What I realize now is that, without thinking, I had instinctively chosen objects that a woman would use. Not a man. My friends, the male painters, were also painting light but they were painting ponds and cathedrals and haystacks, and somehow, I, by being true to my own nature, had chosen objects that were not to be painted and definitely not to be taken seriously.

DOLORES: Clovis, when you were a girl, what was your favorite game?

CLOVIS: You see, I'd chosen the objects I loved. Isn't a painter someone who sets the light free? What does it matter which objects I choose?

DOLORES: When you were eleven, what was your favorite game?

CLOVIS: Sun, Moon, Earth.

DOLORES: How do we play?

CLOVIS: Oh, it's a children's game.

DOLORES: How do we play this children's game?

POLA: How do we play Sun, Moon, Earth, Clovis?

CLOVIS: It was a game I made up. I wanted to know if we see all of the moon or always the same side.

POLA: Show us.

CLOVIS: One of us is the sun, the other the moon, the other the earth.

DOLORES: We can do that.

CLOVIS: I like to be the moon.

DOLORES: I like to be the sun.

POLA: I am the earth. Then what do we do?

CLOVIS: We form a constellation and spin and rotate round each other.

POLA: Who goes where?

CLOVIS: Dolores, you're the sun.

DOLORES: I'm the sun.

CLOVIS: So you go at the center.

POLA: Am I next?

CLOVIS: Yes.

POLA: Is the earth in between the moon and sun or is the moon in between the earth and sun?

CLOVIS: Pola.

POLA: Where do I go?

CLOVIS: You're confusing me.

DOLORES: The earth is in between the sun and moon.

CLOVIS: Yes.

POLA: Here?

CLOVIS: Yes, and I go here. We are in our places. We are a constellation. Turn round each other slowly.

[*The moon doesn't rotate on its axis but it does move around the sun, and it is in the earth's orbit. The earth rotates on its axis and moves around the sun. The sun rotates on its axis. And all is counter clockwise.*]

CLOVIS: [*Cont'd.*] If this is going to work, we need to keep in a steady rhythm.

DOLORES: Like this?

CLOVIS: You're fine, but Pola, you're spinning too fast.

POLA: Better?

CLOVIS: Better.

POLA: I'm growing dizzy.

DOLORES: Slowly, slowly.

POLA: Now what?

CLOVIS: I want to know if we see all of the moon or always the same side.

POLA: Don't you always see the same craters on the moon?

CLOVIS: That's what I'm trying to find out.

DOLORES: They look the same each night.

CLOVIS: Pola, you're turning too fast again.

POLA: I'm the earth.

DOLORES: Move in the steady rhythm.

POLA: You're the Goddess of Delight.

DOLORES: I'm the sun.

CLOVIS: Each time you turn, Pola, are you seeing the same side of me?

POLA: Yes, yes I am seeing the same side of you.

CLOVIS: What are you seeing now?

[CLOVIS *breaks out of the gravitational field and all three women spin freely about the garden.*]

POLA: I'm seeing you. I'm seeing you.

CLOVIS: I'm the moon. I'm the moon.

[THE WOMEN *create a dance, something radiant and flowing. It has a different feeling than the exuberance of the King Dido game.*]

[VICTOR *charges into the garden carrying his painting.*]

VICTOR: What is going on?

CLOVIS: I'm the moon, Victor, I'm the moon.

POLA: And I'm the earth.

DOLORES: And I'm the sun.

VICTOR: It's chaos out here. Chaos all evening.

CLOVIS: What do you want?

VICTOR: We've run out of chicken legs. Marc ate four legs himself. Clive complained he got nothing but breasts and went on and on about how he only likes dark meat and white is too dry. I had no chicken at all. And we never got any glazed carrots. What happened to the glazed carrots?

POLA: Is this your painting, Victor?

VICTOR: I'm returning it to the shed.

POLA: I like the way you have the light on the river reflecting the pink in the sky. Oh, and this is lovely, how the light touches her skin.

CLOVIS: I've never painted a nude.

POLA: Neither have I.

VICTOR: Clovis, could I talk to you? In private.

POLA: We'll run thrugh the woods and gather more berries.

[POLA *and* DOLORES *twirl off toward the woods.*]

POLA & DOLORES: I'm the earth, I'm the sun...

VICTOR: What is going on out here?

CLOVIS: Is that what you wanted to talk to me about?

VICTOR: No.

CLOVIS: Did you accomplish what you set out to with your dinner?

VICTOR: No. Well, yes, we did plan the exhibit. At least that's been organized.

CLOVIS: So?

VICTOR: I've been wanting to say something to you all day long, but I don't know what it is. This whole dinner has been so unsettling.

CLOVIS: Yes, Victor?

VICTOR: They didn't like my painting.

CLOVIS: Oh. I am sorry.

VICTOR: Did you know that Pola wanted to paint portraits?

CLOVIS: No.

VICTOR: Neither did I.

CLOVIS: That would have been difficult.

VICTOR: That would have been impossible.

MAN'S VOICE #1: [*A shout from off.*] Victor, I'm leaving.

VICTOR: [*Exiting.*] I cannot tell you how much I despise that Clive Riviere.

[MARC *rushes out and throws up.*]

VICTOR: [*Cont'd.*] I know exactly what you mean.

MARC: I've had too much to drink.

[MARC *wipes his face.* VICTOR *and* MARC *stand in silhouette in one of the windows.* CLOVIS *turns slowly round in the garden. The men watch her. They hear* POLA's *laughter from the woods.*]

VICTOR: It would've been fun to have Pola in there.

MARC: She would've told Clive Riviere where to hang his paintings.

VICTOR: All during dinner I kept hearing the rattling of a mirror not firmly attached to a wall. I kept waiting for it to crash. I went to look for it and couldn't find it. [*Pause.*] I visited Edouard Bousseau's gallery last week.

MARC: Photography.

VICTOR: Are we the end of the line, Marc? Will photography render us obsolete?

MARC: Painters? I don't believe that.

VICTOR: Some of it's quite good. The color, the light.

MARC: However good, these photographs allow us to see things for the second time. A painter, a real painter, reveals things to us for the first time.

VICTOR: I like to paint, Marc. The physical act of painting. To go down to the pond and watch the light on the water, how it changes. I want to paint that. I cannot imagine my life without it. But it's not everything. It takes a whole lifetime to know just one other person. To know one other person really well.

MARC: I am an intelligent, educated man, Victor, but I cannot fathom my own heart.

[VICTOR *exits with his painting.*]

CLOVIS: [*She turns slowly round.*] I'm the moon. I'm the moon.

MARC: Hello, Clovis.

CLOVIS: Feel the wind.

MARC: Yes.

CLOVIS: Why aren't you inside with the others?

MARC: Now they're arguing wildly about whether it's better to paint in the open air or in the studio. I don't care.

CLOVIS: It's better in the air when you're the moon.

MARC: I've missed you, Clovis.

CLOVIS: Don't. [*She spins away from him.*] Do you want to be the earth?

MARC: What are you doing?

CLOVIS: I'm the moon. Do you want to be the earth?

MARC: I don't understand.

CLOVIS: Do we see all of the moon or always the same side?

MARC: I think we see the same craters.

CLOVIS: Do we? Watch me.

[*He moves with her being the earth.*]

MARC: I've always watched you. All that summer when I painted with Victor, I watched you.

CLOVIS: Are you seeing the same side of me?

MARC: I'm seeing everything.

[*She stops.*]

CLOVIS: Everything?

MARC: Clovis. Clovis, I hate myself for how I hurt you.

CLOVIS: You didn't hurt me.

MARC: I can imagine what you felt when I left like that.

CLOVIS: I didn't feel anything at all.

MARC: Then why were you with me?

CLOVIS: I thought you would help me feel more alive.

MARC: And didn't I . . . help?

CLOVIS: For awhile.

MARC: I didn't know what you wanted from me.

CLOVIS: I wanted what all women want.

MARC: What?

CLOVIS: To be loved as they love. Women drown when in love. This drowning is crucial. Men are able to stand on the shore not getting wet.

MARC: I wasn't on the shore.

CLOVIS: [*Gently.*] You realize, of course, I'm speaking in metaphor.

MARC: You frightened me. I didn't know what you needed.

CLOVIS: What did I have that you needed?

MARC: I felt out of control.

CLOVIS: You were never out of control. Ever. You always held back one little piece.

MARC: And Victor was my close friend.

CLOVIS: He doesn't know. I don't want him to know.

MARC: Of course.

CLOVIS: It would mean nothing now. It was foolish. A mistake.

MARC: [*Breaking slightly.*] I did love you, Clovis.

CLOVIS: No.

MARC: I do love you.

CLOVIS: No.

MARC: I've never finished my paintings of you.

CLOVIS: The painting I remember best was when you wanted to paint me in the midst of a storm. Do you remember?

MARC: Yes.

CLOVIS: And you wanted to age the canvas first. So we wrapped the canvas around ourselves and rolled about the floor of your studio.

MARC: That was the happiest time of my life.

CLOVIS: But you left. The worst year of my life and you left.

MARC: After the accident —

CLOVIS: — It wasn't an accident.

MARC: It was getting messy. After the accident, I felt it was a punishment to us both.

CLOVIS: How were you punished?

MARC: It seemed like an omen.

CLOVIS: What did you lose? What of yourself did you lose that really cost you something?

MARC: I lost things.

CLOVIS: That day I went to the gallery and watched. People stood laughing at my painting. Victor stood with Clive Riviere. Laughing at my painting. I ran to my studio and set fire to all of it. I wanted to build a funeral pyre of all those canvasses and burn like Joan of Arc. When my hair grew back it was like a baby's.

MARC: I'm so sorry, Clovis. I wish there was something I could do.

CLOVIS: Do you know that I've never painted a nude?

MARC: What has that got to do with anything?

CLOVIS: I've posed nude, but I've never painted a nude.

MARC: What do you want, Clovis?

CLOVIS: I want you to pose for me.

MARC: I don't understand.

CLOVIS: Take off your clothes, Marc. I want you to pose for me.

MARC: You're not serious.

CLOVIS: [Deadly serious.] Take off your clothes.

[As some concession to her, he removes his jacket.]

CLOVIS: [Cont'd.] I want you to model for me. You'll need to be nude.

MARC: I can't. Clovis? Where are you going?

[CLOVIS exits. She returns holding VICTOR's gun.]

CLOVIS: I said, take off your clothes.

[MARC unbuttons his shirt. CLOVIS points the gun at each garment indicating which he should remove next. He is in his undershirt and barefoot.]

CLOVIS: [Cont'd.] Naked, Marc. I intend to paint a nude.

MARC: Clovis.

[She shoots the gun in the air.]

CLOVIS: Now, take off your clothes.

MARC: I can't.

[*Hearing the gunshot*, POLA, VICTOR, DOLORES, *and* MYLO *come running*.]

MYLO: Maman! Maman!

VICTOR: What is going on?

POLA: We're painting nudes.

CLOVIS: Marc is modeling for me.

MARC: I don't understand you.

CLOVIS: I want to paint a nude.

VICTOR: Why?

CLOVIS: I want to because I want to.

MARC: You are crazy.

[VICTOR *reaches for the gun.*]

CLOVIS: Get away from me.

DOLORES: Someone could get hurt.

MARC: I don't care if you shoot yourself.

POLA: Clovis.

MARC: I just don't like the mess you're making.

VICTOR: Give me the gun, Clovis.

CLOVIS: No.

POLA: You don't need the gun, Clovis.

CLOVIS: Will all of you please shut up please and stop telling me what to do. I know exactly what I'm doing so please shut up please.

VICTOR: Clovis, I have had enough. I have really had enough.

CLOVIS: I haven't. I haven't had nearly enough.

VICTOR: Clovis.

CLOVIS: [*Steady, direct.*] You can call me crazy, you can say my work isn't good, you can tell other people my work isn't good, you can laugh at me, you can refuse me a place at the table, but you cannot stop me.

VICTOR: Stop you from what?

CLOVIS: From painting my first nude.

[VICTOR *is still for a moment, looking at* CLOVIS. *He moves away from the others and quietly begins removing his clothing.*]

MARC: Is this what you want?

[CLOVIS *turns the gun back toward* MARC.]

MARC: [*Cont'd.*] You want to point guns at men, make us take off our clothes.

CLOVIS: You've done it to us.

MARC: I've never pointed a gun.

CLOVIS: You don't need a gun.

VICTOR: When I was a boy, I had a knack for finding misplaced objects and people in the village would come to me and ask, where did my father leave his eyeglasses, where did I leave my bag of marbles? I would close my eyes and answer, on the red chair, in the café, inside the birdcage at Michel's house.

[VICTOR *has removed all his clothing and stands naked, wide open to* CLOVIS.]

VICTOR: [*Cont'd.*] What pose would you like? [*Softly.*] It's all in your hands, Clovis. Now, what are you going to do?

POLA: Clovis, what are you going to do now?

[CLOVIS *is still for a moment holding the gun. She takes a breath.*]

MYLO: Maman.

[CLOVIS *gently lowers the gun.*]

CLOVIS: My paints. Someone get me my paints.

[MYLO *goes.* CLOVIS *arranges* VICTOR *in the pose she wants.*]

VICTOR: Here I am. Paint me.

[MYLO *returns carrying his mother's paints, easel, and canvas. He helps his mother set up.*]

[*As* CLOVIS *sets up her easel, paints and canvas, the air gradually fills with the radiance of the night butterflies.*]

VICTOR: [*Cont'd.*] After our first time together, I looked over and saw a radiant third body between us, a radiant third body that we had created.

MYLO: Maman, do you know about the night butterfly?

CLOVIS: No.

MYLO: They're from the moon.

CLOVIS: [*She smiles.*] From the moon?

MYLO: Yes, from the moon.

DOLORES: Last night I had a craving for something to eat and went downstairs and opened the kitchen door, and I tell you, I was dazzled. It was full of good things to eat. Chicken steeped in lemon, garlic and white wine, a lentil and sausage salad with fresh parsley and black olives, mandarin oranges, gallons of apple cider and more. What I am saying is that it was bountiful.

POLA: I wore saffron-colored trousers, a purple turban, and carrried a walking stick.

MARC: I touched my face and there was less of me.

POLA: I knew very clearly what I was up against.

MARC: Less muscle, less bone, less hair, less of me.

VICTOR: Tell me about the light.

CLOVIS: I can't paint and talk at the same time.

VICTOR: Yes, you can. Tell me about the light, Clovis, what you see.

[CLOVIS *picks up the paintbrush.*]

CLOVIS: What I see is a complete sphere of the world made of glass. And I can walk through it on a glass bridge that's the equator bisecting the room. When I look up, I see a hemisphere of multi-colored continents and seas lit from outside so that it glows like a cathedral. Below me is another hemisphere. And here I am at the center of the world standing on a glass bridge.

DOLORES: When I opened the door to the kitchen, I tell you, I was dazzled.

POLA: I saw the night moonflower.

MARC: The fact is, I was changed.

CLOVIS: Victor, can you turn your head a bit more to the side?

VICTOR: Like this?

CLOVIS: That glass room, so round and radiant, has become for me an image of wholeness. I wonder whether the patterns of glass have been altered to reflect the changes in the world? I had remembered the hemispheres of that world as being separated by a glass bridge, but I'm wondering now if they were instead joined by that bridge.

POLA: Oh, how marvelous.

[*The train whistle sounds for the last time.*]

MYLO: Look, Maman, it's beginning to get light.

[*As brush hits canvas, there is some light now, and* CLOVIS *begins to paint.*]

THE END

Joyce Carol Oates

BLACK

Black was produced by the Women's Project & Productions under the artistic directorship of Julia Miles at Intar in New York City, March 7-April 3, 1994. It was directed by Tom Polumbo with the following cast:

BOYD	John Wojda
DEBRA	Kristen Griffith
LEW CLAYBROOK	Jonathan Earl Peck

Set Design by David Mitchell
Lighting Design by Jackie Manasee
Costume Design by Elsa Ward
Production Stage Manager: Patty Lyons

CAST

DEBRA O'DONNELL   mid-30s, Caucasian
JONATHAN BOYD   mid-30s, Caucasian
LEW CLAYBROOK   late 30s, Black

Setting: Debra O'Donnell's house in the small suburban town of West Windsor, N.J.

Time: A winter evening, early 1990's

ACT 1

SCENE 1

DARKNESS. Several bars of a classic blues number, "Cry Me a River."

LIGHTS UP on DEBRA O'DONNELL, *who is setting a table for dinner.*

The living room/dining room of DEBRA's *house is the main set. We can see into a kitchen at an angle. If furnished more than minimally, it should contain attractive "modern" furniture; a sofa and chairs in neutral, subdued colors; bookshelves containing both books and CDs; a coffee table; an end table with a German bell-glass clock; a dining room table and chairs; perhaps a large potted plant in the background. On the floor, near the door stage right, are several cardboard boxes (containing* BOYD's *things).*

DEBRA is a beautiful woman, sensuous, self-conscious, accustomed to being looked at; the kind of woman in whom intelligence is not taken for granted, but must be continually asserted. She is dressed for the evening in an attractive cream-colored outfit that shows her figure to advantage, but is in her stocking feet at the moment. She is edgy, nervous; causes one of the candles to topple from its holder.

LIGHTS UP on JONATHAN BOYD, *extreme stage left.* BOYD *is making a telephone call from a pay phone in a café. Cigarette in mouth, perhaps glass in hand. Telephone rings in* DEBRA's *living room.* DEBRA *moves, with some hesitation, to answer.*

DEBRA: Yes? Hello?

[*A pause, as* BOYD *stands unspeaking; café noises in the back-ground.*]

Hello — ?

BOYD: [*Guiltily, yet eagerly.*] Debra? Is that you?

DEBRA: Boyd? Where are you?

BOYD: It's — you?

DEBRA: Of course it's me! Is something wrong?

BOYD: Your voice is — different.

DEBRA: I'm sorry — what? I can't hear you very —

BOYD: I wasn't sure when you wanted me. I mean — exactly.

DEBRA: [*Looking at watch.*] Around seven, didn't we say?

BOYD: Oh, Christ. I *am* late.

DEBRA: No, no — just come. Are you still on the Turnpike?

BOYD: I'm on Route 1, at the Anchor Inn.

DEBRA: [*Puzzled, alarmed.*] You're there? Ten minutes away? Why?

BOYD: I wasn't sure when you — wanted me.

DEBRA: I can't hear you — what's going on there, Boyd?

BOYD: Sorry!

[DEBRA *has grown agitated;* LLEWELLYN CLAYBROOK, *who has been in the kitchen, overhears and comes to her. He may lay a comforting hand on her shoulder or gently embrace her from behind. He is a well groomed Black man in his late thirties; casually but tastefully dressed; an intellectual with a markedly unpretentious style; playful, quick-witted, perhaps somewhat self-conscious; carries himself with grace, dignity. A professor and administrator, he has become accustomed to assuming authority; one of those who display their power lightly, until it is challenged.*]

DEBRA: [*To* BOYD, *more assertively.*] Boyd, just come. We'll be expecting you in a few minutes.

BOYD: But — is it all right?

DEBRA: For God's sake please just come!

[DEBRA *hangs up receiver. Turns to* CLAYBROOK, *and they embrace; she hides her face in his neck. Freeze as LIGHTS OUT.*]

SCENE 2

LIGHTS UP. As doorbell rings, DEBRA *and* CLAYBROOK *open the door to* BOYD, *who is carrying a duffel bag (over one shoulder), a long-stemmed red rose, and a bottle of wine. He appears calm— smiling, charming, keyed-up but seemingly in control. For the briefest moment, he stares at* DEBRA *and* CLAYBROOK *—then takes* DEBRA's *hand, murmuring "Hello" as* DEBRA *in turn murmurs a greeting and, after a moment's hesitation, leans forward and kisses him on the cheek. One should sense they have not seen each other for some time.*

BOYD: God, I'm sorry—I guess I'm late?

DEBRA: [*Just slightly edgy.*] We're so happy to see you. [*She turns to* CLAYBROOK.] Boyd, this is Llewellyn Claybrook—Lew—my friend; Lew, this is Jonathan Boyd—his friends all call him *Boyd.*

[BOYD *and* CLAYBROOK *energetically shake hands.*]

BOYD: Hey! Great to meet you.

CLAYBROOK: Great to meet *you.*

BOYD: [*A moment's confusion.*] Lew.

CLAYBROOK: Some call me Lew, some call me Clay. Some call me [*A chuckle.*] — well, never mind!

DEBRA: [*An arm through* CLAYBROOK's.] Llewellyn is *Lew* to his friends.

BOYD: Well, I'm—relieved to be here, off that damned Turnpike. I mean—Route 1. For you, Debra—[*Hands her the rose.*] and, Lew—[*Hands him the bottle of wine.*]

DEBRA: Thank you, Boyd.

CLAYBROOK: [Peering at label, appreciatively.] Thanks!

[BOYD *swings his duffel bag down and sets it on the floor. There is a certain air in* BOYD *regarding his duffel bag. His back to* DEBRA *and* CLAYBROOK, BOYD *paws through the bag, takes up a camera, turns.*]

BOYD: Like that! *Perfect.* [*Takes a flash photo of* DEBRA *and* CLAYBROOK, *caught off guard*].

[*A beat.*]

DEBRA: Boyd, you should give warning. And ask permission.

BOYD: Hey, sorry! [*Puts camera away, contrite; moves about living room, staring and smiling at objects.*] So warm in here — so nice. I'd forgotten how — *nice.* This — [*Touches sofa, stoops to touch carpet.*] — and this — new? — no sign of damage, in any case.

[CLAYBROOK *exits with rose and wine bottle.*]

DEBRA: [*Uneasy laugh.*] Things aren't much changed.

[BOYD *takes off jacket and gloves.*]

BOYD: The room is larger, though — I'd swear. The walls — [*Pointing into audience, to rear.*] — are farther away than they used to be.

[CLAYBROOK *enters.*]

CLAYBROOK: [*Not certain if* BOYD *is joking.*] What kind of damage —?

BOYD: Storm. Hurricane...

DEBRA: [*Quickly.*] Come sit down, Boyd, and relax.

BOYD: How many times I've seen this — space. From thousands of miles away. You don't know how imprinted a space can be, in the brain... just *there*, indelibly. [*At bookshelves, examines CDs.*] Well, these are new. Mmmm — Ellington, Tatum, Coltrane — the best. [*To* CLAYBROOK.] Let's hear one of these, all right?

CLAYBROOK: What's your preference?

BOYD: How about this? [*As* CLAYBROOK *inserts CD, music starts. Cool, mellow jazz that continues through the scene, gradually decreasing in volume.*] Last month, on one of my assignments, in Africa, I got sick, a fever of 104, I tried to find a space inside

BOYD: [*Cont'd.*] myself where I could hear *this*—exactly *this*. Kept me calm and pulled me back to life.

DEBRA: But—you're all right now, Boyd?

BOYD: [*To* CLAYBROOK.] This music—when you're away from home, it's home. It's America.

CLAYBROOK: [*Sympathetically.*] 104—that's a high fever. What caused it?

BOYD: [*Shrugging.*] Oh, one thing or another. I survived. [*Seeing boxes on floor, smiling.*] I guess those are my things—ready to go?

DEBRA: Well, eventually. Right now, Boyd—would you like a drink? Let's relax.

BOYD: [*Squatting beside boxes. looking through them with childlike interest.*] God, these things!—I'd forgotten all about them. [*Lifts tennis racquet, a pair of shoes, etc.*] What's this? [*A notebook, into which he glances.*]—handwriting of a stranger, brilliant aphorisms—must be mine. [*Tosses the notebook back; lifts a tape recorder, a glove, paperback books, etc.*] It's so considerate of you, Debra, to have packed all this. Another woman might have— [*As he lets an item fall.*]—tossed it out with the trash.

DEBRA: [*Laughing, to disguise hurt or annoyance.*] Yes, but *I didn't*, Boyd.

CLAYBROOK: [*Overlapping.*] Debra isn't "another woman."

BOYD: [*Lifting camera.*] My old Polaroid. So it wasn't lost, after all. [*Examines the camera tenderly, sights through the viewfinder.*]

DEBRA: I'm sure I told you that, Boyd. Nothing was lost. Only just misplaced. [*Pause, warmly.*] Why don't we all sit down?

CLAYBROOK: [*Hospitably.*] There's cold beer, wine, vodka—whatever. And a great single-malt scotch. Not quite as good as the wine . . . [*Indicating the bottle* BOYD *has brought.*] . . . but almost.

[BOYD *sits heavily on the sofa, as if his legs have given out. He seems temporarily disoriented, as if trying to think or position himself.*]

CLAYBROOK: [*Admiring wine.*] That, we'll have with dinner.

BOYD: [*Staring up at him, at first unseeing.*] I'll have a, a — club soda.

CLAYBROOK: [*Doubtfully.*] Club soda? With lemon, lime — ?

BOYD: [*Grinning, indicating that* CLAYBROOK *is tieless.*] Right, man — no tie. That's the idea. [*Removing necktie.*]

DEBRA: Oh, Boyd — that tie.

BOYD: Yeah?

DEBRA: I — always liked it. I'm just now remembering.

BOYD: [*Staring at tie.*] Did you give it to me? — I suppose . . .

DEBRA: I — don't remember.

BOYD: [*Folding tie quickly, stuffing into pocket.*] I don't remember. [*Pause.*] Lemon, lime — anything is fine, thanks, Lew.

[CLAYBROOK *exits with jacket.* CLAYBROOK *and* DEBRA *exchange a meaningful glance ("I love you, let's make the best of this."), which Boyd doesn't notice.*

Jazz continues. A beat. DEBRA *and* BOYD, *abruptly alone, can barely look at each other.* DEBRA *stands beside the sofa, not quite in* BOYD's *line of vision;* BOYD, *sitting, stretches his arms wide in a gesture of both weariness and comfort.*]

BOYD: [*As if making a decision.*] Yes, this is it . . . [*Softly, looking at* DEBRA, *who remains motionless, uncertain how to reply.*] . . . beautiful.

DEBRA: You've been traveling for years, Boyd. One assignment after another.

BOYD: [*Continuing to stare at her.*] And you. Like always. Beautiful.

[DEBRA *sits self-consciously, not beside* BOYD *on the sofa, but in one of the chairs. She is agitated, trying not to show emotion.*]

DEBRA: You had a fever, you said? Were you hospitalized?

BOYD: [*Shrugging.*] Like I said, I survived. In a manner of speaking. [*More zestful, pointing at clock.*] Hey! — I'd forgotten *that.*

DEBRA: [*Looking at clock as if she'd forgotten it, too.*] Oh — I'm sorry, Boyd. I should have packed it with your other things.

[DEBRA *would rise, but* BOYD *makes a quick gesture of dismissal.*]

BOYD: No, no! [*Comic exaggeration.*] It looks terrific right where it is.

DEBRA: I see the clock every day, I don't "see" it — you know?

BOYD: Please keep it, Debra! My mom's "heirloom clock" is as much yours as mine. It belongs here.

DEBRA: Unfortunately, it doesn't keep time. Lew tried to wind it, but...

[CLAYBROOK *is whistling off-stage.*]

BOYD: "Lew" — "Clay" — "Claybrook." That's him? — he sounds happy. [*Pause.*] He isn't what I'd been — led to expect. [*Pause, as* DEBRA *resists the implications of his remark; offhandedly.*] Oh, I caught malaria in Africa. Second time, actually. I'm fine.

DEBRA: You have lost weight...

BOYD: [*Trying not to stare.*] And you — you've regained. [*Pause.*] You've come back to life.

DEBRA: I haven't *re*gained. I've gone back to where I was, when you knew me. [*Calmly.*] Are you back in the country for long?

BOYD: [*Evasively.*] I'm keeping my options open.

DEBRA: I'm glad you could...stop by. To pick up your things after —

BOYD: Three years! —

DEBRA: — more like five, actually.

BOYD: Well, it's sweet of you to invite me. Generous. You and — him.

DEBRA: It was my idea. I thought, well — it's time!

BOYD: Benny is still bartending, at the Anchor Inn. He asked for you, wondered why he hadn't seen us in so long.

DEBRA: And what did you tell him?

BOYD: [*Shrugging.*] The truth.

DEBRA: And tonight you're staying — ?

BOYD: The Marriott on Route 1. I'm fine. [*Pause, boyishly.*] Did you

BOYD: [*Cont'd.*] notice, Debra, at the door, just for a moment he didn't want to shake my hand? [*Laughs.*] Remember that piece I did on Roberto Duran for *Sports Illustrated?* [DEBRA *doesn't seem to remember.*] Duran was being introduced to a boxer he was scheduled to fight, and the other man put out his hand to be shaken, and Duran jumped away, and screamed at him, "Get away! Get away! I'm not your friend!" [*Laughs; pause.*] You let me in the door, Debra — you must have — forgiven me? [*Pause.*] Maybe — that's too generous.

DEBRA: [*Trying to shift to a lighter tone.*] Shouldn't have forgiven you? — or let you in the door?

[BOYD *stares at* DEBRA. CLAYBROOK*'s whistling grows louder; he appears in the doorway.*]

CLAYBROOK: [*Smiling, genial.*] Say there, Jonathan — I mean, Boyd — you're *sure* you want a club soda? I'm having a Heineken.

BOYD: [*As if needing to be tempted.*] Uh — Heineken dark?

CLAYBROOK: Real dark.

BOYD: Well, O.K. — make that two. Thanks!

[CLAYBROOK *signals O.K.; disappears back into kitchen.* DEBRA *laughs, pressing fingers into lips.*]

BOYD: Something amusing, Debra?

DEBRA: Oh, no.

BOYD: You're laughing.

DEBRA: I'm — smiling.

BOYD: I stick to beer, now. This is my first of the day. [*Pause.*]

DEBRA: It's fine, Boyd. It's all right.

BOYD: It *is* fine, I promise. [*Pause.*] I'm not the way — you remember me.

DEBRA: [*Almost tenderly.*] I know that, Boyd.

BOYD: [*Flaring up.*] You don't *know*, I'm telling you.

[DEBRA *stiffens.* CLAYBROOK *returns, cheerful, hospitable. He is carrying a tray with two bottles of beer, two tall glasses, a glass of wine, a bowl of nuts, and the long-stemmed rose in a slender vase. He serves* DEBRA *and* BOYD, *then himself. Sits.*]

BOYD: [*Lifting glass.*] *Chilled.* That's real class! Thanks, Lew.

DEBRA: [*Sipping wine, relieved he has come back.*] Thanks Lew! How is the veal?

CLAYBROOK: Everything's under control. [*Checks watch.*] I'll start the pasta at 9:30. [*As* DEBRA *is about to get up.*] No, sit *still*; I'm in charge.

BOYD: [*Drinking thirstily, scooping nuts out of bowl.*] Driving on those expressways after dark — it's mesmerizing. And the snow falling. And the oncoming headlights. You start to float free— don't know where the hell you *are.*

CLAYBROOK: It can be dangerous at night. Driving alone.

BOYD: Driving alone is always dangerous.

CLAYBROOK: So! [*Slight pause.*] Debra was telling me, you've been traveling?

BOYD: I'm back for good, now. For now.

DEBRA: That isn't very likely.

BOYD: My bones ache. [*As if amused.*] I'm not a young kid any longer.

DEBRA: [*To* CLAYBROOK.] Boyd never said no to any assignment, no matter how dangerous.

CLAYBROOK: [*Looking through a pile of magazines on a table, not finding the one he wants.*] Debra gave me the article you did on the I.R.A., I was impressed.

BOYD: [*Surprised, pleased.*] You read it?

CLAYBROOK: — thought it was here, somewhere.

DEBRA: I may have — put it away.

BOYD: In the *New York Times Magazine.* But that was a while back.

CLAYBROOK: Very powerful, I thought. Man! — you were taking a chance, eh? Those people are desperate.

BOYD: Losers are always desperate. [*Pause.*] That was last year.

DEBRA: This time you were in — Ethiopia?

BOYD: In Addis Ababa mainly. I was starting for the interior when I got sick. I came back — to Europe, I mean — my next assignment was Bosnia, for *Newsweek.* [*Vague, drinking.*] Crossing time zones too often, you can displace who you *are.* [*Pause.*] My best camera was stolen in Budapest. In the Hilton of all places.

CLAYBROOK: I've been there, just once — the Budapest Hilton. Pretty swanky.

BOYD: *You've* been there?

CLAYBROOK: [*Ignoring* BOYD's *condescension.*] Well, not recently. I only go to such places if I'm invited, and my way is paid.

DEBRA: Lew travels, too. To professional conferences.

CLAYBROOK: It's more I used to, when I was a theorist— a teacher.

DEBRA: [*Proudly.*] At Rutgers — New Brunswick, the School of Social Work. That's where we met — Lew was my professor.

BOYD: Professor — !

CLAYBROOK: Now I'm in the real world, trying to practice what I've been preaching in books. [*Shakes head wryly.*] No more *theory.*

BOYD: I guess I've been told some — inaccurate things about you.

CLAYBROOK: [*Coolly.*] Well. People *will* talk. [*Smoothly.*] Yes, I surely do envy you, Boyd. A world traveler. I'd always wanted to visit Eastern Europe, and now it's totally changed. I had a theory about "demonizing" — projecting opposites onto "enemies" — wanted to test it out, first hand. The Berlin Wall, the walled city — I'd have liked to spend time there.

BOYD: Berlin! No, you wouldn't have.

CLAYBROOK: [*Not liking to be contradicted, but lightly.*] Hmmm? Why not?

BOYD: [*As if with authority.*] That Wall — it was a, a hard thing to deal with. If your mind's susceptible to — things.

DEBRA: [*Quickly.*] Well, the Wall's been down a long time now.

CLAYBROOK: What kind of things, Boyd?

BOYD: [*Smiling.*] Debra prefers I not talk about the Berlin Wall be- cause there are bad personal memories associated with the Wall. So O.K., I won't.

DEBRA: It was a nightmare city, West Berlin. All the worst paranoid fantasies.

BOYD: They weren't fantasies, they were real. [*Searching in pockets for cigarettes, without success.*] Those ten days we spent there, I was on assignment for *Life*, it just happened that there was an "incident"—an attempted escape, a kid shot down by the East German guards—they just let him lie there, bleeding. [*Pause.*] I was the man with the camera. [*Drinks, as if a toast to himself.*]

DEBRA: [*To* CLAYBROOK.] *I* came along, I'd always wanted to "see Europe".

BOYD: [*As if defending their trip.*] It might've worked out. [*Pause.*] The fact about West Berlin people don't realize, and most Americans had no idea of, at the time, was that the Wall *sur- rounded* the city. I mean, *surrounded.* [*A gesture.*] So you were walled in, trapped— it wasn't just some East-West wall; and it sure wasn't ideological. It was *real.* [*Has gone to his duffel bag to get a pack of cigarettes.*] Some people freaked if they stayed there too long, and I don't mean just Germans. Like I said, if your mind's susceptible — [*About to light cigarette.*]

DEBRA: [*Quickly.*] Excuse me, Boyd—I'd rather you didn't smoke. If it's all right with you.

BOYD: [*Glancing about, seeing no ashtrays.*] God, you've quit?

DEBRA: I'm in the process. I'm about 85% successful. Lew doesn't smoke — [*Squeezing Lew's hand.*] — so he can give me moral support.

BOYD: [*Awkward with his cigarettes, stuffs them in his pocket.*] Well. I wish you luck, Debra. [*Pause, smiles.*] Remember that Christmas, we just moved here, we both tried to give up?

DEBRA: [*Ruefully.*] For forty-eight hours.

BOYD: Hey, it was longer than that.

DEBRA: For you, maybe. *I* was sneaking on the side.

BOYD: [*Laughing.*] You weren't! I was sneaking on the side.

DEBRA: You were? Oh, Boyd —

[*Both laugh, perhaps a bit excessively.* CLAYBROOK *looks on indulgently.*]

BOYD: [*Laughter turns to coughing.*] Just the thought — see? — I start coughing. [*Strikes his chest with the heel of his hand, rather hard.*]

DEBRA: Please sit down, Boyd — don't hover.

BOYD: [*To* CLAYBROOK.] Debra used to say that all the time — Boyd, don't *hover*. [*Flapping arms.*] I used to be a bat.

[CLAYBROOK *laughs,* DEBRA *smiles faintly.*]

BOYD: [*Cont'd.*] [*Sitting, as before.*] True, you did miss something historic, Lew, I mean Clay — no, Lew — not seeing the Berlin Wall. [*Pause.*] Weird fucking symbol, but *real*.

DEBRA: [*Laughing impatiently.*] Boyd, the Wall's *down*.

BOYD: It's the ones you can't see that kill you. Walls, I mean. [*A significant glance at* DEBRA.] You told Lew about it, eh? — that time?

DEBRA: [*Incensed.*] I certainly did not tell Lew about that sorry episode. Or any other. The past is *past*.

BOYD: [*Glancing from* CLAYBROOK *to* DEBRA, *and back.*] Yes, but you have to share the past, don't you? — good times and bad times? — misfortunes? — happy memories? That's love, right?

DEBRA: [*Interrupting on "love."*] I've told Lew very little. We have plenty of other things to talk about.

BOYD: Oh, I know! — I mean, I can guess. Of course. Sorry to bring it up. [*Has finished beer, drinking from bottle.*]

CLAYBROOK: [*Restless.*] You about ready for another, Boyd? — we've just got time.

DEBRA: [*Not wanting to be left alone with* BOYD.] Wait, Lew, I'll go—

CLAYBROOK: [*Warmly, but also accustomed to having his own way.*]
No, no, no, Debra. You stay with your — guest. [*His hand on
her shoulder, gently but decisively.*] Boyd — another beer?

BOYD: Well — if you are.

CLAYBROOK: Sure thing!

[CLAYBROOK *removes the empty bottles; exits stage left. In his wake
there is a brief silence. Then, startling her,* BOYD *reaches over to
squeeze* DEBRA's *hand.*]

BOYD: He's — nice. I like him, Debra.

DEBRA: [*Almost shyly.*] I thought you might. [*Pause.*] I mean, I
thought you might like each other.

BOYD: You think he likes — me?

DEBRA: [*Withdrawing her hand.*] Oh, Lew likes everyone. He's the
most even-tempered man I've ever known.

BOYD: [*A bit deflated.*] What's he, a Christian or something?

DEBRA: [*Pleased to be talking about her lover.*] In fact, Lew's father *is* a
preacher — in the "African Methodist Episcopal Church." In
Philadelphia.

BOYD: [*Running a hand through his hair, bemused.*] Well — I was certainly misled about all this.

DEBRA: [*Coolly.*] What's "all this" — ?

BOYD: [*Shrugging.*] You, here. And him.

DEBRA: [*Voice rising.*] Who's been talking about me? — our mutual
friends? Whose business is my life but my own?

BOYD: [*Portentously.*] I bear a certain — responsibility. We were together ten years.

DEBRA: We were married eight years.

BOYD: We were *together* ten years — that can't be altered.

DEBRA: Don't think about it, that's all. I've stopped.

BOYD: You've — stopped?

DEBRA: I've *stopped.*

BOYD: [*Bluntly.*] I don't believe that. [*Pause.*] I'm sorry I behaved like a shit.

DEBRA: [*Laughing, genuinely amused.*] Oh, really? When?

BOYD: Just — generally. I believe I lacked perspective. A common failing of American — male — youth.

DEBRA: [*An effort to be both magnanimous and dismissive.*] It's history, now, Boyd. Like the Berlin Wall.

BOYD: Him? Does he have kids?

DEBRA: Ask him.

BOYD: He's so sensitive, isn't he — just now, he left at precisely the right moment, knowing he can trust me with you.

DEBRA: [*Laughing, a bit incensed.*] Of course Lew can trust you with me.

BOYD: He can trust *you* with *me.*

DEBRA: What is that supposed to mean?

BOYD: [*An undertone.*] Is he — moved *in*? Here?

DEBRA: [*Implacably.*] To a degree.

BOYD: I mean — is it serious, permanent? [*When* DEBRA *declines to answer; shrewdly.*] He isn't married, or — ?

DEBRA: [*After a moment's hesitation.*] Ask him.

BOYD: I wouldn't want you to be hurt, Debra — that's all.

DEBRA: [*Laughing.*] From *you* — that's funny.

BOYD: He *has* been married, right? — his age, he must have almost grown children.

DEBRA: [*An air of pride.*] Llewellyn Claybrook is a very special person, and a very private person. He isn't, in some ways, like *us.*

BOYD: Not like White people, or not like *us*?

DEBRA: [*Annoyed.*] With Lew, I don't think in terms of *white* or *black*. [*Pause.*] I'm in love.

[*A painful pause.*]

BOYD: [*Stiffly.*] I see.

DEBRA: I'd hoped you'd be friends with Lew — with us. You and he are both men of — integrity and principle.

BOYD: [*Pulling at his shirt collar, as if warm.*] Are we.

DEBRA: You had some rough times but they're over.

BOYD: [*Sardonic mirth.*] Yeah, like thirty years. [*Pause, glancing toward kitchen.*] You think he's hiding out there? — from me?

DEBRA: He thinks we might want to talk.

BOYD: But we don't, huh? [*Pause.*]

DEBRA: Boyd, Lew was genuinely impressed with that piece of yours on Northern Ireland, and some other things I showed him.

BOYD: Other things? What?

DEBRA: — He said, "Here's a *brother.*"

BOYD: [*Strangely moved.*] "A brother." He said that?

DEBRA: You see, I told him nothing — he knows we'd had some hard times — we were together too young, and married too young — we fell out of love — we got divorced. And that's all.

BOYD: [*Wincing.*] That's . . . all. [*Pause.*]

DEBRA: It's not as if it's an uncommon story. Every one of your friends — I swear, they've all gotten divorced.

BOYD: *Our* friends. [*Pause.*] You keep in touch?

DEBRA: No.

BOYD: As long, as you're happy, Debra. That's what I'm trying to determine.

DEBRA: I am very happy. Don't try to change that.

BOYD: I would never — !

DEBRA: Yes. Yes you would.

BOYD: [*After a pause.*] The scar isn't visible — is it?

DEBRA: [*Quickly touches her upper lip, as if ashamed.*] That depends on how close you are.

[BOYD *gets to his feet, restless. Glances toward kitchen as if fearful* CLAYBROOK *might be overhearing.*]

BOYD: I'd heard some — upsetting things — about him, and you. That's one of the reasons I'm here tonight.

DEBRA: Well, you were mistaken. [*Sharply.*] Who's been talking about me?

BOYD: Oh, you know . . . guys I run into. [*Pause, then plunges in.*] Someone said he thought you were involved with a jazz musician mixed up in drugs; someone else swore he was an ex-cop, mixed up in drugs. [*Not noticing* DEBRA's *mounting anger.*] Burt Weidel, I ran into him in Frankfurt, said he'd heard you were living with a breeder of pit bulls. He swore. [*Laughs, as if to suggest the gullibility of these others.*] The one consensus was — your lover was *Black*.

[DEBRA *rises, advances upon* BOYD, *slaps his face.* BOYD *grabs her hand to still her; stares at her; a beat.* BOYD *unexpectedly sinks to his knees, encloses* DEBRA's *ankles with his hands, embraces her legs and presses his face against her legs in a reckless, romantic gesture of contrition.*]

BOYD: These are so lovely — your shoes, your lovely shoes, Debra — oh, God, I'm so sorry!

[CLAYBROOK *enters with tray and drinks, an apron knotted around his waist. He stares at* DEBRA *and* BOYD.]

LIGHTS OUT.

SCENE 3

LIGHTS UP. An hour or so later. There is evidence of drinking; empty beer bottles on the coffee table, a nearly depleted bottle of wine. Low-key jazz in the background. DEBRA *and* CLAYBROOK *are seated together on the sofa . . .* BOYD, *his sport coat removed, is eager, happy, showing his portfolio of photographs to them.*

BOYD: — You think you've seen the worst, but it goes on, and on! — in Africa. This is Ethiopia — [CLAYBROOK *frowns at the photos,* DEBRA *can barely bring herself to look.*] — I was sent to cover the

BOYD: [*Cont'd.*] war but there was also the drought —famine— starvation— oh, Christ, the AIDS epidemic—it wasn't the first time it caught up with me, but it was the worst. Made me sick to my guts. [*A bit of bravado, watching* CLAYBROOK *and* DE-BRA'*s faces.*] But I filed the story anyway. One of "Boyd's best."

CLAYBROOK: [*Moved.*] God have mercy!—these are powerful images. You really got to know these people, Boyd, did you?

BOYD: There is that assumption.

CLAYBROOK: It surely makes the heartbreak I deal with, in my job, what you'd call *negotiable*. [*Showing a photo to* DEBRA, *who stares at it.*] Look at those eyes!—poor beautiful child.

DEBRA: How did you get such a picture, Boyd?

BOYD: [*Shrugging.*] I'm a professional.

DEBRA: If you can't do anything to help, it seems wrong to get so close. To look.

BOYD: Right! You're absolutely right. But—some of us have to look.

CLAYBROOK: Where's the piece coming out, Boyd?

BOYD: [*Evasively.*] It's—pending. An editor and I don't quite see eye to eye. [*Leafing through photos.*] I spent Christmas photographing families. Children especially. Lost my translator halfway through the jungle, then I lost my guide. To get close-ups like these. Imprinted on film. To sell. [*Pause.*] Why else?— to sell. And there's the byline—"Jonathan Boyd."

DEBRA: [*To* CLAYBROOK.] Boyd won a Pulitzer, did I tell you?—

BOYD: [*Quickly, dismissively.*] I was a kid, twenty-six years old. It was a fluke.

CLAYBROOK: Fluke or not, congratulations!

BOYD: [*Vehemently.*] It was a fluke. An accident. I didn't know shit, I just happened to be at—the right place at the right time.

CLAYBROOK: And where was that?

BOYD: [*Ignoring this, looking at photos.*] Back in New York, the rap is my shots are "too graphic"—or "not graphic enough, too

BOYD: [*Cont'd.*] artsy." [*Pause.*] The closer the spark of life is to extinction in these kids' eyes, the more valuable the photo; but if the spark of life is actually *out*, and all you have is a kiddy corpse — no, thanks!

DEBRA: [*Upset by the photos.*] Oh, Boyd, let yourself *be*. It's all about you, isn't it?

BOYD: [*Hurt.*] About *me*?

[DEBRA *shakes her head, turns away.* CLAYBROOK *puts the photos back carefully, hands the portfolio to* BOYD.]

CLAYBROOK: Now's not the proper time, maybe. For these.

BOYD: When is the proper time, then?

CLAYBROOK: [*Seriously.*] Well — some sacred time.

BOYD: Some what?

CLAYBROOK: [*Holding his ground.*] Sacred time.

[*A beat.* BOYD *returns the portfolio to his duffel bag, a bit carelessly.*]

BOYD: Yeah, well. "Sacred time."

CLAYBROOK: There's true courage there, Boyd. In that work. And artistry, too. I'd have to say beauty — cruel beauty. [*Trying to be congenial.*] Like Hell might be beautiful. If you've got the eye.

BOYD: If you've got the perspective.

CLAYBROOK: [*To* DEBRA, *in his professional — arbitrating manner.*] It's true what you say, Debra — it does seem wrong to *look* if you can't act, — like *knowing* and *acting* shouldn't be separated. But there's a need to bear witness — that's a true course of action, too.

BOYD: [*Drinking.*] Debra doesn't buy that, Lew. She knows we're in it for the dough. "Media" men.

DEBRA: Please don't put words in my mouth, Boyd.

CLAYBROOK: [*Glancing at watch.*] Man, it's getting on past 10:00 — how'd that happen?

DEBRA: [*Moves to get up but sinks back, as if dizzy, laughing.*] Wow. We'd better get dinner on the table before it's too late.

[CLAYBROOK *helps* DEBRA *to her feet. They confer together, checking watches;* BOYD *watches them covertly.*]

CLAYBROOK: [*Murmuring intimately to* DEBRA.] Sweetheart, you let me make the pasta, no need us both fussing—

DEBRA: Hey c'mon, I'm not drunk—

CLAYBROOK: You toss the salad.

DEBRA: [*Moving off, to* BOYD, *by way of teasing* CLAYBROOK.] He doesn't trust me, fears I'll make a mush of his pasta. *His* pasta—made it himself.

[DEBRA *takes up some of the empties.* CLAYBROOK *hands tray to* DEBRA. DEBRA *exits.*]

BOYD: [*Trying to retain their attention, aggrieved tone.*] I guess I thought that reporting injustice, atrocities, suffering—I could make a real difference in the world. But one day I had to see, I was only just *reporting*. Just a cog in the media—consumer machine.

[*But the moment is lost.*]

CLAYBROOK: Say, honey—you need some help there?

DEBRA: [*Offstage.*] Honey, no.

[BOYD *is hurt, offended; for the remainder of the scene, it is all he can do to suppress his deep rage. Even as, left with* CLAYBROOK, *listening to jazz, the men appear to be on congenial terms.*]

BOYD: Man, that's terrific. The greatest.

CLAYBROOK: [*Keeping time with the music.*] Mmmm.

BOYD: Ellington, right?

CLAYBROOK: Peterson.

BOYD: Who?

CLAYBROOK: Oscar Peterson.

BOYD: Oh, right! [*Listens.*] That's what I meant—it's American

BOYD: [*Cont'd.*] music. Not "Black"—American. [*Pause.*] When you're away from home, I mean. [*Pause.*] I mean—hell, you know what I mean.

CLAYBROOK: [*Noncommittal.*] Hmmm.

BOYD: The farther you get from home, the more you know you're *American*. Once, I was in Rangoon sitting in a café and I heard Coltrane and it brought back...[*Pause.*] The color of a man's skin becomes irrelevant.

CLAYBROOK: [*Listening, to music, inscrutable.*] Hmmmm.

BOYD: You probably have a larger collection, eh?—than just these CDs?

CLAYBROOK: [*Bemused.*] I have records—must be hundreds!—I prefer them to CDs. Drop the needle in the groove—pop—hiss—static! I can't go by a used record store without parking my car and going inside—buy 'em every chance I get. Over at the other place.

BOYD: The other place?

CLAYBROOK: Down the 'pike, in Trenton. Where I'm located 'til things get worked out.

BOYD: Legal things?

[CLAYBROOK *shrugs, inscrutably.*]

BOYD: [*Cont'd.*] My divorce—seemed to take forever. [*Pause, when* CLAYBROOK *still evades a response.*] So—you're living in Trenton?

CLAYBROOK: Since I'm working for the state right now, I figure I best live in the capital. You're living in Washington?

BOYD: I'm living in—[*Shrugs, smiling.*]—my car.

CLAYBROOK: [*Not having heard.*] Where's that?

BOYD: [*Drinking, voice slurred.*]—living in my bag. [*Kicking gesture toward duffel bag on floor.*]

[CLAYBROOK *laughs uncertainly.*]

BOYD: [*Almost hesitantly.*] So, um, Clay—I mean, Lew—my wife was your student, huh?

CLAYBROOK: [*Carefully.*] "Debra O'Donnell" was my student, yes.

BOYD: Looks like, now, she's graduated.

CLAYBROOK: Debra's getting her degree in May, up at Rutgers. But she's been working with Mercer County Services since last fall.

BOYD: That's where you work, too?

CLAYBROOK: [*Mildly annoyed.*] I'm in Trenton. Like I said — the capital. I direct Family Services for the State of New Jersey.

BOYD: [*Impressed.*] The State! [*Pause.*] Why'd you leave the University?

CLAYBROOK: The Governor appointed me. [*Shrugs.*] Took a salary cut, in fact.

BOYD: [*A bit ironically, yet admiring.*] *That's idealism.*

[CLAYBROOK *chuckles, as if to say "call it what you will."*]

BOYD: I bet — you're going into politics.

CLAYBROOK: I've been approached, yes.

BOYD: "Approached" — what's that mean.

CLAYBROOK: Exactly what you'd think.

[BOYD, *subtly rebuffed, takes a new tack.*]

BOYD: [*An Irish accent.*] "Debra O'Donnell" — not "Debra Boyd." That's how she identified herself?

CLAYBROOK: That's the woman's name, friend.

BOYD: How'd you two meet? — I'm curious.

CLAYBROOK: As Debra said, I was her "professor" — for a large lecture course, "Inequality: Class, Race and Gender." But we met — became acquainted — on neutral territory, off campus. I never went out with Debra while she was my student.

BOYD: [*A joke.*] Well — I hope you gave her an "A."

CLAYBROOK: I don't "give" grades. Grades are earned.

BOYD: [*As if conceding a point.*] Debra has — changed. A lot.

CLAYBROOK: Debra is a fine, strong, good-hearted woman. She just needs more faith in her spiritual *self.*

BOYD: I'm—happy for her. [*Not looking happy at all.*]

CLAYBROOK: [*Following his own line of thought.*] A human being, beneath his or her skin, has got to realize the spiritual self. The outward self, economic political—it's just preparation for the inward. [*Pause.*] That's why the outward self *is* crucial. [*Pause.*] "The Kingdom of God is within."

[*A beat.*]

BOYD: [*Subtle irony.*] That's real—Christian. [*Pause.*] That tiny scar on Debra's upper lip, sickle-shaped—ever noticed?

CLAYBROOK: [*Taken by surprise.*] A bicycle accident, she said—when she was a little girl.

BOYD: [*Evenly, relieved.*] Well. O.K. 'Cause that's the truth, it was an accident. [*Pause.*] My wife—ex-wife—is a, a somewhat destructive person—you know? [*As* CLAYBROOK *frowns, noncommittally.*] You saw us—before—sort of fooling around?—[*Gestures toward the spot where he and* DEBRA *had been standing when* DEBRA *slapped him.*]—I was complimenting her on her new shoes. Beautiful new shoes, and expensive. [*Pause.*] That wizened little black nail on her smallest right toe—you ever noticed?

[CLAYBROOK *seems to be shrugging "no."*]

BOYD: Next time, you'll notice. [*Pause.*] *That* was no accident, the toenail. How it happened was—[*Leaning forward, confidentially.*]—we'd just moved here, to West Windsor—had to get out of Manhattan—and things were sort of strained—y'know how married life can get, sometimes—[*Trying to draw* CLAYBROOK *into agreement, but* CLAYBROOK *remains noncommittal.*]—my father told me, at my mother's funeral, he was drunk and sick but he knew what he was saying, "Son," he said "days can be damned long but life goes fast and you never learn a thing"—[BOYD *breaks into laughter, succumbs to coughing.*]—so anyway, we'd moved here, into this house we were actually buying, on a twenty-year mortgage—and Debra had the idea that I was involved in a "secret infidelity" at the time with a woman in New York but I was *not*—I swear, I was *not*—[*Pause, a moment of anguish, anger.*]—it was just, just—the weight of daily,

BOYD: [*Cont'd.*] domestic life — how love's like a bright flame flaring up and this other, this weight, is like a concrete sky pushing down, crushing your chest — so you can *love* a woman but can't, sometimes, stand her? — to be in the same room with her? — to hear her brush her teeth, flush the toilet, blow her nose? — walk across the floor? — *breathe?*

[DEBRA *has reappeared in the kitchen doorway, to call* CLAYBROOK; *but now pauses, listening.*]

[*Maudlin, though earnest.*] I'd blow out my brains before I'd hurt that woman, I swear, I loved that woman, I never stopped loving her but it sort of — wore thin — not *out*, but *thin* — she believes I stopped loving her but I swear I never did — *never.* It was more I was so close to her, she was me, y'know? — and around that time, about six years ago, my work wasn't steady — editors were always double-crossing me — never mind! — that's a whole other story — and, anyway, Debra had a job at a mall on Route 1, God-awful place, she hated her job and hated her life and hated me I guess and every day, God knows why, for this job at a travel agency she'd wear a pair of fake crocodile shoes, spike-heeled shoes with a strap — good-looking shoes, sort of sexy, sluttish — showing her legs the way high heels are designed to do — and it turned out Debra was in pain wearing them — I mean *pain* — they were cheap, and they fit badly — almost, like, Debra was wearing them deliberately? — these glamorous slutty shoes? — and the nail on one of her little toes turned black — blood had collected beneath it — till finally she was in so much pain she couldn't walk, so I examined it — [*Laughs, exasperated, perplexed.*] — and I was so — stunned, kind of — couldn't imagine why she'd done it, how she could be so stubborn — hurtful to herself. I tried to hold her, I guess — I could feel the terrible rage in her just trembling. [*Pause, as if he recalls; then in a different tone.*] At first it looked as if the toenail would have to be surgically removed. The podiatrist said he'd never seen anything quite like it.

[*Through* BOYD's *monologue,* CLAYBROOK *has been listening sympathetically, looking down.* DEBRA *has withdrawn discreetly; and now reappears, smiling, to fetch* CLAYBROOK. *She is carrying a glass of wine. Supressing her anger and humiliation, she enjoys the attention of both men, who stare at her.*]

DEBRA: Professor Claybrook—your expertise is required. In the kitchen.

[*LIGHTS OUT.*]

SCENE 4

LIGHTS UP.

Dining room area. Candlelight; candles have burnt part way down. DEBRA, BOYD, CLAYBROOK *are seated at the table amid wine bottles, glasses, dishware. The rose in a vase.*

CLAYBROOK: I'm optimistic—basically. My position has always been: I start with myself, a Black man in America, O.K., and I am responsible for myself. Meaning I don't pity myself and I don't make excuses for myself. The only way to help my brothers and sisters—or anyone—first I must help myself, and no excuses. [*Pause.*] Certainly I know the "history of my race"— but now *I'm making history.*

DEBRA: Lew has a plan, a work-study program for young welfare mothers, he's making a presentation to the state legislature next week. He's got support there, even among the conservatives, so maybe...

BOYD: [*Interrupts, words slightly slurred.*] If this was the Sixties, we'd know how to proceed.

CLAYBROOK: Yeah, how?

BOYD: BLOW IT ALL FUCKING SKY-HIGH!

[*A beat.*]

CLAYBROOK: Then what?

BOYD: The Sixties, man. People had the courage of their despair.

CLAYBROOK: [*Not wanting to sound puritanical, but annoyed.*] Despair? Huh! Despair never helped anybody. You got to be optimistic, in the public sector.

BOYD: That's right — things can always get worse. The fucking sun could come unhinged. [*Laughs.*] Serve *Homo Sapiens* right.

DEBRA: [*Part teasing, part critical.*] Boyd is always looking to the Apocalypse, to set things right.

BOYD: [*Pleasantly, as if rebuked.*] That's how you'd sum me up? "Looking to the Apocalypse, to set things right" — ?

DEBRA: I'm not in the habit of "summing people up."

CLAYBROOK: [*Thoughtfully.*]   Yeah — "Looking   to   the Apocalypse" — that's a temptation. Man, where I come from, is it ever.

BOYD: Where's that?

CLAYBROOK: North Philly.

BOYD: With a faint trace of — North Carolina? Bet your folks came up, say, 1940?

[CLAYBROOK *laughs, admitting it's so.*]

BOYD: [*Pursuing it, big smile.*] I bet you got the highest grades in your high school class, Lew — hell, I bet you were valedictorian. [*As* CLAYBROOK *acknowledges it.*] I bet the hot-shot Ivy League schools were pursuing you — the way the Big Ten pursues the Black athletes — begging you to accept their scholarships, eh? And you had a hard time choosing between Harvard, Princeton, Yale, but you chose —

CLAYBROOK: [*Wanting to cut it off.*] Yale.

BOYD: [*Snapping fingers.*] Right! [*Pause.*] *I* was rejected.

DEBRA: [*Eager to change the subject.*] There's more arugula salad — anyone?

BOYD: It's O.K., Lew — I went to Cornell. No scholarship, but my folks could afford it. [*Pause.*] And I worked.

CLAYBROOK: We all worked, man, scholarship or not.

BOYD: I never resented it — "affirmative action." I saw the justice of it — the history behind it.

DEBRA: [*Sharply.*] It isn't "affirmative action," is it, when the student's grades are in the highest percentile?

CLAYBROOK: [*Hoping to change subject, offering salad bowl to* BOYD.] Boyd? — greens're good for you.

DEBRA: Lew insists on real olive oil, from Italy. The dressing we used to use — Lew poured it down the sink. [*Laughs.*]

[*A beat.* BOYD *shakes his head. He's not hungry or too distracted to eat.*]

CLAYBROOK: Your talent for photography, Boyd — you never

CLAYBROOK: [*Cont'd.*] learned that in school. True talent, you either have it or you don't.

BOYD: [*Slowly*] You either have it . . . or you don't.

CLAYBROOK: Trouble is, we all know how photographs can lie.

BOYD: The photograph never lies.

CLAYBROOK: No?

BOYD: The photograph never lies. As a photograph.

CLAYBROOK: C'mon, man. Some photographs are just trickery.

BOYD: Compared to — [*Gesturing.*] "Reality"?

CLAYBROOK: Your subject is the outsides — surfaces — of things, people's faces, skin. What's inside, isn't showing. Most of what we see is accidents of light, fleeting impressions, moments — but, on film, it becomes permanent. And that's false.

DEBRA: [*Trying to lighten tone.*] We've all seen photographs of ourselves we can't even *recognize*.

BOYD: That's just vanity.

DEBRA: Yes? It is?

BOYD: A photograph isn't *you*; it's a separate entity. A composition - a formal work of art — has nothing to do with the subject's perception of himself, or herself. Who cares if Modigliani's female model recognized herself? You don't judge art by such trivial standards. [*Contemptuously.*] People can't bear it, yes, I've been called a soul-stealer. I seize the essence before the mask comes on. But that's "art."

CLAYBROOK: [*Chuckling.*] The way you describe it, it sounds like a mugging.

DEBRA: Boyd's the quintessential photographer, Lew — he refuses to allow his own picture to be taken. [*Teasing.*] You should see him, he actually gets...scared.

CLAYBROOK: [*Amused.*] Why's that?

BOYD: She's exaggerating.

DEBRA: Oh — yes?

[*Goes to get* BOYD's *camera; playfully; as* BOYD *follows anxiously after, hoping to make a joke if it.*]

DEBRA: [*Cont'd.*] Let's see! How's this work? [*Holding up camera, aiming at* BOYD.]

BOYD: [*Ill-at-ease.*] Debra, hey — c'mon.

[CLAYBROOK *remains at the table, looking on.* DEBRA *is very much enjoying her power over* BOYD. *One senses how* DEBRA *and* BOYD *are still attracted to each other.*]

DEBRA: [*Giggling.*] How's this damn thing work? [*Fussing with camera.*]

BOYD: [*Reluctantly.*] You push down here, you wait for the little red light —

DEBRA: What is it — Japanese?

BOYD: [*Exasperated.*] That's what you always ask! [*Turning to* CLAYBROOK, *as if he is fearful of* DEBRA.] Anything the least bit complicated, she asks — "Is it Japanese?"

DEBRA: C'mon, c'mon! Smile for the camera, Boyd!

[BOYD *steps back, trying to smile.*].

DEBRA: [*Laughing*] Boyd, you look ghastly! C'mon *smile.*

[BOYD *manages a grimace,* DEBRA *takes the picture, and* BOYD *takes back the camera, puts it aside.*]

BOYD: [*Getting revenge.*] Debra's father was an Army officer. It comes out sometimes — she was an Army brat.

DEBRA: [*Startled.*] Boyd, that's — silly. [*Pause.*] I haven't seen my

DEBRA: [*Cont'd.*] father in years.

CLAYBROOK: Well, I have yet to have the pleasure of meeting him.

DEBRA: Boyd had the pleasure.

BOYD: Once! Does he know about—us?

DEBRA: [*Quickly.*] Somebody in the family probably told him, *I* didn't.

BOYD: Lieutenant Colonel "Buck" O'Donnell. [*He makes a mock salute, shuddering.*] Color-blind, they said of ol' Buck—treated Whites and Blacks equally: like shit.

DEBRA: [*To* CLAYBROOK.] I've seen my father three times since I left home as a teenager. It's all ancient history.

CLAYBROOK: He's retired?

DEBRA: [*Laughs ruefully.*] Retired from the human race, just about. He never did do that well in the Army, as he'd wanted.

BOYD: Slight drinking problem, as I recall.

DEBRA: Boyd, it's ancient history.

BOYD: Debra dislikes the military, sometimes it spills over into disliking men. [*Pause.*] Or, the obverse—you know how opposites "attract"—liking them too much.

DEBRA: When have I ever disliked men!—that's ridiculous.

BOYD: I could think of a few times.

[DEBRA *moves off from* BOYD; BOYD *and* CLAYBROOK *watch her. She is the apex of a triangle that joins them.*]

DEBRA: [*Recollecting, both bitter and nostalgic.*] All through my childhood we moved from one Army base to another...Texas, Florida, Minnesota, South Carolina...I'd make friends, we'd move. I never gave up. The Army bases were the same base. The flag was the same flag. The day was the same day. Always at the same time the enlisted men marched out to the artillery range. The gunfire from the range was like thunder. Rolling and dark sounding so you'd think the sky was black with clouds. So it was a shock to look up and see the sky blue. [*Pause.*] I'd think, my Daddy is out there: I can hear him. [*Pause.*] I've been

DEBRA: [*Cont'd.*] gone from that world since I've been fifteen. I didn't run away, I walked. My mother said, "Keep in touch. I won't let him know where you are." [*Pause.*] *She* stayed.

BOYD: There's a faithful woman! [*Pause.*] Debra used sometimes to confuse me with Lieutenant Colonel O'Donnell. I mean subliminally.

DEBRA: [*Trying for a light tone.*] Boyd, I've never confused you with anyone but yourself.

BOYD: I'll drink to that. [*Drains glass.*] Hey—I brought a second bottle of wine, let's open it.

DEBRA: [*Quickly.*] Oh, no—

CLAYBROOK: [*Overlapping.*] A second bottle of *this*? [*Indicating original bottle.*]

BOYD: Pretty good stuff, eh? 1982 Ponte Canet.

CLAYBROOK: A little too good, man, for now. Best save it for another time.

BOYD: Maybe there won't be another time.

DEBRA: Of course there will be . . .

CLAYBROOK: Sure there will!

BOYD: [*Almost too vulnerable.*] You mean that?

DEBRA & CLAYBROOK: Yes!

[BOYD *looks searchingly at them.*]

BOYD: I'm—I'm grateful. [*Pause.*] When I called Debra last week, I expected—[*Pause.*] Instead, she invites me here. "Come and have dinner with us, I want you to meet my friend Lew Claybrook. [*Pause.*] I have to admit, I wasn't expecting such—kindness.

DEBRA: [*To* CLAYBROOK.] Boyd is always expecting people to behave the way, in their positions, *he* would. So he's always being surprised.

CLAYBROOK: Well—we all do a bit of that, don't we?

BOYD: She doesn't really mean that.

DEBRA: [*Pushing it.*] "You don't really mean that," he'd say. "You think you do, but you don't." [*Laughs, though she's angry.*] "You do not like those people." "You *do* like these people" — meaning *his* friends. Always imagining he understood me, from above.

BOYD: [*Stricken.*] Debra...

DEBRA: [*Not hearing, a contemplative voice.*] Once, I was thirteen years old, just starting to get filled out — there was a traveling

DEBRA: [*Cont'd.*] carnival in Ft. Lauderdale near where my father was stationed, and a bunch of us from the base went, and one of the acts was a hypnotist... he invited subjects up on stage and my girlfriends pushed me up and... there on the stage, I was so scared, I thought I'd faint! All those people in the audience looking at me, some of the guys whistling... "Dr. Night" told me to relax, he was going to demonstrate the "higher powers of the intellect" and it would be "painless," I'd never know a thing. So he waved his fingers in front of my eyes and intoned in this deep gravelly voice, "When I count to ten you will be a little girl again, five years old," and he started counting, and everything began to swim about me, I could feel my... consciousness... getting smaller and smaller like a candle flame about to go out, he gets to "eight, nine, ten," but I was still awake... I saw "Dr. Night" was wearing orangish pancake makeup and I could smell his whiskey breath, I knew I wasn't falling under the spell, I wasn't hypnotized like I was supposed to be, and "Dr. Night" saw it too, he was sweaty and angry and tried again, "When I count to ten you will be a little girl, five years old," so the poor man tries it again I'm... [*Pause.*]... in my own mind. [*Pause.*] I couldn't be hypnotized.

BOYD: [*Hurt.*] You're saying that's what I did, Debra — hypnotized you?

DEBRA: Tried to.

CLAYBROOK: [*Quick to change subject.*] Folks, what we need is a little nightcap.

[DEBRA *and* BOYD *have been staring at each other.* DEBRA *turns away, as if with an effort, to* CLAYBROOK.]

DEBRA: Oh, Lew—should we? I'm drunk...

BOYD: I'm *not drunk*. I'm stone cold sober. Terrifying prospect at this hour of the evening. [*Sits heavily.*] Actually I'm Boyd. Rhymes with "void."

CLAYBROOK: What kinda talk's that, man?

BOYD: You're a void if you don't have a soul. There's lots of us in that category. [*Laughs.*]

CLAYBROOK: [*Just a bit preacherly.*] God is inside you—whether you know it or not. Trying to keep His sense of humor. [*Moves toward kitchen.*] Enough of this kind of talk, I'm gonna make us a Claybrook special.

[DEBRA *follows* CLAYBROOK *carrying glasses, dishware.*]

DEBRA: Excuse us, Boyd! Be right back.

BOYD: [*Clumsily.*] You want some help—? [*He would take something from the table, but* DEBRA *slips it from him.*]

[DEBRA, CLAYBROOK *exit to kitchen and out of sight.*]

BOYD: I'm the *ghost* here! [*Boyd runs his hands over himself.*] Ghost. That's it.

[BOYD *has circled his duffel bag as if something attracts him powerfully. Gives in, goes to the bag and, glancing over his shoulder to make sure he's unobserved, removes an object from the bag, wrapped in a towel: a revolver. He checks the chamber, squints along the barrel, shoves it into his trouser pocket. The object is too bulky, so he shoves it into his belt, hiding it with his shirt.*]

BOYD: [*Cont'd.*] [*Breathless, excited.*] The Kingdom of God is within. THE KINGDOM OF GOD IS WITHIN.

[*LIGHTS OUT.*]

ACT II

SCENE 1

LIGHTS UP. The living room area, some minutes later. [The candles have been extinguished on the table, and the dining room is in semi-darkness.] DEBRA, BOYD and CLAYBROOK are back in the living room, though seated differently. DEBRA and CLAYBROOK are on the sofa, affectionately close; BOYD is in a chair to their right. His shirt tails out, BOYD looks disheveled but not dangerous; DEBRA has kicked off her shoes [and, as if unconsciously, moves and stretches her legs, even smooths the stockings with slow fingers — if she behaves in a sensuous, provocative way it should be very subtle]; CLAYBROOK has removed his sport coat and appears to be quite warm, perspiration glistening on his face. The long-stemmed rose in its vase is still on the coffee table.

CLAYBROOK has brought in a tray of the ingredients for the nightcap — bottles, glasses, a tall shaker, a container of ice cubes, etc. He is genial, relaxed, expansive, hospitable; one of those people whom alcohol makes warm and childlike, yet volatile emotionally. His "Black"/North Carolina accent is distinctly perceptible.

CLAYBROOK: Friends, this is a Flintlock I'm gonna conjure up, from my days tendin' bar on Seventh Avenue, workin' my way through *N.Y.U.* [*Stressing each syllable of N.Y.U.*] for the *Ph.D.* [*Stressing each syllable of Ph.D. — making the sounds comic.*]

DEBRA: Bartender? You never said.

CLAYBROOK: [*Hand on her knee.*] Lots of things I ain't said, honey. [*Preparing the drinks, CLAYBROOK moves his hand in magician-style, basking in the attention.*] First — three and three-quarters ounces bourbon: like so. [*Into shaker.*] Next — two and one-quarter ounce apple-jack brandy: like *so.* Then — li'l bit Creme de Cacao. Li'l bit lemon juice. Li'l bit grenadine. O.K., now shake. [*Shakes liquid, eyes shut; both DEBRA and BOYD watch attentively.*] O.K., friends, now pour over your ice cubes, and here y'are — straight from yo' man's hands.

[BOYD, DEBRA, CLAYBROOK *touch glasses ceremonially, and drink.*]

DEBRA: [*Between a sigh and a cry.*] Oh. God.

BOYD: [*Trying to sound sober.*] Man, this is *good*. What's it called?

CLAYBROOK: Flintlock.

BOYD: [*Enunciating word.*] "Flint-lock."

DEBRA: Some kind of old-fashioned gun? — musket? [*Laughs.*]

BOYD: A bartender, too.

CLAYBROOK: Among my many dazzlin' gifts.

BOYD: [*Almost boyishly.*] Are there — other things about you, too? — I mean —

CLAYBROOK: [*Dismissive gesture of his hand.*] Nah, what you see is what you get.

BOYD: Well — that was the finest meal I've had in, in — [*Wipes at eyes.*] — my *life*.

[CLAYBROOK, DEBRA *laugh. They speak simultaneously:*]

DEBRA: Oh, Boyd, *c'mon*.

CLAYBROOK: Listen to the man jivin' us!

BOYD: No, seriously, it was *good*. The meat, the sauce, the spices, the pasta —

DEBRA: [*Proudly, but a bit teasingly.*] Lew insists on everything fresh, and I mean fresh — no canned tomatoes, no oregano or marjoram or basil out of jars. He's the real thing!

CLAYBROOK: The veal got overcooked, some. But the pasta turned out pretty good.

BOYD: You made the pasta yourself — didn't just *buy* it. [*As if marveling.*]

CLAYBROOK: Only way you can control quality, it's to do as much as you can, yourself.

BOYD: In food as in life! [*Pause, not mockingly but a bit ingenuously.*] You take it all seriously, don't you? Making a meal, setting the table, coordinating the wine — all that.

CLAYBROOK: [*Laughing.*] Man, I take *everything* seriously. "We don't pass this way but once."

BOYD: [*Seeming non sequitur.*] A condemned man. A friend of mine did an article — interviewed Death Row prisoners and officials, in Texas. Number One favorite last meal is T-bone steak and French fries. Some ask for lobster — first time in their lives. [*Laughs.*]

DEBRA: [*Shuddering.*] *I* couldn't eat, knowing I was to die!

[*A beat.*]

BOYD: Right. It's better not to know. [*Pause.*] Veal Marsala and Angel-hair pasta and a good Bordeaux — that's for me.

CLAYBROOK: You buy that wine by the case?

BOYD: [*Laughs.*] Are you kidding?

CLAYBROOK: Some folks do. Like, an investment.

BOYD: Folks you know in Trenton, New Jersey?

CLAYBROOK: Nah, hell. Guys I used to keep in contact with, from Yale.

BOYD: How come you're out of contact, now?

CLAYBROOK: [*Shrugs.*] Ask them, man.

BOYD: [*To* DEBRA.] So! — "Debra O'Donnell" — you're getting a college degree, after all. *I* couldn't talk you into it.

DEBRA: I wasn't ready. Then.

BOYD: What kind of a job do you have? — "Mercer County Services"?

DEBRA: [*Enthusiastically.*] I'm assisting a case worker. After May, I'll be a case worker myself. I help clients with all sorts of things — budgets, leases, dealing with landlords. And within a family, say one member is dominating or exploiting the others — I help them deal with that. [*To* CLAYBROOK.] Lew, that woman Marina that I told you about? — the one whose husband broke her arm, threatened to kill her? I got her into the Womanspace Shelter, her and her children.

CLAYBROOK: Good!

DEBRA: I drove her myself. . . [*Laughs sadly.*] Imagine! Twenty-two

DEBRA: [*Cont'd.*] years old, with four children under the age of six. I love my work. I'm just learning...It's exhausting, but it's worth it.

BOYD: [*As if humoring her.*] You "want to do some good in the world."

DEBRA: Yes, I do.

BOYD: Putting a Band-Aid on severed arteries, people bleeding to death...

DEBRA: [*Holding her own.*] There's a time for tourniquets and there's a time, yes, for Band-Aids. We help individuals as we can — as individuals, not statistics.

BOYD: Hmmm.

CLAYBROOK: You got a better agenda, Boyd? Cynicism's easy.

BOYD: Cynicism is *not* easy. Cyn-i-cism hurts like hell.

CLAYBROOK: We all pass through it — cynicism. On our way to growing up.

BOYD: Well! That's telling the rest of us, who didn't go to Yale.

CLAYBROOK: My life hasn't been all Yale, I assure you.

BOYD: [*Abrupt semi-drunken ebullience or its simulation.*]. So, Clay my man! Dogs.

CLAYBROOK: Eh?

BOYD: Dogs! You breed pit bulls, huh?

CLAYBROOK: [*Staring.*] Say what, Boyd?

BOYD: [*As if confused, smiling foolishly.*] Uh — I mean — you *don't* breed pit bulls. [*To himself.*] He *doesn't* breed pit bulls.

[DEBRA *pokes* BOYD *in the ankle, annoyed. An awkward moment.* CLAYBROOK *might let it go, but for some reason takes it up.*]

CLAYBROOK: *Pit* bulls? Hell no, man, where'd you pick that up? Those are killer dogs, mean and dangerous. I'd vote to make the breed extinct.

DEBRA: [*Alert, slightly provocative, like a bright student.*] Extinct? An actual breed of animal? Can that be done?

CLAYBROOK: [*Shrugging.*] Anything can be done.

DEBRA: But —

CLAYBROOK: Pass a law. The U.S. Congress can pass a law. Civilized folks can do *anything*, passing the right laws. Look what Abe Lincoln did, finally, freeing the slaves, the Abolitionists put enough pressure on him.

[*Pause*]

DEBRA: But, Lew, how can a breed of animal be outlawed? Isn't that — like genocide? There's a law, isn't there, to protect endangered species?

BOYD: A pit bull isn't a species, it's a breed.

DEBRA: So? What's the difference? The poor creature doesn't choose its nature!

CLAYBROOK: [*An air of patience.*] Look, Debra, pit bulls ain't your specialty, how's about dropping the subject?

DEBRA: They're some kind of bulldog, obviously. Something to do with — [*A bit vague.*] — pits.

BOYD: They're part terrier and part bulldog —

CLAYBROOK: English bulldog. [*Innuendo.*] That's the nastiest kind.

BOYD: [*To* DEBRA.] A pit bull is bred and trained to attack — to kill. They've been known to kill unprovoked — children, elderly people — whoever. And they don't bark. They give no warning, just leap at your throat.

DEBRA: That may be how they're trained, but I can't believe that's their nature.

CLAYBROOK: [*Curtly.*] The training *is* their nature, and the pit bull isn't natural, it's a hybrid.

DEBRA: But the individual animal — how can it be its fault? All animals are innocent.

CLAYBROOK: Who brought this up? Let's drop it.

DEBRA: I just feel —

CLAYBROOK: Enough! [*Pause, then with contempt.*] Look, the pit bull

CLAYBROOK: [*Cont'd.*] is a macho breed, *Black* macho breed, get it? That's what this is about, get it? — they give the word, the fucker's gonna tear somebody apart, Real baaaad-ass.

DEBRA: [*Hurt, confused.*] But that isn't the point —

CLAYBROOK: [*Interrupting.*] You want the sociology, the subtext, O.K. the prof will provide it: the pit bull helps compensate for the male nigger in America being a dog himself but not a killer-dog, no way, man, just a runty ole mongrel not worth kickin'. You got it, honey? You takin' notes for the final? Like having a big cock is s'posed to compensate for not havin' nothin' — including, in fact, the cock. [*Pause, coolly contemptuous.*] You got it now, honey?

[DEBRA *is stunned into silence.*]

BOYD: [*Excited, trying to assert control.*] You d-don't have to be rude to Debra, Clay — you don't have to be — rude —

CLAYBROOK: [*On his feet, moving off.*] Wasn't being *rude* to her, man, was just *explicatin'.*

BOYD: [*On his feet.*] — sounded rude to me.

CLAYBROOK: Well, fuck you, man — whose problem's that?

BOYD: Just a —

CLAYBROOK: [*Overlapping.*] Don't you fuck with me —

BOYD: [*Overlapping.*] — a minute —

CLAYBROOK: [*Overlapping.*] Don't none of you fuck with *me.*

[CLAYBROOK *exits. In his wake, a stunned silence.*]

BOYD: He *has* got a temper. Man! [*Admiringly.*] Nobody gets in his face. North Philly. That's where he comes from. You can say about a man like that, he's no hypocrite.

DEBRA: God damn you, Boyd! Bringing up pit bulls! Who told you about pit bulls? Which one of your "friends"?

BOYD: [*Taking* DEBRA'*s arm, gently.*] If that's what the man is like, Debra —

DEBRA: That isn't what the man is like. Lew Claybrook is a man of

DEBRA: [*Cont'd.*] pride, and we offended his pride. Is that — ? The back door? He wouldn't just leave — would he?

BOYD: [*Annoyed.*] If he did, where would he go? — Where does he live?

DEBRA: Here! He lives here.

BOYD: I don't think so, Debra.

[DEBRA *goes to the window, looks out but seems to see nothing.* BOYD *approaches her as if he's stalking her; touches the butt of the gun through his shirt.*]

BOYD: He's been married, right? — *is* married?

[DEBRA, *at window, ignores him.*]

BOYD: He has a family, right? — kids? How do they feel about you — "Debra O'Donnell"?

DEBRA: Boyd, take your things, please, and *go.*

BOYD: I didn't come back for my fucking things, Debra.

[*A beat.*]

BOYD: [*Looking at her, with longing.*] Tonight, I'm here, I came back for — you.

DEBRA: What are you saying, Boyd?

BOYD: I was — wasn't — myself, then. Those months. You know what I was like. I said things I didn't mean, and I did things I didn't mean. So did you.

DEBRA: [*Half-sobbing, pleading.*] The people we were then, we're not now. That's over.

BOYD: Remember that marriage counselor? She said it wasn't just your husband you were angry with, but —

DEBRA: I hate "anger" — it isn't purging, it only makes things worse.

BOYD: Telling the truth? That makes things worse?

DEBRA: What Lew said just now wasn't *him*, it was what we made him say. [*Voice rising.*] Two Whites, speaking in ignorance.

BOYD: You can't rise above the color of your skin, in his eyes — no matter what he says.

DEBRA: Never mind Lew and me, Boyd. It has nothing to do with you.

BOYD: Nothing is over, Debra, until it's — over.

DEBRA: Look, you can see. I have a new life now.

BOYD: You know it.

DEBRA: No.

BOYD: As soon as I walked in that door — you knew.

DEBRA: *No.*

BOYD: The connection between us, it's like — the roots of trees, tangled underground. You remember... [*Sexual pleading, coercion.*]

DEBRA: [*Backing away, frightened.*] No! I, I have a certain regard for you, Boyd — I respect and honor you, I *like* you, yes —

BOYD: I want — the way it *was.*

DEBRA: The way it was — when? The last few months you were living here?

BOYD: No, the way it was. [*Almost tenderly.*] *You* know.

DEBRA: [*Quickly.*] No! That's over, that's gone.

BOYD: Why'd you invite me here, then?

DEBRA: *You* called — and — I thought — [*Pause, confused.*] I wanted you to meet — Lew and you, to —

BOYD: Wanted to show him off to me, eh? Make me jealous?

DEBRA: [*Guiltily.*] No! I wanted to — bring the two halves of my life into — balance — [*Voice trails off.*]

BOYD: Make *him* jealous?

DEBRA: No!

BOYD: Come *on!* Admit it! I'm the one who loves you, I've loved you since you were just a girl. I know you; need you. I'm your *husband.* I need to come home.

[LIGHTS DIM.]

SCENE 2

LIGHTS UP, immediately following Act II Scene 1. DEBRA *has turned from* BOYD, *searching out her shoes, putting them on, as* CLAYBROOK *appears from kitchen, in a manner that might be described as rueful, yet not repentant.* BOYD *is alert, cautious.*

CLAYBROOK: *[In stiff, "White" diction.]* I started some coffee — it should be ready shortly.

DEBRA: *[Almost shyly, with infinite relief.]* What a good idea, Lew! Thanks!

CLAYBROOK: *[Humbly.]* To sober us all up.

BOYD: Well, it's time — I guess. *[Laughs awkwardly.]* Please accept my apologies, Lew — [BOYD *extends his hand but* CLAYBROOK *discreetly ignores it.]*

DEBRA: *[Approaching* CLAYBROOK.] *I'm* to blame, I guess — I feel like such a fool.

CLAYBROOK:*[Touching or squeezing her arm, a quick almost unconscious gesture of intimacy.] I'm* the fool. Let's forget it.

BOYD: I guess — I don't really need any coffee. I should just be —

CLAYBROOK: *[Trying to speak normally, though still in his "White" diction.]* When you leave, Boyd, I'll help you with those boxes. But have some coffee first.

BOYD: *[Eagerly.]* Thanks!

DEBRA: I smell — is it Mocha Java?

CLAYBROOK: Right. A fresh package.

[CLAYBROOK *tidies up the coffee table;* DEBRA *takes tray from him, preparatory to moving off.]*

DEBRA: Thanks, honey. I'll take care of everything.

[DEBRA *exits to kitchen.]*

BOYD: *[Nervously lighting cigarette.]* Man, man, *you're* sure not to be messed with.

[CLAYBROOK *shrugs or grunts a reply. Straightening cushions on the sofa; adjusts the German glass-bell clock by a fraction of an inch.*]

BOYD: [*Cont'd.*] It was those dynamite Flintlocks — that's what it was.

CLAYBROOK: [*Bemused.*] Maybe.

[CLAYBROOK *indicates that* BOYD *should sit. The men face each other. A beat. (No music is playing).*]

BOYD: [*Realizing he shouldn't be smoking.*] Oh — sorry. [*Looks for an ashtray, grinds out cigarette finally in a crumpled up napkin in the palm of his hand.*] Forgot. [*Pause.*] Well, it certainly was — is — generous of you, and Debra. Having me here tonight. The ex-husband, the ghost.

CLAYBROOK: O.K., man, that's O.K.

BOYD: She's a good woman and she deserves the best. I'm happy for her. [*Pause, smiling.*] I'm not *happy*, but I'm *happy* for her.

CLAYBROOK: O.K., man.

BOYD: If you've been divorced, you know. [*A pause;* CLAYBROOK *doesn't take this up, so* BOYD *continues cautiously.*] You think it's over but — she tried to call me. She hasn't told you, I guess ... that's just as well. [*Pause.*] She'd try to call me, but I was out of the country, mostly, on assignment; out of contact. "The Kingdom of God is within" — that's something that needs to be said. Thanks!

CLAYBROOK: That's nothing more than what everybody knows. Or don't know.

BOYD: The time she got pregnant ... It was a, a mutual decision ... [*Pause, with anguish.*] She never forgave me, said I forced her ... to, to ... [*Pause.*] Fuck it. [*Pause, laughs.*] I wasn't even *here*, how'd I force her? [*Pause.*] Your father's a minister, Debra said? African Episcopal Baptist Church?

CLAYBROOK: African Methodist Episcopal Church.

BOYD: [*Leaning forward eagerly.*] I wasn't "jiving" you. Clay. About "The Kingdom of God." It doesn't require a supernatural

BOYD: [*Cont'd.*] belief, does it? or anything theological? — just, y'-know, *psychological?* "Psyche" meaning "soul?" [*Pause.*] I was thinking, you and I, maybe, with your experience — with — "welfare" —

CLAYBROOK: [*Correcting.*] Family Services.

BOYD: — the kinds of things you see first-hand — the two of us could collaborate some time — a book of photographs with a text — [*Seeing* CLAYBROOK's *negative expression.*] — No?

CLAYBROOK: In my profession you don't exploit the people.

BOYD: [*Hurt.*] This wouldn't be "exploiting."

CLAYBROOK: You don't use the people as material, that's all.

BOYD: [*Deflated.*] I see. [*Pause.*]

[DEBRA *enters, with coffee things on a tray. More composed, has freshened herself up: hair, makeup; may be wearing, not the high-heeled shoes, but flatter-heeled, more comfortable sandals.*]

CLAYBROOK: [*Smiling.*] Smells *good.*

DEBRA: [*Seating herself between the men, speaking brightly and conversationally to Boyd.*] There's a new food store, on Third Street — remember, where the Italian Bakery was? It specializes in all sorts of coffee.

BOYD: Sounds like West Windsor's been gentrified. Since I left.

[BOYD *grabs an empty coffee cup. Pours a shot of bourbon.*]

DEBRA: Boyd, no.

BOYD: [*Smiling.*] You know that sign you see, sometimes—aimed at commuters: "If you lived here, you'd be home by now." [*Laughs.*]

DEBRA: You're not serious.

BOYD: I'm always serious! [*Pause.*] Like Clay. I mean — Lew. [*Pause.*] Since you have a Ph.D., Lew, from N.Y.U., I guess you're *Dr.* Claybrook?

CLAYBROOK: Only when necessary.

BOYD: [*Overlapping, to* CLAYBROOK.] I appreciated your response, Clay, to my photographs. That meant a lot to me.

CLAYBROOK: Well — it's good work.

BOYD: Too bad you don't want to collaborate with me.

CLAYBROOK: Eh? I said I *couldn't.*

BOYD: [*To* DEBRA, *teasing.*] Clay snubbed me, just now. I suggested we collaborate sometime on a major project. I'd do the art, he'd provide the text. "An unflinching look at America's underclass."

CLAYBROOK: [*Trying to be pleasant.*] I didn't *snub* you, friend. I said I *couldn't,* for professional reasons.

DEBRA: Boyd, Lew doesn't have time.

BOYD: Oh, I know! I can imagine. [*Pause.*] *I* don't have time, either. Right now.

CLAYBROOK: I'm not working just with the "underclass" — whatever journalists mean by that. Family Services deals with all kinds of folks — [*Smiling.*] — middle-class White folks not excepted.

BOYD: That's what our book could do — refute stereotypes.

DEBRA: Maybe you could discuss it with Lew some other time, Boyd.

BOYD: [*Eagerly.*] I'd like that. [*Pause.*] You know, *you* can perpetuate stereotypes, too. [*Meaning* CLAYBROOK.] It isn't just us.

CLAYBROOK: [*Smiling.*] Who's *me?*

BOYD: Talk of "Whites" — "Blacks" — like you did, before — *that's* hurtful. That's irresponsible.

DEBRA: Now, Boyd — don't start this again.

BOYD: [*Overlapping.*] Let's be reasonable, all right? This vocabulary of "Black" — "White" — it's reductive, it's illogical, and it's hurtful. *You* aren't Black — I mean, not *Black.* Even a really dark-skinned person is not *Black,* so why insist upon Black, then?

[CLAYBROOK *stares at* BOYD *for a long moment, his expression neutral. He is sitting very still.*]

DEBRA: [*Overlapping.*] Boyd! — What are you doing this for?

BOYD: [*Overlapping, speaking frankly, ingenuously.*] I mean — why not speak the truth? From the heart? For once? Midnight's the hour for truth, yes? A man like you, Clay, with your skin tone, it's absurd to designate you *Black*. I know, I know — there are historical factors — but it's so extreme, distorting. Like South Africa, . . .

DEBRA: That's it, Boyd. It's time for you to go.

[DEBRA *exits as* BOYD *keeps on talking, taking no notice.*]

BOYD: . . . apartheid, a lone drop of blood and you're Black — bullshit! Primary colors — primary ways of — thinking — no subtleties. Am I "White?" [*Extending hand.*] Hell, no. Somebody from another planet, arriving on Earth, would think we were all color *blind*.

DEBRA: [*Enter with* BOYD's *coat.*] Enough, Boyd! Go!

CLAYBROOK: [*Shaking head, droll smile.*] Man, you sure are one, aren't you?

BOYD: One what?

CLAYBROOK: One asshole-cracker-sup-*reme.*

DEBRA: He doesn't mean . . .

BOYD: [*Protesting.*] You're not addressing the issue! It's a, an epistemological issue! — how can we *know* what we believe we know, when it turns out we don't know it because it's wrong.

CLAYBROOK: [*On his feet.*] Say what, man? — I'm tuning out.

BOYD: Don't go! Sit down! Don't — [*Pleading, yet with a threat implied.*] — condescend to me.

DEBRA: Lew, honey, Boyd doesn't mean any insult, he isn't like that, truly. He's always questioned, doubted — [*Embarrassed.*] He just means what he — well, *says* —

CLAYBROOK: I don't give a shit what he *says* long as I don't have to listen to it.

BOYD: You're afraid! You're afraid! Man, you surprise me — you're

BOYD: [*Cont'd.*] *afraid*! To talk man-to-man, friend to friend, to speak the truth for once — "to bear witness."

CLAYBROOK: Friend-to-friend? [*Laughs.*] Get away, man, you're not my friend!

BOYD: Cause you shut me out. That's why.

CLAYBROOK: Oh shit! [*Genuine laughter.*]

BOYD: What's so funny? What the fuck's so funny?

CLAYBROOK: Ma asshole bleeds for the poor White man. People of color have got to JUMP UP AN' DOWN WITH JOY they get invited at last to the White-folks' house — my, my! Ain't we lucky! Must be, we've been *good*, to be so *lucky*! You're nice to me so you don't have to be nice to my sister, my brother, my grandparents. They be shakin' our hands like our hands was *White*. Sayin', skin color don't mean nothin' to me, I'm color blind, I ain't like these other redneck bastards, real nasty an' prejudiced — *I'm* a brother! [*Laughs.*] Sure, I was the "scholarship" boy — the "good Black boy" — got my ass kicked when I was a kid for acting "White." Figured it was worth it, maybe. So one day I'm "the highest ranked Black appointee in the State of New Jersey" — man, *that's* luck! *That's* bein' "a credit to the race!" Except — I best take care where I drive my new-model Lexus in New Jersey — like, for instance, in Princeton, coming home late one night from a party — one of these "private roads" — and the police stop me and just about put the cuffs on me,

[*Claybrook kneels with hands behind his head.*]

. . . askin' who're *you*, boy? What're *you* doin' here? Where'd you get that car? What's your business in this neighborhood, boy? Could be, I was imagining I could "pass" — huh? Could be, I was deluded?

DEBRA: [*Touching his arm.*] Oh, Lew, when did that happen? I didn't know —

CLAYBROOK: [*Throwing off her hand.*] There's plenty you don't know, honey. Like some of my colleagues, they see me coming so they cross the street until they realize it's me.

CLAYBROOK: [*Cont'd.*] [*To* BOYD.] You — why're you looking at me like that? Could be, you was deluded? Thinking I'm a "brother"? — Your "brother"? Pit bull, eh? Pit bull — they're real ferocious, man, but their lives are short. If somebody don't put a bullet through their heads, they kill one another. You know that? [*Savage sarcasm, indicating* BOYD's *portfolio.*] Like that Third World victim shit you're peddling. Share your income with your "tragic" victims — pay them for your pictures. Share your fucking Pulitzer prize!

[CLAYBROOK *goes to CD player.* BOYD *crosses to the table and takes out his gun and sets it on the table.*]

BOYD: I'm not going to use this — I'm not a man of violence — [*Pleading.*] I just want to explain, I want you to listen, I want respect —

[*He picks up the gun.*]

CLAYBROOK: [*Frightened, trying to be reasonable.*] Hey, man, put that down — no need for that — hey?

BOYD: [*Interrupting.*] I've seen human beings die. [*Snaps his fingers.*] "Natural" causes — and not so "natural" — like, for instance, bullets. But I never aimed a gun at anyone before tonight. This is the — exigency! — you've brought me to! You — a stranger — in my house — with her — sleeping with her — that's a, an outrage. Another man, he'd lose it completely — shoot you both dead —

DEBRA: Boyd —

BOYD: You said I'm not your friend — well I *am*! I am your friend! I want to be. God damn it, how can you shut me out? I'm fighting for my life.

CLAYBROOK: Nobody's shutting you out —

DEBRA: Oh Boyd, my God —

BOYD: [*Swinging barrel toward* DEBRA.] It isn't me, it's you, and him, it's both of you shutting me out.

CLAYBROOK: Boyd, don't point that at Debra. O.K., man? Don't point that at her — please.

BOYD: [*Excited, frightened.*] I'm not, I'm not pointing it at anyone, I don't want to hurt anyone, don't push me! [*Swinging barrel in* CLAYBROOK's *direction.*]

CLAYBROOK: Man, nobody's pushing you — we're just sitting here talking, we're O.K., we're cool, nobody's pushing you, O.K.?

BOYD: Just don't push me, O.K.?

CLAYBROOK: Nobody's pushing you, Boyd, you're cool.

BOYD: [*To* DEBRA.] See? — his hands? — the insides of his hands? — no blacker than I am. It's just crazy. It's tearing us all apart and it's just crazy, the craziest shit! [*Points gun at* DEBRA.] Tell him! C'mon tell him! How it really was, you and me — like it was — right here — *right here in this house.* [*A pause.*] Tell him.

DEBRA: [*Shrinking.*] Boyd, no —

BOYD: Do it! Tell the truth! For once! For once tonight! Tell him how it *was,* and how it never will be again — with any other man.

CLAYBROOK: Don't point that gun at her —

DEBRA: Lew, it's all right!

[*Rises, to comply with* BOYD's *command, comes forward, frightened, and in a dilemma, her back to the men who stare at her.*]

BOYD: [*Almost pleading.*] Tell him!

[DEBRA *must convey to the audience that she is willing to risk death for* CLAYBROOK's *sake — though, perhaps, what she says is not true.*]

DEBRA: I... I can love another man. [*Pause.*] I *do* love another man. As much ... more ... than I did you.

BOYD: [*Stricken.*] That's a lie!

[CLAYBROOK *makes a motion as if to protect* DEBRA, *and* BOYD *wheels upon him, the gun in his raised hand shaking. All freeze.*]

BOYD: You're lying, Debra — you remember how it was for us, the two of us — in that room back there — [*Gesturing toward bedroom.*] — those nights — Tell him the truth.

DEBRA: I'm not the woman you knew. You don't even know me now. I love another man . . . I love Lew.

BOYD: Liar!

[DEBRA *hides her face in her hands.*]

BOYD: [*Cont'd.*] [*To* CLAYBROOK.] She's lying! She'd die for you. [*Emotion draining from him, still holding the gun on* CLAYBROOK, *then weakens, gives up.*] O.K. I'm fucked. I'm *over.* [*Laying revolver on coffee table.*] You win, Clay my man.

[*A beat of silence.*]

CLAYBROOK: What're you saying, man?

BOYD: Take it, it's yours. [*Shoves gun toward him.*] Here's "Whitey" —blow me away.

[BOYD *tries to force* CLAYBROOK *to take the gun.* CLAYBROOK *backs away.*]

BOYD: [*Terrified but reckless, goading.*] C'mon! Your turn!

CLAYBROOK: [*Managing to speak calmly.*] Just get your things, and get out of this house, man!

BOYD: C'mon!—pull the trigger. You scared?

[BOYD *pushes* CLAYBROOK. DEBRA *tries to interpose herself between them, and* BOYD *pushes her aside.*]

CLAYBROOK: Don't touch her!

[CLAYBROOK *takes gun,* BOYD *has his hands over* CLAYBROOK's *hands, pointing it at himself, then falls to his knees.*]

BOYD: O.K., pull the trigger, it's loaded, black boy, big-shot nigger, c'mon *you* ain't scared, North Philly *you* ain't scared . . . GOD DAMN YOU, PULL THE FUCKING TRIGGER! [CLAYBROOK *aims gun in* BOYD's *face,* BOYD *is lying on the ground, willing* CLAY *to shoot him.* CLAYBROOK *removes the bullets from the gun, drops them into his pocket, tosses the gun into one of* BOYD's *boxes, as if its touch is repellent.*]

CLAYBROOK: [*Panting.*] Now get your ass out of here like it never *was* here!

[*BLACKOUT.*]

SCENE 3.

LIGHTS UP. A few minutes later. CLAYBROOK *takes two boxes off as* BOYD *puts his coat on, looking at* DEBRA. CLAYBROOK *then watches as* BOYD *exits with bag, portfolio and remaining boxes.* CLAY *exits after him. Door remains open.* DEBRA, *shaken, comes forward, her fingertips to her eyes. She drops her hands.*

DEBRA: [*Slowly, emphatically.*] I'm happy. I'm happy. I'm not going to cry—I'm happy.

[*A beat.*]

[CLAYBROOK *returns. They regard each other in silence. Lights slowly out.*]

THE END

Anna Deavere Smith

AYE AYE AYE I'M INTEGRATED

Aye Aye Aye I'm Integrated was produced by the Women's Project & Productions under the artistic directorship of Julia Miles in A Festival of Six One-Act Plays at American Place Theatre, New York City, March 20-April 1, 1984. It was directed by Billie Allen with the following cast:

CYPRIENNE	Seret Scott
NURSE	Elba Kenney

Sound Design by Tim Roberts
Lighting Design by Jane Reisman
Costume Design by Judy Dearing
Production Stage Manager: Lue Morgan Douthit

CHARACTERS

CYPRIENNE A doctor, Black, light-skinned
NANCY   A nurse

A nurse's station in a pediatric cancer ward in Sloan Kettering, New York City. A nurse, white, is upstage behind the desk. There is a radio on upstage, very faint. There are sounds of children squealing and applauding, off right. A doctor, Black, woman, light-skinned, approaches. She speaks to the audience throughout. The nurse is oblivious to that.

CYPRIENNE: Did you see the float?

The troopers have come to entertain the troopers!

This

is a pediatric cancer ward.

I admire the generosity of entertainers.

I gave thought to becoming an actress,

when I was a child and also

also

in my teens

[*She writes something on the clipboard and hands it to the nurse. The radio is becoming more audible. Piano music.*]

One summer

my next door neighbor and best friend and I

started a theater.

I grew up in integration

and my best friend

Roderick Sawyer

and I brought a lot of joy to a very racially confused neighborhood

The Sawyers were White,

we were Black.

You'd know Roderick if you saw him

he's made commercials all his life

and although he fashioned himself after all the angry young
   men,

in literature and movies,

I think he describes himself as the Daddy type

very open

very expressive kind of face,

had freckles as a boy.

[*The other external noise is completely gone, the music on the radio
is* Rachmaninoff's Suite for Two Pianos, No. 1 op 5 Third
Movement. *Cyprienne peruses a sheet of paper and signs it
quickly.*]

When Roderick was eight

he got himself run over by a Good

uh

a Good Humor truck

and I being the daughter of a physician,

and rather nurse-like

renounced all summer activities and dedicated myself exclu-
   sively to

the recuperation of Roderick.

Lucille,

Lucy,

Mrs. Swayer,

Roderick's mother,

made me a nurse's outfit and my mother couldn't have been
more pleased about buying me a pair of white sturdy oxfords
in lieu of flimsy P.F. Flyers.

Roderick was quite a tyrant in his wheelchair

he led me fully with my clothes *on* into the shower and then
he made me get into the clothes dryer,

my nurse's uniform having been soiled with a grape popsicle.

Lucille . . . *entered,*

horrified

to find me a flash of white cloth and high yellow flesh and
wild summertime Negroid hair flipping across the glass of the
clothes dryer,

"What on earth are you doing?" she said.

"We're playing laundry," Rod said.

"LAUNDRY!!!!" She said and she stormed into the garage

got all her Goodwill bags and dumped them in the swimming
pool

just tons and tons of clothes because Mrs. Sawyer was one of
those people who would buy something at a *garage* sale for
the Goodwill. . .

[*She signs another paper.*]

and an *enormous* box of Tide

the Tide was about as *big* as a wagon

"Here play laundry," she said.

And we did.

Roderick

gets an idea to hang all of the clothes on a *line*

which we hung up

it was a long piece of string strewn from the

elderberry tree they had

to the pool cabana

and from *that*

we began to build an *enormous* ENORMOUS

tent

of Goodwill clothes and we started putting on little *shows*

in there

and people would come and see the plays

and we were both *really* now that I think back,

really like ambassadors. . .

for our parents and for the neighborhood and for integration,

because Roderick was White and I was Black

and in order for people to get *in* to our plays

they had to bring a piece of dirty laundry!

And our tent expanded and we developed a very

sophisticated costume collection and sometimes

the admission charge would be more specific

like bring shoes,

you see

or *boots*,

and we became increasingly shrewd inasmuch

as we were able to collect things like fur *coats*

in the summer time,

and winter *things*,

leggings and Halloween costumes,

and in the *fall*,

we'd get sailor hats,

goggles,

flippers,

or sunglasses,

or old Mexican hats,

or organdy dresses,

and summer petticoats and little sort of summer girls socks.

And lots of these nice,

Washington D.C. *adult*,

party dresses!

One night Roderick's uncle,

big advertising name

came to Silver Springs and *saw* one of our shows and he

said to Lucille, to Mrs. Sawyer,

"Lucy," he said,

"You ought to bring these kids on up to New York,

I'll put ya up at the Plaza

and maybe I can get 'em some work."

He did!

And Roddy and me

were the voices on one of those the old perhaps you remem
ber

the old Good and *Plenty* commercials.

Those commercials, don't laugh, helped put me through medical school.

Now while we were *there*,

Bill,

this is Rod's uncle,

Bill

makes arrangements for us to meet an *agent*

a woman by the name of Phoebe Something or other

British woman,

prematurely white haired,

and English somehow,

English,

and very very tastefully *dressed*.
She signs Roderick im*me*diately,
barely even looked at him.
Mrs. Sawyer im*me*diately says, "Well
What
What about Sissy?"
That's what everyone called me
Sissy short for Cyprienne,
uh,
Cyprienne is my mother as well —
uh
So the *agent* stared at me for a uh
few minutes and a few minutes and
"Well what do people think she *is*," she says.
"She's an actress," says Lucille, "and she dances. . ."
"Where is she *from*?"
"She lives next door to us in . . . Maryland."
"What's her *back*ground?"
Now Roderick,
Roderick now cuts in
"She's colored."
"I see." Says this Phoebe,
uh woman.
"Didn't Bill make that clear?" says Mrs. Sawyer,
"Oh yes, indeed, yes indeed he did he was quite clear,
but
when *Bill* said a *colored* person I expected a much *darker*
person

I think of a *colored* person as a very *dark* person and this is *not*
a very *dark* person this is a very *light* person."
"Wait till you see her Lady Macbeth." Roddy says,
he was uh *precocious* then
"Bring her back when she's darker," this Phoebe says.
Rod and I were taken out of the office as we sat in the waiting
room we couldn't hear every word that was said,
but voices were raised.

I went home.
And I was so upset.
Roddy moved to New York it all worked out perfectly for him
his father had gotten assignment to the U.N. and
Rod started serious acting school and ballet and
the only time I saw him was on T.V. in commercials
and my *mother* wouldn't let me join any
of the theater groups in D.C. she said I was too emotional
to be an actress
Oh it was awful
it was the most difficult three years of my life
even now as I look back I can see that the circumstances were
less than
well
finally
they decided to send me to prep school and lucky me surprise
surprise I end up within commuting distance to New York
Don't you know I was on that train every weekend
and Roddy and I took acting together and we'd go see shows I
took *ballet*
[*RADIO: You have just been listening to Rachmaninoff's* Suite for

Two Pianos No. 1 Op 5, *the last two movements, Andre Previn
and Vladimir Ashkenazy. The last two movements, 3 and 4 . . .
The nurse gives her something else to review which she does as she
talks, and signs it.*]

Now my *father*

Is a very very kind very

generous very soft spoken never

pushy

man

and he started sending me

subscriptions

to medical journals

and I'm no fool I knew what that

was all about, a long line of

physicians in the family,

first Black physicians—New Orleans and so forth and here I
am the only child,

no sons. . .no nephews my father had been an only child also,

I *did* read the journals,

voracious reader that I was,

[*RADIO: You have just heard the Third Movement and will continue with the Fourth Movement after this message. "Hello this is
Lauren Bacall (Etc. — Fortunoff.)*]

[*The nurse leaves, the music resumes, commercial over.*]

and there was an article about a man who was doing research
in New York

to find a cure for vidaligo which is a disease that Blacks and

East Indians get in which the patient suffers a loss of

pigmentation in spots all over the skin

and the physician conducting the experimenting was looking
for
*sub*jects,
you had to take a medication,
all effects
were to be temporary and it was so harmless in fact,
that
many White girls,
wanting a tanned look,
signed up—
and you would even get paid.
The next time I went to New York, I paid a visit to the
clinic.
I was scared
but Roddy came with me and held my hand through the
whole thing.
I went for ten visits.

May rolls around,
May Day at my school was a huge event
with a Maypole and athletic competitions and awards and
prizes and Parents weekend—*parents* would come.
When
my
mother
laid
eyes on me. . .
Now my *mother* is a very very delicate very serious very
pretty

but very strong, very wiry and very strong, very petite
quarter French, quarter German, half Black
"Well what has happened to your skin?"
"I've been lying in the sun."
"You've had nothing but rain all spring.

My *father*, "Cyprienne, I think it's her liver I'm taking her to
see"
"I went to the Bahamas over Spring Break," I blurted out.
"We thought you were in New York with the Sawyers."
"I *lied*," I said.
"How did you get to the Bahamas?"
"Who paid for it?" my mother said.
"A man." (I lied.)
"*WHAT* man???" my mother says.
"My *lover*," I said (*lover* I hadn't even been kissed.)
My mother just uh just
began
to
to hi hi hi
hit me
with a purse,
like a wild person!
So I took off and ran away from her across the lacrosse field,
don't you dare tell her I told you this
to this little stream that ran through campus.
It was very
dramatic.
Sure, I got punished but worst.

My *father*

I tell my own daughters,

they're only four and I say crime-does-not-pay!

Crime-does-not-pay! My *father*

had gone to a medical convention in New Orleans

and Dr. Branch, the

one who was conducting the experiment

delivered a paper

and whose face pops up on the screen

when he showed slides. . .

Within twelve hours Dad and the Headmistress

were taking me over the carpet

Dad:	Sissy I can barely speak
Headmistress:	Cyprienne don't you know the color of your skin is given you by God and you can't change it?
Dad:	Sissy, you must not ever do this again.
Headmistress:	Cyprienne, has anyone *here* made you dislike the color of your skin?
Dad:	Sissy, there is a fifty percent chance his treatment causes skin cancer now we've got to get you in a warm sunny climate fast.

And he broke down crying and shook all over.

[*The Nurse reenters very bouncy, light on her feet.*]

Once again Mrs. Sawyer,

old Lucy came to the rescue

somehow between she and my Dad and Mr. Sawyer some strings

got pulled and before I knew it I was in an

exchange program in the Ivory Coast and that

is where I completed high school.

Now. . .

Nobody

was more excited about my return to the states than Roderick

he picked me up at the airport looking like the proud father.

We're driving into Manhattan

"Sissy," he says, "I'm starting a theater company

and I want you in it

and just to get you back on the track I have set up

an appointment with my agent for you. . ."

"You're crazy," I said, "your agent almost ruined my whole

life."

He said, "You got to make a *living*,

and my theater company won't

pay much to start,

you gotta be *tough* kid don't take these guys serious!"

"Roderick," I said, "I've changed."

"Oh *Sissy*," he said, "this company is going to be great! For

admission you bring your *pain*, your *joy*

instead of dirty laundry."

He grabbed my hand with this way he had,

sort of like a minister and tore off down the Highway,

"Roddy," I said, "if anything I'm lighter

now than I ever have been,

all the medication wore off and. . ."

"Color, my dear Cyprienne," he said,

"goes in and out of fashion

like hem lines go up and down."

3:15 a Friday afternoon in May

[*Cyprienne is talking at the same time as Radio.*]

we're in Phoebe's office	Where else can you hear Brahms
Phoebe is twirling around a	Rachmaninoff, Steve Reich,
mirror made of ivory which	Phillip Glass and Charles Ives
she had been showing us, gift	on the same program? WNYC Music for

[*The Nurse has turned the radio off and has the phone to her ear and is talking on the phone.*]

of a client who, like myself,

had been in Africa.

"Well, what do people think she *is*?" Phoebe said

Sound familiar?

"I'm Black," I said.

Now no one was excited or anything,

Phoebe was twirling the mirror and Rod was sitting on the edge of her desk,

dipping his fingers in and out of the paper clip container,

playing with the magnet.

"Well. . .when I think of a Black person, I think of a very dark person and this is not a very you are not a very dark person you are a very light person, dear."

"Phoebe Phoebe Phoebe" Roderick said, "you haven't seen her *act*."

"Well I mean," said Phoebe,

"now seriously,

who would you be,

I mean what would you *go* as would you be Lena Horne is that what you'd be?"

I said, "Lena is an incredible singer and I"

"You see," she said, "there simply is *nothing* for you.

I wish,

I desperately wish there were,

but I didn't make these circumstances,

the Lord did for some reason unbeknownst to me."

"God doesn't make circumstances," I said, "People do."

"In America," she said, "*either* you're Black or White and there's nothing in between,

we simply haven't got time for racial ambivalence."

"Give us a break Phoebe,

with that accent you have the nerve to talk about *America*,

you're not gonna *get* more American than me and Sissy!"

"Oh *Rod really* the next thing I know you'll come in here and try to get me to sign fauns and centaurs and sphinxes and sirens. . ."

"Are *you* calling Sissy a half *animal*?!"

They were both on their feet.

"For the last time, Roderick, this is a business I'm not playing *doctor* here!" she said.

And with that I was at the door,

and I said very very quietly

very quietly I said

"And I'm not playing person."

[*Radio is back on. Steve Reich music for six pianos is on.*]

As I was walking out of the offices,

first thing that

popped into my mind was my *mother*

I thought of her and I thought of her telling me I was too emotional to be an actress.

She was right!!!

She was right!!!

In the Ivory Coast I had seen I had been with the midwives

and I had seen children born all the time and every time a child

was born I would weep!

And yet. . .walking out of that office and hearing Rod argue

with Phoebe in the background,

and hearing what I later found out

was the mirror breaking,

and seeing all of these kids,

black

kids white kids *Chinese* kids in baseball caps waiting to

try out for a McDonald's ad,

I thought,

it was so clear

if I cried everytime a child was born I'd never be tough enough

for this three ring circus.

I *flew* down thirty-four flights of stairs and went to the first phone booth,

and the first sane words I said on American

soil were

"Hi Dad,

I've decided to act like I have some sense and be an obste*tri*cian,

yeah Dad," I said, "I wanna birth babies!"

[*The Nurse gives her another sheet of paper which she reviews and signs.*]

Several thousand birthings later,

I am not

above crying

but I have altered a bit,

I'm

a pediatric surgeon,

here,

in this oncology unit,

and

never be timid about bringing your child to see

[*She reads more carefully.*]

me if you suspect that anything isn't quite

right,

[*She is now becoming engrossed in her chart.*]

nothing is too small or too large

a problem. . .

do I sound like a commercial?

Excuse me.

Nance. . .would you. ..

[*Lights down. Music of Steve Reich up and then fading out with Radio: "Hello this is Lena Horne for National Public Radio, won't you help us in our fight to help find . . ." Sound goes suddenly down.*]

ABOUT THE PLAYWRIGHTS

HILARY BLECHER emigrated to the U.S. from South Africa in 1981, where she was a resident director at the world renowned Market Theatre and taught at the University of the Witwatersrand. She made her New York debut with the Obie, Drama Desk, and Laurence Olivier (London) award-winning production of *Poppie Nongena*. (She was nominated as the most promising newcomer to the London stage for her conception and direction of the work.) Other American productions include: *Frida* (conception, book/Director), which opened BAM's 10th Anniversary Next Wave Festival and was selected as the best realization of "opera/music theater" by *The New York Times* in 1991; *Sacrifice of Mmbatho* (Writer/Director), commissioned and produced by BAM and the Market Theatre at BAM in 1994; *Trio*, a jazz opera by Noa Ain presented at Carnegie Hall; *Brightness Falling* (Writer/Director); *Black Novel* (Adapter/Director) with Argentine author Luisa Valenzuela; *Slain in the Spirit* with composer Taj Mahal and writer Susan Yankowitz, and *Many Moons* (Librettist/ Director), adapted from the James Thurber story with composer Rob Kapilow. Hilary has long been associated with The Women's Project, for whom she has done numerous staged readings both of her own and other playwrights' work.

CLAIRE CHAFEE received her B.A. in theatre from Oberlin College and studied acting and directing in New York and London. Her work has been given numerous readings and productions, at theatres including: The Women's Project, Lincoln Center, Manhattan Theatre Club, The Magic Theatre, Finborough Hall in London. Her play *Why We Have a Body* won 5 Dramalogue Awards, and earned her Newsday's George Oppenheimer Award for Best Emerging Playwright in 1995. She recently completed her M.F.A. at Brown, in fiction.

MIGDALIA CRUZ is the author of over twenty-seven plays, musicals and operas produced in the U.S. and abroad in venues as diverse as Playwrights Horizons (NY), Houston Grand Opera, Old Red Lion (London), Steppenwolf Studio

(Chicago), and Foro Sor Juana Ines de la Cruz (Mexico City). Her awards include: two NEA fellowships, a McKnight, a 1996 Kennedy Center Fund for New American Plays award, a runner-up for the 1997 Susan Smith Blackburn Prize, and a PEW/TCG National Artist in Residence award at Classic Stage Company (NY). She was a '96 member of Steppenwolf's Play Lab and has been writer-in-residence and Director of Theatre Programming at Latino Chicago Theater Company since September 1996. Migdalia has taught in the Dramatic Writing Program at NYU, Princeton, and Amherst College. An alumna of New Dramatists, she was born and raised in the Bronx. Recent productions include: *So...*(Part of the series *Pieces of the Quilt*), Magic Theatre (CA), Oct '96; *Dylan and the Flash*, Citylights Youth Theater (NY)/Oddfellows Playhouse (CT), November '96, March '97; *Fur*, Latino Chicago/Steppenwolf Studio, January '97; *Another Part of the House*, CSC (NY), March '97. Upcoming productions include: *Fur*, CampoSanto Theater (CA), October '97; *Che-Che-Che!*, Latino Chicago, October '97; *Another Part of the House*, Latino Chicago, April '98. She has been commissioned to write another in her series of political history plays for the Papp/Public Theater (NY) and for the University of Connecticut, Storrs, a piece based on her experiences with Children of War.

HEATHER McDONALD's most recent play, *An Almost Holy Picture*, premiered at the La Jolla Playhouse in 1995, and was named Best New Play of the Year by the L.A. Times. It has since been produced at the Round House Theatre, The McCarter Theatre, and, most recently, at Berkeley Repertory Theatre. Her other plays include *The Rivers and Ravines*, *Available Light*, *Faulkner's Bicycle* and *Rain and Darkness*. Her work has been produced at Berkeley Repertory Theatre, Arena Stage, Yale Repertory Theatre, Actors Theatre of Louisville, The Round House Theatre, The Magic Theatre, and The Joyce Theatre/American Theatre Exchange. For theatre of the First Amendment (Washington D.C.) she directed *Dream of a Common Language* which was nominated for eight Helen Hayes Awards and won four including Outstanding Resident

Production. She has twice been awarded NEA Playwrighting Fellowships.

JOYCE CAROL OATES's *Black* has also been performed at the Williamstown Summer Festival in Williamstown, Massachusetts, at the Contemporary American Play Festival in Shepherdstown, West Virginia, and in Cambridge, Massachusetts (under the title *Cry Me A River*); a new production is planned for Philadelphia in 1998. Other recent plays by Joyce Carol Oates have been performed by Circle Rep. in New York, The Attic Theatre in Los Angeles, the Voltaire Theatre in Chicago and the Annenberg Theatre in Philadelphia under the auspices of the Philadelphia Festival of New American Plays, the McCarter Theatre in Princeton, New Jersey, and the Théâtre du Rond-Point, Paris. Her plays have been collected in *Twelve Plays* and *The Perfectionist and Other Plays* and *New Plays* is scheduled for 1998. An opera adapted from her novel *Black Water* with a libretto by the author premiered in Philadelphia in April 1997 under the auspices of the American Music Festival Theatre.

ANN DEAVERE SMITH, as a playwright and performer, has, over the past thirteen years, created a body of theatrical works which she calls *On the Road: A Search for American Character*, and which includes *Fires in the Mirror: Crown Heights, Brooklyn and Other Identities* and *Twilight: Lost Angeles, 1992.* Ms. Smith received two Tony nominations for *Twilight*, as well as an Obie, a Drama Desk Award, two NAACP Theatre Awards and numerous other honors. Her next installment in the series will emerge from an in-progress residency at the Arena Stage in Washington, D.C. and will premiere in the fall of 1997. In addition to her new play, Smith is also writing a book based on her observations and impressions of her time in Washington and on the road, to be published by Random House in 1998. Smith is also currently serving as the Ford Foundation's first artist-in-residence, as part of the Foundation's effort to strengthen the role of artists and cultural leaders in public dialogue on contemporary civic issues. As an actor, Smith has had roles in Ivan Reitman's *Dave* and Jonathan Demme's *Philadelphia*.

Most recently she was seen in Rob Reiner's *The American President*, starring Michael Douglas and Annette Bening, in which she played the White House Press Secretary. In addition to her roles as actor, playwright and performance artist, Ms. Smith teaches at Stanford University, where she is Ann O'Day Maples Professor of the Arts. A native of Baltimore, she lives in San Francisco.

WOMENSWORK
Five new Plays from the
Women's Project
Edited by Julia Miles

The voices of five major playwrights offering a
vibrant range of styles and themes can be heard here
as they resound from the stage of The Women's
Project. The dramas which converge here from
Maria Irene Fornes, Cassandra Medley, Marlane
Meyer, Lavonne Mueller and Sally Nemeth emanate
with international character and universal allure.

MA ROSE Cassandra Medley
FIVE IN THE KILLING ZONE Lavonne Mueller
ETTA JENKS Marlane Meyer
ABINGDON SQUARE Maria Irene Fornes
MILL FIRE Sally Nemeth

paper • ISBN: 1-55783-029-0

WOMEN ON THE VERGE:
7 Avant-Garde American Plays
Edited by Rosette C. Lamont

This APPLAUSE anthology gathers together recent work
by the finest and most controversial contemporary
American women dramatists. Collectively, this
Magnificent Seven seeks to break the mold of the well-
wrought psychological play and its rigid emphasis on
realistic socio-political drama. The reader will imbibe the
joyous poetry flowing in these uncharted streams of
dramatic expression, a restless search that comes in the
wake of European explorations of Dada, Surrealism and
the Absurd.

THE PLAYS:

Rosalyn Drexler Occupational Hazard
Tina Howe Birth and After Birth
Karen Malpede Us
Maria Irene Fornes What of the Night?
Suzan-Lori Parks The Death of the Last Black Man in the
Whole Entire World
Elizabeth Wong Letters to a Student Revolutionary
Joan M. Schenkar The Universal Wolf

paper • ISBN: 1-55783-148-3

APPLAUSE

I AM A WOMAN

THE JOURNEY OF ONE WOMAN AND MANY WOMEN
A Dramatic Collage Conceived and Arranged by Viveca Lindfors & Paul Austin

"Lindfors delivered a revelation...her essential subject was not morality but love. It is precisely this sort of theatre that they ought to bring all people to these days."
—NEWSWEEK

"Miss Lindfors is excellent as she mercurially brings to life a cavalcade of 36 women, from Shaw, Ibsen, Colette, Shakespeare, Sylvia Plath, Brecht, a battery of women's liberation journalists and many other sources."
—THE NEW YORK TIMES

Among the excerpts:

Colette IN MY MOTHER'S HOUSE
Hellman PENTIMENTO
Frank DIARY OF ANNE FRANK
Lawrence CHATTERLY'S LOVER
Merriam A CONVERSATION AGAINST DEATH
Seaman THE LIBERATED ORGASM
Giraudoux THE MADWOMAN OF CHAILLOT

paper • ISBN 1-55783-048-7

PLAYS BY AMERICAN WOMEN: 1900-1930

Edited by Judith E. Barlow

These important dramatists did more than write significant new plays; they introduced to the American stage a new and vital character—the modern American woman in her quest for a forceful role in a changing American scene. It will be hard to remember that these women playwrights were ever forgotten.

A MAN'S WORLD Rachel Crothers
TRIFLES Susan Glaspell
PLUMES Georgia Douglas Johnson
MACHINAL Sophie Treadwell
MISS LULU BETT Zona Gale

paper • ISBN: 1-55783-008-X

PLAYS BY AMERICAN WOMEN: 1930-1960

Edited by Judith E. Barlow

Sequel to the acclaimed *Plays by American Women: 1900-1930* (now in its fifth printing!), this new anthology reveals the depth and scope of women's dramatic voices during the middle years of this century. The extensive introduction traces the many contributions of women playwrights to our theatre from the beginning of the Depression to the dawn of the contemporary women's movement. Among the eight plays in the volume are smart comedies and poignant tragedies, political agitprop and surrealist fantasies, established classics and neglected treasures.

THE WOMEN Clare Boothe

THE LITTLE FOXES Lillian Hellman

IT'S MORNING Shirley Graham

THE MOTHER OF US ALL Gertrude Stein

GOODBYE, MY FANCY Fay Kanin

IN THE SUMMER HOUSE Jane Bowles

TROUBLE IN MIND Alice Childress

CAN YOU HEAR THEIR VOICES? Hallie Flanagan and Margaret Ellen Clifford

paper • ISBN: 1-55783-164-5

WOMEN HEROES
Six Short Plays from the Women's Project
Edited by Julia Miles

The English Channel, the United States Government, Hitler, cancer—these are a few of the obstacles which these extraordinary women hurdle on their way to ticker tape parades, prison cells and anonymous fates.

COLETTE IN LOVE Lavonne Mueller
PERSONALITY Gina Wendkos & Ellen Ratner
MILLY Susan Kander
EMMA GOLDMAN Jessica Litwak
PARALLAX Denise Hamilton
HOW SHE PLAYED THE GAME Cynthia L. Cooper

paper • ISBN: 1-55783-029-0